WHAT CEOS EXPECT

FROM

CORPORATE TRAINING

WHAT CEOs EXPECT

FROM

CORPORATE TRAINING

Building Workplace Learning and Performance
Initiatives That Advance Organizational Goals

William J. Rothwell
John E. Lindholm
William G. Wallick

AMACOM

American Management Association

New York • Atlanta • Brussels • Buenos Aires • Chicago • London • Mexico City
San Francisco • Shanghai • Tokyo • Toronto • Washington, D. C.

Special discounts on bulk quantities of AMACOM books are available to corporations, professional associations, and other organizations. For details, contact Special Sales Department, AMACOM, a division of American Management Association, 1601 Broadway, New York, NY 10019.
Tel.: 212-903-8316. Fax: 212-903-8083.
Web Site: www. amacombooks.org

This publication is designed to provide accurate and authoritative information in regard to the subject matter covered. It is sold with the understanding that the publisher is not engaged in rendering legal, accounting, or other professional service. If legal advice or other expert assistance is required, the services of a competent professional person should be sought.

Library of Congress Cataloging-in-Publication Data
Rothwell, William J.
    What CEOs expect from corporate training : building workplace learning and performance initiatives that advance organizational goals / William J. Rothwell, John E. Lindholm, William G. Wallick.
        p. cm.
    ISBN 0-8144-0679-3
    1. Organizational learning. I. Lindholm, John Edwin. II. Wallick, William G. III. Title

.
    HD58.82 .R673 2003
    658.3'124—dc21

                                                                        2002011719

Printing number

10 9 8 7 6 5 4 3 2 1

William J. Rothwell dedicates this book to his wife, *Marcelina Rothwell*, and his daughter, *Candice Rothwell*. Without their loving support, this book would never have been written. They are my inspiration.

John E. Lindholm dedicates this book to his loving wife, *Mary*, and to his children, *Benjamin, Emilie, Luke,* and *David*.

William G. Wallick dedicates this book to his wife, *Judy Wallick*, and his two children, *Kelly* and *Zachary Wallick*, the most important people in his life.

CONTENTS

PREFACE

Sitting atop the pyramids of vast organizations that sometimes wield more economic clout than many nations, CEOs are the embodiment of the American dream. They are usually rich, powerful, and influential. As a result, many people are fascinated by CEOs and want to learn from them.[1] This fascination has made bestsellers of books by (or about) former General Electric CEO Jack Welch,[2] former Chrysler Chairman Lee Iacocca,[3] and even former Remington Chairman Victor Kiam.[4] The general public wants to know what CEOs, company presidents, and chairmen of the board think on a range of issues. Of course, so do employees who work in organizations controlled by these influential leaders.

For many years, CEOs and board members have used a version of the politically correct phrase "people are our most important assets" in board meetings, stockholder meetings, and annual reports. Research has generally proven this statement to be true.[5] Organizations investing more than their competitors in training and innovative human resource practices tend to outperform their competitors.[6] (And yet, in the words of the CEO of a Pennsylvania-based manufacturer, *training really suffers when we go through some tough economic times. It is an easy expense to slash. Everybody gives lip service to it.*[7])

Although research has been done on CEO opinions of human resource management (HRM) practitioners,[8] general manager opinions of HRM practitioners,[9] and CEO roles in organization-sponsored training,[10] relatively little research has focused on CEO opinions of Workplace Learning and Performance (WLP) professionals.[11] For readers unfamiliar with the term WLP, suffice it to say that this phrase represents the most recent, research-based thinking about the roles that should be played and the competencies that should be demonstrated by those whose job titles were once "trainer," "training and development practitioner," or "human resource development (HRD) professional."[12]

In recent years, WLP has been the focus of much attention.[13] Trainers and HRD practitioners play an important role in national workforce development, a topic of keen interest to government policymakers because of its key role in job creation and continued employment. As interest has spread among corporate leaders on important and cutting-edge issues such as learning organizations, intellectual capital, and knowledge management—topics naturally associated with WLP and workforce development—many people naturally wonder what CEOs think about the roles that should be played and the competencies that should be demonstrated by WLP professionals in today's organizations. For the growing number of people interested in careers in WLP, and for the students and faculty in the more than 300 graduate programs in the United States and other nations that are geared toward helping people enter or advance in the WLP field,[14] CEO opinions are crucially important because CEOs exercise the ultimate control over their organizations' resources. Their support for, or opposition to, organizational initiatives like WLP often spell the difference between success and failure.

As this book goes to press, CEOs have been the target of even greater scrutiny as public opinion reveals concerns about how well—and how honestly—CEOs are managing their organizations.[15] Indeed, at this writing trust in CEOs has plummeted to the low level with which Americans regard lawyers.[16] And yet no one doubts that CEOs are more important than ever in the minds of investors,[17] and their reputations can increase or decrease company stock prices.[18] One public relations firm commissioned a study that revealed that 40 percent of a company's reputation may be attributable to the CEO's reputation.[19] And few can doubt that learning—key to the role played by WLP professionals—is receiving growing attention as critically important to the success of the long-term strategic direction of organizations,[20, 21] an issue for which CEOs are primarily responsible.

The Purpose of This Book

What do CEOs think of training and development, human resource development, and workplace learning and performance in their organizations? This book is intended to answer this question. It furnishes trainers, HRD practitioners, WLP professionals, workforce developers, and other interested readers with useful perspectives from CEOs about the increasingly important WLP function. It can also provide WLP professionals with compelling background information to help plan a dialogue with CEOs about what they think of this function and its role in organizational settings.

Sources of Information

As we began to write this book, we decided to base it on the first-hand opinion of CEOs. To that end, we conducted over seventy interviews with CEOs from a broad cross-section of organizations.[22] We also referred to a previous research study that encompassed some fifty additional CEO interviews.[23] Further, we conducted literature searches on CEO opinions about training, HRD, and workplace learning and performance, as well as broader literature searches about the perceived roles, competencies, and outputs for specialists in WLP and in such related fields such as human resource management (HRM).

This book is primarily based upon three research studies. The foundational study was *ASTD Models for Workplace Learning and Performance: Roles, Competencies, and Outputs*.[24] This groundbreaking study redefined the field that has been variously called—at different stages in its evolution—training (or training and development), human resource development (HRD), and, most recently, workplace learning and performance (WLP). This study presents the results of research about the most contemporary roles, the competencies needed to perform those roles, and the suggested outputs from enacting the roles. The highlights of the study are addressed here to help you understand the roles and competencies that can help you to achieve success in WLP practice. The findings of the study indicate that WLP professionals need to shift their focus away from formal training events to a variety of learning experiences and performance improvement interventions that can solve organizational problems and ultimately improve business results.

First, it is important to recognize the most contemporary competencies required for success. The study examined the competencies—as perceived by training/HRD practitioners and line managers—needed for success in workplace learning and performance now and five years into the future. Although formal training still occurs, the focus now is on creating conditions in the workplace where managers and employees alike can become more responsible and accountable for learning and improved performance. The traditional view of training was as an activity rather than a method of producing results in work settings. WLP represents a paradigm shift in the field once called training and development, and later human resource development, and is designed to stimulate a shift toward bridging the gap between activity and results.

The researchers in *ASTD Models for Workplace Learning and Performance* posed two major research questions:

1. What competencies do WLP professionals, senior WLP professionals, and line managers perceive as currently required for success in workplace learning and performance?

2. What competencies do WLP professionals, senior WLP professionals, and line managers perceive will be required in five years?[25]

More than 1,000 individuals from twenty-eight nations participated in the study. They represented three groups—WLP professionals, senior WLP professionals, and operating managers. The six major competency groupings identified in the study are analytical, technical, leadership, business, interpersonal, and technological.

From these six major competency groupings seven WLP roles emerged. As we mentioned earlier, *roles* represent a grouping of competencies targeted to meet specific expectations of a job or function. As you read the seven roles, be careful not to equate roles with job titles. Remember that, for example, the director of HRD in an organization can play multiple roles as analyst, intervention selector, designer, developer, and so forth. However, that title in particular may be most closely aligned to WLP professionals who enact the manager role.

The second piece of research upon which this book is based, *A Study of CEO Perceptions of the Competencies of Workplace Learning and Performance Professionals*,[26] sought responses from CEOs to three questions:

1. What are the major business challenges CEOs perceive to be impacting their businesses?
2. How do CEOs perceive workplace learning programs to be linked to business challenges?
3. What competencies do CEOs recognize to be most important for the person responsible for workplace learning?[27]

The third study, *CEOs' Perceptions of Trainer Roles in Selected Multihospital Health Care Systems*,[28] examined how CEOs perceived the roles of WLP professionals, compared their perceived roles against the seven suggested WLP roles, and further compared these WLP roles to the formalized job descriptions from the surveyed organizations. Sixteen CEOs from the largest health care systems in the United States were interviewed, and a total of forty-eight WLP or WLP-related job descriptions were received from the participants. All of the health care systems had dedicated WLP functions. Curiously, seven CEOs did not meet at all with their WLP professionals, while seven others met one to three times per month, and only one CEO met four to six times per month with the WLP professional. One CEO opted not to respond to the question.

Another interesting question dealt with the placement of the WLP function in the organizational structure. Six CEOs reported that the leaders of their WLP functions were part of senior management and contributing at a fully strategic level in their organizations. Five other CEOs reported that their leaders of the WLP function were part of upper management and were functioning at both a strategic and operational level. Four CEOs considered their WLP leaders to be part of middle management or strictly operational. One CEO opted not to answer the question.

The Organizational Scheme of This Book

Chapter 1 explains why CEO opinions are important and worthy of examination. Chapters 2 through 8 focus on CEO opinions about WLP roles as they are currently defined.[29] The seven WLP roles identified by a recent study are[30]:

1. Manager
2. Analyst
3. Intervention selector
4. Intervention designer and developer
5. Intervention implementor
6. Change leader
7. Evaluator

Chapter 9 summarizes the key themes of this book. The chapter also offers advice about what readers may wish to do based on the lessons learned from this book.

The book ends with three appendixes. Appendix A provides a list of questions you can use to interview your own CEO. Appendix B is an activity that is intended to help you, as a WLP professional, start a process of self-reflection about what the CEO quotations mean for you. And Appendix C contains twenty-eight self-assessment worksheets that you can use to evaluate your own competencies in the various WPL roles and to assess how you measure up to your CEO's expectations.

ACKNOWLEDGMENTS

Writing a book is always an adventure. And the Acknowledgments section is our opportunity to thank those who helped us undertake that adventure. Accordingly, we wish to express our thanks to:

Our AMACOM acquisitions editor, *Jacquie Flynn*, who showed patience in working with us to prepare this book for publication.

Xeujun Qiao, research assistant of William Rothwell, who tracked down many articles, books, and other sources to add to the reference list of this book and *Faye Hickman*, also research assistant of William Rothwell, who helped with securing copyright permissions.

Sean Mahoney, who offered useful editorial comments on the first draft of the manuscript.

The CEOs who participated in our interviews. Without their help and willingness to discuss Workplace Learning and Performance, this book would not have been possible.

To these people, we owe a special debt of gratitude.

William J. Rothwell
John E. (Jed) Lindholm
William G. Wallick
July 2002

WHAT CEOS EXPECT

FROM

CORPORATE TRAINING

CHAPTER 1

Why Examine CEO Opinions of Corporate Training?

> **N**o longer can a company survive by producing goods and services that are commodities. In order to remain profitable, competitive, and a growing business, a company's work culture has got to embrace its customers' needs, wants, and desires.
>
> A CEO INTERVIEWED FOR THIS BOOK

Why Training Isn't Enough: The Case for WLP

The training field has evolved over the past sixty years from a primary focus on training individuals to improve their job performance to a more comprehensive focus on individual, group, and total organizational performance improvement. There are major differences between training, human resource development (HRD), and workplace learning and performance (WLP). Training and HRD are the most widely practiced approaches to improving performance in organizations today. However, they are not the most effective approaches to improving performance through learning: workplace learning and performance is.[1] Though people who work in corporate training have many titles—from trainer to HR developer—we will use the term "WLP professional" throughout the book to signify the new, proactive "trainer" who uses any and all interventions to get results. To make an effective shift from practicing training and HRD to practicing WLP, you must first examine the major differences among the definitions, goals, and nature of all three fields. Exhibit 1-1 provides a snapshot of these key differences.

Training focuses on equipping individuals with the knowledge or skills they need to refine their performance to meet current work conditions. However, training will not cure unsatisfactory work that results from deficient incentives or rewards, unsuitable tools, or other obstacles that are not under the employee's control. Training is essentially a short-term learning intervention designed for immediate performance improvement. Training is implemented for a variety of purposes, such as orientation training for new hires, qualifying employees for special assignments within an organization, or cross-training, which prepares employees to support critical activities in the absence of employees who regularly perform specialized work.[2]

Human resource development (HRD) seeks to move from implementing isolated solutions, such as training, into managing organizational change processes and individual career growth. Development is one key distinction between training and HRD. *Development* focuses on identifying, ensuring, and helping evoke new insights through planned learning. It gives individuals opportunities to grow and can provide organizations with employees who work smarter rather than harder. Development can be individually initiated, organizationally initiated, or jointly initiated by the employee and the organization. An example of jointly initiated development would be a situation in which an employee volunteers for a special assignment to learn new insights into a problem. The employee's supervisor might allow the employee to perform the assignment during the normal workday to encourage employee development while providing a benefit to the organization.[3]

The evolutionary step of HRD was important in that it

Exhibit 1-1. A Comparison of the Key Differences Among Training, HRD, and WLP

Meaning, Goals, & Nature	Training	HRD	WLP
What do the terms mean?	Through planned learning interventions, training focuses on identifying and developing key competencies that enable employees to perform their current jobs.	HRD is the integrated use of training and development, organization development, and career development to improve individual, group, and organizational effectiveness.	WLP is the integrated use of learning and other interventions for the purpose of improving individual and organizational performance. It uses a systematic process of analyzing and responding to individual, group, and organizational needs. WLP creates positive, progressive change within organizations by balancing human, ethical, technological, and operational considerations.
What is the major goal of each field?	The major goal is improved knowledge, skills, and attitudes about the job.	The major goal is the integration of training and development, organization development, and career development for the purpose of achieving improved performance through planned learning.	The major goals are: • Improving human performance • Balancing individual and organizational needs • Building knowledge capital within the organization • Improving financial return
What is the nature of each field?	Training and development focus on planned learning events.	HRD focuses on the three-fold purposes of giving individuals the knowledge and skills they need to perform, helping them to formulate and realize career goals, and helping them to interact effectively in groups.	WLP focuses on progressive change in the workplace through learning and other performance improvement strategies or interventions.

SOURCE: William J. Rothwell, Ethan S. Sanders, and Jeffrey G. Soper. *ASTD Models for Workplace Learning and Performance: Roles, Competencies, and Outputs* (Alexandria, Va.: The American Society for Training and Development, 1999), p. 9. Used by permission of ASTD. All rights reserved.

moved the field beyond training and development to include career development and organization development. *Career development* focuses on assuring an alignment of individual career planning and organization career management processes to achieve an optimal match of individual and organizational needs.[4] In other words, career development means structured interaction between an organizational representative and an individual, in which mutual expectations are negotiated.[5] Organization development focuses on assuring healthy inter- and intra-unit relationships and helping groups to initiate and manage change.[6] *Organization development* assumes that people want to belong to work groups, that openness and interpersonal trust are essential to group performance, and that willingness exists to see others as creative and useful.[7]

WLP is the most recent paradigm shift to define and describe the roles, competencies, and outputs that you, the WLP professional, should be practicing in your organization. The terms *workplace learning* and *performance*, when linked together, dramatize the key role that learning plays in achieving results. Workplace learning and performance (WLP) has been defined by the American Society for Training and Development as follows:

> WLP is the integrated use of learning and other interventions for the purpose of improving human performance, and addressing individual and organizational needs. It uses a systematic process of analyzing and responding to individual, group, and organizational performance issues. WLP creates positive, progressive change within organizations by balancing human, ethical, technological, and operational considerations.[8]

WLP uniquely combines the talents of organizational members from many disciplines to improve human performance through learning and other interventions. This is an important statement because, as you will see later in the book, CEOs are firmly dedicated to sharing the talents of other organizational members to improve performance.

As workplace learning and performance (WLP) professionals, you have many customers or stakeholders both inside and outside of your organizations. One important stakeholder is your CEO. Obviously, the top leader of your organization holds perceptions, perspectives, and opinions about you and the work that you effect as a WLP professional. How much thought have you given lately to what your CEO really thinks about the work you do? Are you satisfying his or her needs, wants, and desires? How do you know that you are living up to your CEO's expectations? This is a realm in which it is dangerous to make assumptions. The importance of examining your CEO's opinions about WLP is undeniable. Knowing the perceptions that some CEOs hold regarding the WLP field can guide your thinking to stay one step ahead—or at least keep pace.

Think about this: Regardless of your personal circumstances, your CEO is evaluating what you do regardless of the roles you play, the competencies you possess to enact those roles, and the resulting outputs you achieve. Before we move further ahead, let's take a moment to clarify the definitions of roles, competencies, and outputs.

ROLES, COMPETENCIES, AND OUTPUTS

Roles represent a grouping of competencies targeted to meet specific expectations of a job or function. The roles you will encounter in this book relate very specifically to WLP. The WLP roles identified by *ASTD Models for Workplace Learning and Performance*[9] and discussed in this book are:

1. *Manager*: Plans, organizes, schedules, monitors, and leads the work of individuals and groups to attain desired results; facilitates the strategic plan; ensures that WLP is aligned with organizational needs and plans; and ensures accomplishment of the administrative requirements of the function.

2. *Analyst*: Troubleshoots to isolate the causes of human performance gaps or identifies areas for improving human performance.

3. *Intervention selector*: Chooses appropriate interventions to address root causes of human performance gaps.

4. *Intervention designer and developer*: Creates learning and other interventions that help to address the specific root causes of human performance gaps. Some examples of the

work of the intervention designer and developer include serving as instructional designer, media specialist, materials developer, process engineer, ergonomics engineer, instructional writer, and compensation analyst.

5. *Intervention implementor*: Ensures the appropriate and effective implementation of desired interventions that address the specific root causes of human performance gaps. Some examples of the work of the intervention implementor include serving as administrator, instructor, organization development practitioner, career development specialist, process re-design consultant, workspace designer, compensation specialist, and facilitator.

6. *Change leader*: Inspires the workforce to embrace the change, creates a direction for the change effort, helps the organization's workforce to adapt to the change, and ensures that interventions are continuously monitored and guided in ways consistent with stakeholders' desired results.

7. *Evaluator*: Assesses the impact of interventions and provides participants and stakeholders with information about the effectiveness of the intervention implementation.

Competencies are any characteristics people possess that lead to results. They include the knowledge or skill that is critical for producing your key work outputs. But they are also more than knowledge or skill and could include motivation, innate ability, and other characteristics linked directly to results. Competencies are sometimes referred to as internal characteristics that people bring to their jobs. These may be expressed or demonstrated in a broad, even infinite, array of on-the-job behaviors.[10]

Competencies are often mentioned in terms of *competency groupings*—such as business competencies, technical competencies, or leadership competencies. Each competency grouping can have numerous "sub-competencies," which relate to the larger grouping. For example, under the business competency grouping, you might find knowledge of your company's business, industry awareness, or cost/benefit analysis.

Outputs are products or services that an individual or group delivers to others, especially to colleagues, customers, or clients.[11]

THE IMPORTANCE OF CEO PERCEPTIONS

Some of the perceptions your CEO holds about the work that you do may surprise you. Others may cause you to feel uneasy or unsettled. If, as you read further, you feel a bit uncomfortable about what your CEO might be thinking, it is imperative that you remain open to taking on the challenges and capitalizing on the opportunities offered by current thinking about WLP. The first question to be addressed is found in the title of this chapter: "Why is it important to examine CEO opinions about corporate training?" We hope to provide you with new insights about the perceptions some CEOs hold about corporate training—and the newest ideas about this field now known as WLP. Along the way we will provide you with a map of behaviors and relationships needed by WLP professionals in creating and sustaining a learning organization. The information provided should serve as a springboard from which to dive into analyzing and evaluating the expectations of your CEO. We want to help you to shape and frame your own thinking. This process necessarily requires a certain amount of soul-searching, which can be daunting. It is, however, necessary. The results of good soul-searching—which some people call self-reflection—will give you the opportunity to develop a competitive advantage over those who have not dedicated any thought to what the CEO or other key stakeholders might be thinking about the work you perform every day.

For organizations, competitiveness is about maintaining and gaining market share and meeting or exceeding customer expectations. But for individuals, competitiveness is about maintaining or gaining enough credibility to be productive. This definition is expanded with the phrase "competitive advantage": advantage is gained when you are maintaining and gaining market share by focusing on the needs and the desires of your customers. As stated earlier, CEOs are significant customers of WLP efforts, since their perceptions can spell success—or failure—for those efforts. This book will give you the tools to focus on the needs and desires of this important customer.

You know, of course, that your CEO expects you to perform many tasks related to your work in assisting your organization's members to perform their jobs well. These expectations may be written into your job description. However, your duties as stated in your job description might not even come close to what your CEO thinks you should be doing. To excel, you must first become sensitized to your CEO's actual expectations.

Your CEO holds tremendous power over the learning that occurs in your organization and can exercise his or her authority to restrict or expand the scope of practice of the WLP function at any time. If your perceptions of the roles you play are inconsistent with those of your CEO, you might be leaving yourself open to a great deal of criticism—or the need for another job. It is encouraging, however, that absolute agreement about your roles and competencies is not necessary. As you will find later in this chapter, agreement alone does not necessarily mean success. According to some CEOs, dynamic tension can be healthy; synergy and inventiveness might be squelched when you cease to challenge each other's thinking. Though the focus of this book is on CEO perceptions, it is important to remember that all of the constituents you serve hold perceptions of what you do or should do. These other constituents must not be forgotten. Building strong relationships within your organization will help you to gain the respect you deserve as a WLP professional and the respect that the WLP field in general deserves.

In addition to analyzing your relationship to the CEO, it is also important to consider the nature of learning in your organization. This is because the principles that drive organizational learning run in tandem with the relationships that you create to facilitate learning and increased organizational performance. Exhibit 1-2 compares the principles that drive learning in organizations and the desirable relationship between you and your learners.

Perhaps the most significant information for you as a WLP professional lies within the desired relationship between you and your learners. Both you and your learners must share responsibility for improving organizational performance. All stakeholders have at least one role to play in improving the

EXHIBIT 1-2. A COMPARISON BETWEEN THE NATURE OF LEARNING IN ORGANIZATIONS AND THE RELATIONSHIP BETWEEN THE PERFORMANCE IMPROVEMENT PRACTITIONER FROM THE TRAINING, HRD, AND WLP PERSPECTIVES

Topic	Training	HRD	WLP
Drivers of Organizational Learning	Learning should be focused on the job performed by the individual. The results of training should be immediate, and their relationship to the job should be readily apparent.	Increased skill and knowledge about a particular set of tasks will lead to greater organizational effectiveness. Pairing an individually focused intervention (such as training) with other interventions (such as organizational development and career development) best facilitates learning.	1. Learning interventions may or may not be appropriate for solving specific performance problems. The appropriate intervention depends on the root causes of the performance problem. 2. Continuous learning is an important organizational strategy because it builds the intellectual capital that is crucial to individual and organizational performance.
Desirable Relationship between you and your learners	The focus of training is on making people productive in their jobs. Training seeks that end with a short-term focus. The trainer/trainee relationship is akin to the teacher/student model. The teacher/trainer is responsible for teaching the student/learner what he or she must know, do, or feel to be successful in the job.	HRD adopts an integrated approach to change through planned learning. It integrates the individually focused short-term learning initiative of training with group-focused learning initiatives (organizational development) and with longer-term learning initiatives (career development) intended to prepare individuals for future work requirements. Since training is not the sole focus of HRD, the relationship between trainer–trainee is	WLP does not focus exclusively on learning interventions. However, workers and stakeholders have major responsibility in planning instruction and, more importantly, in focusing on ways to support and encourage learning. Everyone has a role to play in that effort. The full-time WLP practitioner is a resource, enabling agent, and learning specialist who facilitates the process but does not take sole ownership of it. The learner is responsible for tak-

(continues)

Exhibit 1-2. *(continued)*

Topic	Training	HRD	WLP
		more complex and varies with the type of change effort and with the results sought.	ing initiative to pursue his or her own learning efforts. In WLP, the WLP practitioner and learner are partners in the learning endeavor, and both are seeking improved performance.

SOURCE: William J. Rothwell, Ethan S. Sanders, and Jeffrey G. Soper. *ASTD Models for Workplace Learning and Performance: Roles, Competencies, and Outputs* (Alexandria, Va.: The American Society for Training and Development, 1999), p. 9. Used by permission of ASTD. All rights reserved.

overall performance of your organization. One role that is clearly yours is that of being an expert resource, enabling agent, and learning specialist who facilitates the performance improvement process. The CEO is a key customer and stakeholder of workplace learning, and he or she sets the tone for what others will say and do.

Not only do you have to recognize your role, but you must also inform and educate your stakeholders about the role(s) they need to play when it comes to workplace learning and performance. Facilitating such a transition is indeed easier said than done. As there are inherent difficulties in making a transition from training and HRD to WLP, knowing your CEOs' opinions and perceptions will help to make the transition easier for you. To get to know your CEO's opinions and perceptions, you need to ask and observe the example your CEO sets.

Having a basic understanding of the most contemporary competencies and roles in the WLP field is critically important in understanding and comparing the perceptions of CEOs with the work you currently perform. In Exhibit 1-3 we present some sample outputs for each WLP role. Although not an exhaustive list, the outputs listed are intended to provide you with an idea of the types of outputs that could be completed in your current work circumstances. The exhibit lists the seven workplace learning and performance roles and some sample outputs.

EXHIBIT 1-3. SAMPLE OUTPUTS ASSOCIATED WITH THE SEVEN WLP ROLES

Manager	Intervention Implementor
• WLP plans for the organization or unit • Strategies that align WLP efforts with organizational and individual need • Work plans for WLP efforts • Plans to secure the human talent to carry out WLP efforts • Objectives that support desired results	• Plans and schedules for implementing interventions • Facilitation methods that will deliver the intervention appropriately • Consulting services • Contributions to business goals and objectives • Measurable return-on-investment

Analyst	Change Leader
• Analytical methods that uncover the root causes of performance gaps • Results of assessment • Reports to key stakeholders of individual, group, or organizational change efforts about directions of such efforts • Reports to executives that highlight the relationship between human performance and financial performance	• Revised implementation plans that reflect changes in the original intervention strategy • Periodic reports to key stakeholders of interventions about their progress • Written illustrations of successful implementation cases

Intervention Selector	Evaluator
• Recommendations to others about selecting interventions to address or avert problems or seize opportunities • Recommendations to others about ways to combine interventions • Assessments of the expected impact of interventions • Objectives for interventions that are aligned with desired business results	• Reports that show the evaluation results • Recommendations for future WLP interventions • Reports that determine if intervention results caused a positive impact on business objectives

Intervention Designer and Developer

• Intervention designs
• Action plans for interventions
• Lists of stakeholders and participants for interventions
• Links intervention design to business objectives

As you will soon see, CEOs recognize that they and their organizations are under ever-increasing pressure to find ways to sustain or increase their competitive advantage. Issues such as global competition, finding and retaining excellent performers, and rapidly changing technology require almost nanosecond responses. These and other business issues are causing a shift in the way work needs to be accomplished. To get work accomplished in the most cost-effective and expeditious way requires a new way of managing the knowledge capital in organizations. That's why traditional training and HRD methods need to be questioned and new methods, such as those inherent to WLP, need to be introduced. WLP offers the possibility for a broader range of solutions. It embraces the understanding that you not only need to close any performance gaps in your organization but simultaneously maintain or increase corporate profitability and capacity as well.

In the pages that follow we intend to help you to increase your awareness of the growing complexities of the workplace through the eyes of some very savvy CEOs. At the same time we'll show you the value that workplace learning and performance can offer you as a contemporary practitioner.

Let's look now at some of the CEOs' responses to several important questions:

1. What are the major business challenges CEOs perceive to be impacting their businesses?
2. How do CEOs perceive workplace learning programs to contribute to meeting business challenges?
3. What competencies do CEOs recognize to be most important for the person responsible for facilitating workplace learning?[12]

The first question sought to learn about the most important business challenges facing organizations now and in the next two to three years. Obviously, this information is pertinent to you as a WLP professional because knowledge of the business challenges your organization is facing positions you to help better prepare your organization to meet the challenges through workplace learning, leading to overall improved individual, group, and organizational success. Once again, accomplishing this goal is easier said than done. Such knowledge of the business challenges and subsequent actions on your part will quite probably lead to your gaining more respect from others.

As you read the statements from CEOs, we hope you will reflect on their relevance to your current situation. We suggest that you jot down a few of your own thoughts as you read these CEOs' statements. Use the self-reflection worksheet in Exhibit 1-4 to compare the various business challenges as perceived by the CEOs to your own situation. Indicate your perceived importance of these business challenges, and then think about and write in your ideas about how you can help your organization meet the business challenges. Don't hesitate to add business challenges from your own experience that are not mentioned in the study.

Exhibit 1-4. Comparison of Business Challenges Worksheet

Directions: Use this worksheet to compare the business challenges your company is facing with those mentioned by the CEOs. First, examine the business challenges presented by the CEOs. Add any business challenges that you see facing your organization that were not mentioned by the CEOs. Then indicate your own level of perceived importance for your organization using the scale from 1 to 5. Finally, list some ways you think you, as a workplace learning and performance professional, might help your organization deal with the business challenges. Add additional paper as necessary.

(1 = Not Important, 2 = Somewhat Important, 3 = Important, 4 = Very Important, 5 = Extremely Important)

Business challenges	Your perceived level of importance	Ways that I can help my organization deal with the business challenges
Financial	1 2 3 4 5	
Recruiting	1 2 3 4 5	
Technology	1 2 3 4 5	
Knowledge management	1 2 3 4 5	
Globalization	1 2 3 4 5	
Customer satisfaction	1 2 3 4 5	
Add your own perceived business challenges	1 2 3 4 5	
	1 2 3 4 5	

CEO-Identified Business Challenges

Based on our interviews of CEOs, the six major business challenges of concern to them are: customer satisfaction; technology; globalization; profits/cost reduction; knowledge management; and attracting, retaining, and improving the performance of their employees.[13] Exhibit 1-5 summarizes these six challenges and some of their accompanying characteristics as perceived by CEOs.

The following statements from CEOs—as well as those reproduced throughout the rest of this book—are direct quotations from interviews we conducted with them.

EXHIBIT 1-5. CEOs' PERCEPTIONS OF THE SIX MOST IMPORTANT BUSINESS CHALLENGES

Financial Challenges	Globalization Challenges
• Reducing operating costs to increase production efficiency • Developing and implementing business strategies that result in profitable return • Maintaining operating profits in an increasingly competitive business environment	• New employee skills to deal with a global economy • Cultural issues • New ways of doing business

Recruiting Challenges	Customer Challenges
• Attracting and retaining an appropriate number of qualified and competent staff • Filling key skill positions • Improving our current employees	• Ability to partner with customers • Helping customers understand how to shop and buy • Deploying technology for greater customer satisfaction

Technology and Internet Challenges	Corporate Knowledge Challenges
• Improving the use of technology to keep ahead of the competition • Gaining new knowledge and employing those available technologies • Matching the latest technologies to customer requirements	• Shared understanding of the organization's objectives • Command of products and services to deepen customer relationships • Open communications and linkages between and among departments

CUSTOMER CHALLENGES

We begin with comments that focus on customer satisfaction. In the words of one CEO:

● "The first and foremost [business challenge] is what I'd call the *customer satisfaction* quotient, which is our ability not only to satisfy our customer base, but to bring them in as a partner in the businesses that we run. What does the customer want...quality, delivery, price, technical assistance? We must change our culture from a manufacturing business to a customer orientation and still have return on investment and growth."

Related to this comment above is a similar one from another CEO that emphasizes the need to keep abreast of new technology to satisfy customer needs.

● "[A key challenge we face is] to make sure that we're staying aligned with an integration of our *rapidly changing customer requirements and also quickly changing technology* to make sure we've matched the latest technology with the new customer requirements. New things come out every month, and customers always want the latest."

TECHNOLOGY CHALLENGES

The most efficient use of technology appears to be another concern for CEOs. They see technology as vital to enhancing customer service and products and achieving efficiencies with other operations. At the same time they recognize how quickly technological advances occur, and they know that trying to stay ahead of that accelerating curve is not easy to do. About these issues, several CEOs offered the following remarks:

● "*Technology* will be our challenge in two respects...how to take advantage of the emergent Internet capabilities that are generally available for all of us in business and then to capitalize on the emerging technologies that are available...to become more successful practitioners."

● "[Our key challenge is the] *utilization of technology* to improve our operating efficiencies plus offering the technology that our customers expect and are looking for."

- "Our [most important business challenge] is dealing with e-commerce...equipping our company to compete in the cyberspace world."
- "[Our biggest challenge is] to continually improve our *technology* to keep ahead of the competitors and be able to develop a profit in the company."
- "What comes to mind is general *e-commerce*...finding ways to maximize our opportunities to interface with customers, suppliers, and distributors electronically to provide more efficient supply chain management, better and more efficient communication in general, and faster access to key information."

RECRUITING CHALLENGES

Finding the "right" people to staff and support organizational growth and prosperity is considered by many CEOs to be a major, and continuing, business challenge. Simply attracting people to work in their organizations is just a part of the concern. Many CEOs believe that two even more pressing issues center around retaining the workforce they have and improving their current workers' skills. To quote our CEO respondents directly:

- "Without a doubt [our most important business challenge] is *recruiting* high quality people that are self-starters...people that have the initiative and ability to grow and learn with the organization."
- "The greatest challenge right now is to *attract and keep qualified people*, without question."
- "Just the ability to *attract and retain* the best and the brightest people."
- "Number one is finding, keeping, and improving the people that you have...the human capital side of the business is going to be critical."
- "I think it's attracting and maintaining the appropriate number of qualified and competent staff, both from a technical and support perspective. Second, I think it's developing new managers who have the expertise to meet the chal-

lenges that lay ahead of us. And third, maintaining a linkage between our departments so that we can break down any barriers that might interfere with our ability to do our work."

- "Number one would be *attracting and retaining* growth managers...individuals within the company that may be involved in either research for new products and/or developing new products."

- "One challenge would be *filling key skills positions* in the organization."

GLOBALIZATION CHALLENGES

A common concern voiced by many CEOs we interviewed is the impact that globalization is having on their businesses and the businesses of their competitors. Countries are very rapidly becoming indistinguishable. Yet within the various countries of the world there are unique cultures that employees must learn about so that companies will not only survive but also gain a competitive advantage. In making this point, CEOs said:

- "The biggest challenge we face is dealing with the *impact of globalization* in our business...resulting in a shift of business mass from the traditional areas of North America to emerging parts of the world, most specifically in the Far East and in South America."

- "The *global market*...we've moved from running a company that had services and products only in the United States and in only two years we've moved into over 140 countries...so there are cultural issues to deal with."

- "I think business has changed more in the last three to four years than it had in the previous fifteen....*Business has become truly worldwide*, and there've been new skills that people have had to acquire and new ways of doing business."

FINANCIAL CHALLENGES

Maintaining financial viability is also an important challenge facing organizations today. Financial challenges were the most frequently mentioned of the business challenges, which should not be surprising because the cost of organizational ineffectiveness can quickly drain company financial resources and human initiative. This dimension includes increased operating efficiency, company growth, increased profitability, and increased shareholder value. The quality and knowledge of the workforce is one clear ticket to financial success, as stated eloquently by one CEO:

● "[Of key concern to the organization is the] pricing and positioning of products...and to do that, you need talented people who are always on top of the leading edge and who are continually learning to change what we do and how we do it to keep up and compete in that kind of environment."

Other CEOs commented about the importance of financial viability in similar ways:

● "Our key challenge is to continue to *reduce cost.*"
● "The greatest challenge is *profitable growth.*"
● "Enhancing shareholder value..."
● "The one which is all important is *protecting profit margins.* Buyers are committed to squeezing suppliers and manufacturers for improved products and services at lower prices. This is going to be an on-going trend, and as e-commerce and other types of tools become more user friendly, I think it will create transparencies for buyers and allow them to become smarter, putting more pressure on margins."

● "Increased competition necessitates that *we lower our cost structure* dramatically while making sure that we attract, obtain, retain, and develop the talents necessary to run the company."

● "The challenge we face is how to present the collective knowledge of the organization on every project, and collective knowledge means that people must interact in the workplace in a very strong way so that a synergy with the whole organization comes to bear."

CORPORATE KNOWLEDGE CHALLENGES

Finally, CEOs regarded the way knowledge is managed within

organizations to be critically important for organizational success. We found it gratifying to find out how much CEOs recognize the value that workplace learning and performance efforts can have if properly managed.

- "The first category is team building...the creation of one team with a common goal and common purpose...to build a very clear identity for our company and its team members."

- "The biggest challenge is to motivate and *change the culture* of the people to work to a high growth capacity."

One CEO neatly summed up nearly all the business challenges mentioned directly or indirectly by the other CEOs by asking some very thought-provoking questions:

- "The biggest issue will be the changes necessary in the structure and the process of business in order to stay viable and competitive from the United States in this global economy. What are the jobs that need to be done? How will the tasks be done? What skills are we going to need in our people to do them well? Where should we be located? Which jobs will disappear or be swamped by technology? What kind of presence should we have around the globe?"

Knowing the challenges that CEOs perceive to be critical to the success of their organizations is only one piece of the puzzle. Figuring out how WLP can contribute to meeting these challenges is the next piece of the puzzle. The CEOs we interviewed provided their perceptions about how WLP professionals might contribute to meeting their business challenges, and their suggestions are described below.

How Can Workplace Learning and Performance Contribute to Meeting Business Challenges?

We now invite you to compare your own ideas from Exhibit 1-4 with the perceptions of CEOs as to how WLP can contribute to meeting an organization's business challenges. We've divided several of the CEOs' comments according to the six most important business challenges.

FINANCIAL

- *"[WLP professionals can best help to meet this challenge] by helping our associates understand the mission of the organization* and their role within the organization and convince them that it's in their best interest to try to help us be the low cost producer and create additional services and support for our customers."*

CEOs perceive that you should have a working knowledge of the products and services that your organization provides and an understanding of the financial issues your organization faces. With knowledge of these business components, you can facilitate the learning of others about any changes to your organization's current business model. Ideally, you can also inspire others in the organization to live the new business model.

RECRUITING

CEOs have consistently commented that the amount and quality of workplace learning efforts play an important role in attracting employees to and retaining employees in your organization:

- "The more you have people learning in the workplace, the more *attractive it is for people to come to work for you and stay."*
- "I think that workplace learning is a critical piece of the people side...*finding, keeping, and improving people.* At the end of the day our knowledge curve is much steeper...*we need to keep up with the knowledge curve.* I think that companies that find a way to capture, share, and use knowledge—particularly better than their competitors—will have a significant competitive advantage in the future."
- *"Putting on appropriate job fairs...*providing an opportunity for people out in our communities who may be prospective employees to come and see us and learn what we have available. Once we get the employee here, the educators are important to ensuring that the employee develops appropriately."

The role WLP professionals play in educating the community about the organization is another way CEOs thought WLP professionals could contribute to meeting the business challenges of their organizations. Bear in mind that "community" refers to not only the people who live within a geographic radius of your organization but to the global community.

TECHNOLOGY AND THE INTERNET

- "The *Internet* is radically changing our entire business model and the way we conduct business. Almost everything that we do has got to be reinvented over the next few years. We need *to stay on top of those trends, figure out how it's going to change our organization, and communicate* that throughout the organization because it's going to change people's jobs."

- "I think that even though fundamental skills are learned prior to someone joining our company, I think that people are not thoroughly versed in what's happening with *technology* changes. *[Employees] need to understand what's happening [with technology]*. So many people are generating new solutions...we need to figure out how to apply and adapt those [solutions] to our needs."

Advancing technology has simultaneously simplified and further complicated the jobs of WLP professionals. On one hand, we can now deliver learning interventions to many locations around the world using distance learning via satellite linkages. Addressing many employees concurrently can reduce the frequency of programs. Technology should result in greater efficiency and cost-effectiveness. However, the proper and effective use of various technologies requires new skills. Although no WLP professional is expected to be an expert in all available technological tools, you should at least know the range of technologies that exist to make informed decisions regarding their most appropriate use.

GLOBALIZATION

CEOs find it imperative that you clearly understand your own organization's culture if you are to help the organization meet the challenge posed by globalization. In the words of one CEO:

- "Number one, people need to *understand our company culture*.... Number two, *enhance specific technical skills and job knowledge*.... Number three, *teach soft skills*, whether it be confrontation skills, communication skills, or delegation skills. All those are examples of how we can do a better job of workplace learning to equip our people to do a better job."

How could you facilitate the transformation of your organization's business model or the way your organization conducts its business if you aren't intimately aware of, and involved with, the culture in which you work? The shift to WLP requires participation from everyone to provide an environment in which all employees can learn and grow.

CUSTOMER

CEOs recognize that customer expectations will continue to drive the way business is conducted for the foreseeable future. In the words of one CEO:

- "The *ability to use learning systems, training systems, and involvement systems* will be a major part of making the culture shift to customer orientation. Some systems would be conventional, and others nonconventional—like going to the customer and learning his business and his needs and his concerns. Then organizing the company to blend the two [conventional and nonconventional]."

The CEOs expect innovative learning interventions to occur, such as visiting your customers. You should learn as much as you can about the customers' businesses so that you can anticipate their needs and concerns. In other words, customers' needs should be discovered firsthand so that the learning interventions you plan will meet customer needs.

CORPORATE KNOWLEDGE

- "In terms of knowledge *management* it's a way of *facilitating the sharing of knowledge*. That's what a great deal of learning is—passing on knowledge from one person to another."

● "First by *continuing to provide specific skills* in performing various functions necessary to operate the existing businesses. But I think the second area is more important... *to broaden the thinking processes of our people such that they are proactively identifying opportunities on a continuing basis* to build our infrastructure but not be limited by our infrastructure. In other words, build on our experience but think outside the box for new opportunities."

● "In our case it's *providing high technology advice, consultation, prototypes, and research, and the ability of workplace learning to have everyone take a piece or part of that.* Each of our jobs is the most important ingredient of the company."

Corporate knowledge encompasses all of the business challenges listed in this section and probably many more ideas than the CEOs suggested. Corporate knowledge challenges deal with finding ways to facilitate the sharing of knowledge, providing skills training, developing the thinking and creative processes of your organizational members, using technology effectively, and assisting your organization in finding and retaining competent employees. Of course, keeping your customers in the forefront of planned learning for your organization is all-important.

The challenges faced by WLP professionals are indeed daunting. But the more advanced knowledge we have of the trends that will most likely affect our individual jobs and the WLP field in general, the more manageable the trends will be.

We've shared with you some of the suggestions we heard from CEOs during our interviews about how WLP professionals can help organizations meet their most important business challenges. Exhibit 1-6 summarizes CEOs' suggestions as to how WLP might contribute to the six major business challenges.

We've challenged you to suggest your own ideas about how you can help your organization meet its current and future business challenges and provided you with our thoughts as we interpreted the statements made by the CEOs.

EXHIBIT 1-6. SUMMARY OF CEOs' SUGGESTIONS FOR WLP PROFESSIONALS TO HELP MEET THE SIX MOST IMPORTANT BUSINESS CHALLENGES

Financial Challenges	Globalization Challenges
• Understand the products of the company • Understand the company's business issues • Facilitate business model changes	• Understand the company's culture

Recruiting Challenges	Customer Challenges
• Increased workplace learning to attract new people to the organization • Job fairs designed to educate the community about the organization	• Regularly consult with customers • Keep customers in the forefront of planned learning

Technology and Internet Challenges	Corporate Knowledge Challenges
• Evaluate technological trends • Use the trends to help change the business • Communicate the trends to the organization	• Manage company-wide transitions • Create a continual learning environment • Provide mentoring

SOURCE: John E. Lindholm. *A Study of CEO Perceptions of the Competencies of Workplace Learning and Performance Professionals.* Unpublished doctoral dissertation (University Park, Pa.: The Pennsylvania State University, 2000). Copyright 2000 by Dissertation Abstracts International. All rights reserved.

CEO-Identified Competencies for WLP Professionals

Now that you have an idea of the business challenges CEOs perceive and how WLP can contribute to meeting the challenges, we next turn to the competencies CEOs regard as necessary for WLP professionals to assist their organization in meeting its challenges. Seven competencies were identified from our CEO interviews as the most salient for increasing organizational performance as an output of learning interventions. The seven competencies are:

❐ Business knowledge

❐ Communication

❐ Broad perspective

❐ Assessment

- ❑ Delivery systems
- ❑ Innovation
- ❑ Drive

Each competency area is described below. We've also included some of the CEOs' comments related to each competency area.

1. *Business knowledge*: aligning training to company strategy, keeping abreast of industry trends and company performance, and demonstrating the transfer of learning to individual performance. CEOs expect that you will help ensure financial profits from company activities and assist in implementing an effective company strategy.

- "The first thing [WLP professionals] need to do is to really understand the business that we're in and understand what the talent needs of the organization and business are."

- "...to be an integral part of the strategic plan, understand what the business needs are and how training can affect it."

- "It's very important that [WLP professionals] truly understand the requirements of business. It's hard to understand what kind of training and people development you need to do without understanding the business."

- "The key aspect is understanding the mission of the business...and then develop programs in an organized fashion that facilitate the accomplishment of that mission."

- "[WLP professionals] have to understand the business that their specific company is in...they have to understand what makes the business tick, how it makes money, what's important and what's not important."

2. *Communication*: communicating effectively throughout the organization, advocating on behalf of the organization and the individual, and facilitating group processes.

- "The ability to effectively communicate is the number one attribute that [WLP professionals] have to have."

- "I think [WLP professionals] need good communication skills. They need the ability to sit down and talk with people, understand what their problems are, and understand the best way to develop some type of training program to fit their needs."

3. *Broad perspective*: assimilating numerous experiences into learning approaches, demonstrating open-mindedness, viewing employees as assets, possessing empathy, and possessing an awareness of the organization's culture.

- "[The WLP position has] grown...very broad based. For example, [WLP professionals] must understand completely this cultural change to customer service, then go out and find out where the deficiencies are in the organization by integrating [themselves] with the management and with our customers to create a series of developmental needs over a broad spectrum, and then create a learning environment where they can be most easily learned. In many cases that is not traditional classroom work."

- "...the ability to be able to empathize with employees and their situation...who are capable of putting themselves in the shoes of our employees, understanding their particular situation and developing programs with that in mind."

4. *Assessment*: measuring, assessing, and guiding both individual and organizational workforce learning needs, forecasting and preparing for training needs, and identifying performance problems.

- "[WLP professionals] need the ability to sit down and talk with people, understand what their problems are, and understand the best way to develop some type of training programs to fit their needs."

- "Understanding what people need to be able to perform their jobs, and that's different than what people want."

- "I think they need to have a very good understanding of assessments and measurement tools to determine where people have weaknesses and where they have strengths."

- "The ability to do an accurate and honest assessment of the capabilities of the organization they are a part of. They also have to make an honest assessment of what [WLP professionals] have in terms of workforce knowledge and of what they may be missing or what they need. This up-front assessment is all critical and all-important because until they really have a sense of the answers to the assessment, they can't even begin to put together a realistic budget to get at the needs."

5. *Delivery systems*: assessing, designing, and implementing effective training delivery systems.

● "I think it's very important that [WLP professionals] stay on top of all the new technologies and opportunities and ways that there are to deliver education. This is a fast changing field."

● "They got to be good at developing systems that are easily understood and easily implemented in an environment that is not [always] ideal to learning. For example, our stores average 3,000 customers a day...that's not a great place to sit around and learn."

6. *Innovation*: conceptualizing, designing, developing, and applying new learning interventions to business needs while simultaneously modeling strong values and openness to change.

● "[WLP professionals] need a strong willingness to try new things, to try new ideas, to experiment quite a bit...and then clearly someone who has a strong values orientation and who is willing to be a model in values and then a strong desire to win."

● "You need somebody [for WLP] who has general leadership skills, who is entrepreneurial in nature, and who has a good business sense—particularly as to the company's needs— and who has very good interpersonal skills."

● "We've looked for [WLP professionals] that care about people, that are empathetic, enthusiastic, smart, and creative."

7. *Drive*: demonstrating energy and enthusiasm for programs and building bridges across barriers for learning program acceptance.

● "One of the most important attributes is energy...it's a matter of having energy and drive to develop the right programs and then convince managers to get their people to the programs."

● "They can provide initiative...the real value in their [WLP professionals] positions is unleashing the thinking potential of employees and the ability to raise new ideas to solve problems in nontraditional ways. They have to be change-oriented people comfortable with new ideas, new thinking, and sponsoring approaches that give people more latitude as opposed to less latitude."

These interviews, then, provided many useful insights into what some CEOs viewed as the most important business challenges facing their organizations.[14] CEOs are very concerned about the financial performance of their organizations. The increasing pace of change in customer expectations also appears to be a major driver of CEOs' financial concerns. Technology is rapidly changing our working environment and is creating opportunities to develop new products and services. CEOs are concerned with positioning their companies to invest in new technology that will keep up with customer demand, while simultaneously using technology to increase their operating efficiencies and profits. These issues impact the types of assessment and learning interventions that must be offered, the skill sets needed by current and future employees, and the infrastructure to support a company's workplace learning programs.

It is important to examine CEO perceptions of how WLP professionals might assist their organizations to meet current business challenges. CEOs thought that workplace learning and performance could best address business challenges when interventions were designed to increase personal awareness of the company's current state of affairs, using a process that distributes the awareness throughout the organization. The use of technology was mentioned as one way to coordinate such an effort throughout the organization. The challenges facing the WLP professional here are to understand how to personalize company knowledge and culture and to ensure the information is useful to employees.

There was strong agreement among the CEOs that job-specific technical training and general business skills are critically important to organizational success. Also of interest is the CEOs' conclusion that workplace learning programs are important for recruiting and retaining a competent workforce. They seemed to indicate that learning interventions aimed at developing individual skills and supporting the sharing of knowledge were highly valued as a way to attract and retain employees.

The final piece of the study addressed perceived application and process competencies needed by WLP professionals. CEOs identified the most important *application competencies* (competencies that result in the accomplishment of a specific task) as communication, assessment, and delivery systems. *Process competencies* are those competencies that demonstrate an ability to process disparate, but relevant, information to guide workplace learning programs that are company specific, creative, and broadly used by a workforce. CEOs thought that the most important process competency was the ability to understand the business. As business changes, CEOs think that WLP professionals should provide programs that use company-specific content to help employees gain a solid understanding of the company's business.

To determine how CEOs perceive WLP roles in their organizations, we sought comments about their past perceptions of WLP. Although some CEOs held positive perceptions by saying that the WLP was a vital, essential, and key part of their organization's success, others didn't view WLP in such a positive way. Some saw the WLP function as ineffective and functionally oriented with little or no broad-based organizational foci. Following are a few comments about CEOs' past perceptions of WLP:

- "[WLP] played a key part in the success of organizations in the past."
- "I would say a very essential part of any learning organization."
- "In the more distant past I think [WLP] was usually pretty ineffective...probably not top-driven in the organization and many times not consistent from year to year."
- "My perception of the past has been that WLP was a functional activity....It's not been my experience that there's been a lot of focus on broad-based organizational development."

How were these perceptions formed? Virtually all CEOs' perceptions were formed by observing programs, participating in programs, or by actually facilitating programs themselves. Involvement in training, HRD, or WLP efforts was evident in shaping CEOs' current perceptions. In response to a question about how they had formed their opinions, two CEOs responded with these observations:

- "Predominately personal interaction...when I've been either involved in attending a training session or participating as an instructor. Personally I do participate in different training exercises for our organization and so I would say direct observation predominately, and secondarily through general feedback from our management structure and our employee group."
- "I've been in training programs all of my career and been a participant and a trainer myself."

CEOs provided some insights into the knowledge, skills, and abilities they perceived to be most appropriate for WLP professionals to possess. From a knowledge standpoint, CEOs thought that a strong educational background in WLP was important but qualified this by saying that education alone was not enough. Practical, real-world experience was seen as an equally important component. In the words of one CEO interviewed:

- "Ideally the person will have some real-world experience so they have some credibility from an operating standpoint. They would have been practitioners in the field in which they now work and would have the appropriate educational background and development to match their experiences."

Communication skills, listening skills, and facilitation skills were also viewed as necessary.

- "Ability to communicate to a given audience...and good listening skills."
- "I think they would need to be able to be very effective in front of a group, be innovative in how they presented and talked, and be effective in training trainers."

In addition, CEOs want to see their WLP professionals exhibit enthusiasm for improving organizational performance, the ability to pull workers together to improve performance, and to be partners with the CEO, managers, and staff to effect improved performance. As the CEOs themselves said:

- "I think [WLP professionals] should be somewhat of a cheerleader for the organization...someone who is very enthusiastic, someone that can develop some esprit de corps, someone who can get excitement surrounding whatever the topic is that they're focusing on, someone who can generate enthusiasm for the project."

- "I think they would be able to pull in workers to help get the work done."

- "I'd say learning to partner with directors and managers of the departments so that you can create what literally is a structure where the trainer is on a peer level with directors and managers as opposed to being a subordinate."

A few CEOs offered interesting comments about why WLP professionals might not have been as effective as possible. Some faulted themselves for not making the desired outcomes clearly known.

- "The only thing I can think of was probably in a situation where we were not specific about the outcomes we wanted."

When CEO expectations were not met, they most often thought that inadequate needs assessment and poor quality programs were at the heart of the problem.

- "I think that [WLP professionals] didn't focus on solving real issues...they focused on perceived problems."

- "[WLP professionals] really have not done enough background work and talking to people about what they really need to have...not enough assessment."

- "When programs were too lengthy and were seen by employees as having too little relevant content to justify the length of time that the programs consumed..."

- "I think the areas of disappointment have been the lack of follow through...the lack of continuity of the training with the strategic plan or goals of the organization, so that the training is not integral to the day-to-day operations but it's kind of a sidebar activity as opposed to reinforcing the goals and objectives in the organization."

One CEO offered a particularly moving comment related to the WLP professional's need to be open to change and willing to change themselves to remain credible in their organizations.

● "[WLP] professionals can become very comfortable with what they do and do not want to change any more than the people they are trying to change. They are resistant to doing anything different. When times begin to change, the people that are in the organizational development roles really have to be the leaders in facilitating change by changing themselves. When they tend to be no better in making that adjustment, they lose credibility."

A look at past CEO perceptions about the knowledge, skills, and abilities that WLP professionals should have possessed is important for understanding their current perceptions. Next, we summarize the key competencies that the CEOs we interviewed thought were essential for WLP professionals to possess today.

ESSENTIAL COMPETENCIES

1. Exposing new employees to the values, mission, and culture of the organization

● "I feel it is important the first day somebody walks in here that they are exposed to the values and the culture and the mission of the organization, and that should be a very important part of the WLP role."

2. Understanding the business needs of the organization

● "Understanding the role of operations, understanding the perceived efficiencies of today, understanding where we need to be tomorrow, and then assisting directors and man

● "I would say the key role is really understanding the organization and how it works."

3. Serving as an expert resource to others in the organization for human performance improvement efforts

● "To provide expert advice and support to operational managers who are involved in transforming the organization."

4. Serving as mentors, teachers, and facilitators of discussion about appropriate interventions to increase organizational performance

● "Facilitation of discussion of interventions that might need to be done with people or groups to effectuate different behavior patterns..."

● "I see [WLP professionals] as teachers, mentors, and as someone who would be attentive to the needs of the organization."

● "[WLP professionals] tend to be consultant/mentor types."

5. Creating an atmosphere where perpetually learning on the job is the norm

● "I would say the first role is to create an appreciation for the need to perpetually learn on the job so that it creates that climate."

6. Demonstrating flexibility to creatively solve organizational issues

● "...flexible enough, the flexibility being such that [WLP professionals] can roll with the punches..."

7. Helping others to identify needs and opportunities for improvement

● "Being able to assess real opportunities for improvements...differences between what we're doing now and how we're doing it."

8. Designing educational efforts that are relevant, meaningful, and productive

● "...assisting various directors and managers in creating a curriculum or a program that will assist our people in meeting challenges."

● "...to design the educational efforts in ways that are productive for the organization, productive meaning that [WLP professionals] adequately educate the workforce [in such a way] that the result is a change in behavior of the workforce."

9. Involvement in the selection process of new employees to hire the skill sets needed by the organization

● "Being more involved in the selection process of new employees to make sure that we're doing as good, job of screening as we can for the skill sets that we're looking for."

Many contributions that CEOs believed to be essential in this study were closely correlated with the perceptions of the CEOs from ASTD's competency study of WLP.

Despite their views about how WLP professionals should perform and the necessary knowledge, skills, and attitudes that they perceived to contribute to exceptional performance, CEOs did not see WLP as an island unto itself. They viewed the work of the WLP professional to be one of collaboration in which WLP professionals would ideally work with many organizational constituents to jointly solve organizational problems.

Some CEOs expressed their desire to meet with their WLP professionals to express their perceptions about the work that WLP professionals routinely perform. When your perceptions of the work you do are congruent with your CEO's perceptions, there is, according to these CEOs, an increased likelihood for success, a real opportunity to optimize performance, synergistic results, and overall, a more successful organization.

● "I think that matching perceptions increases the likelihood for success."

● "...the organization has an opportunity to really optimize its efforts and performance."

● "I think you develop some synergy that pays off for the organization...there's a definite synergy and a greater return on investment when perceptions of the CEO and the WLP professional are in sync."

Yet you must not become too complacent when your perceptions about your role *are* consistent with those of your CEO. Both you and your CEO might be setting your sights too low, allowing creativity to be suppressed, or simply doing the wrong things. Without some creative tension, a continuous, constructive questioning of your roles and competencies, you might meet some organizational objectives but might not achieve quantum leaps in productivity improvement.

- "We shouldn't always match [in our perceptions]...there should always be a dynamic tension there....If you match, then inventiveness sometimes is squelched."

- "It could be a situation where we all agree and we're doing exactly the wrong thing...agreement alone is not necessarily success. I'd rather work in a place where there is some dissonance where people are pushing the envelope and challenging each other's thinking....We might all be in agreement, holding hands, and walking each other down the wrong garden path."

- "Oftentimes I found that if you agree exactly you're setting your sights too low.... I would challenge that. I would try to lift my horizon a few centimeters off the future scale to see if we can really push it, expand the role or scope of it. It's almost not a good thing to be too much in tune together... you don't create synergy when everything is perfectly equal.

Unexpected Results

When questioned about how the seven WLP roles were being carried out in their organizations, CEOs provided comments that were somewhat unsettling. Some CEOs thought that all seven WLP roles belonged to someone other than the WLP professional. Others saw the roles of manager, analyst, intervention selector, intervention designer and developer, intervention implementor, and evaluator as roles that should be shared among WLP professionals, managers, and the organization's top leadership. No CEO thought that all seven WLP roles were exclusive to the WLP professional. The CEOs' comments support the view that everyone has a role to play in using learning to achieve results.

In Chapters 2 through 8 we'll discuss very specific information received from CEOs about the seven WLP roles, and each role will be discussed in complete detail. One bottom-line issue for you is that CEOs generally believe that managers are responsible for their own departments and should perform WLP roles most often. The perception was that those who are closest to the situation should be the ones who carry out the WLP roles. The matter in question is not whether the CEOs' perceptions are right or wrong, but why the perception exists that WLP professionals might not be fitting most appropriately and effectively into the mainstream of human performance improvement efforts of their organizations. At the same time, however, many WLP roles were inherent in job descriptions of WLP professionals:

- ❐ Plans, organizes, directs, and supervises management and staff development
- ❐ Selects WLP staff and evaluates their performance
- ❐ Develops goals and objectives, establishes and implements policies
- ❐ Provides leadership and strategic oversight

The job descriptions that we reviewed for most WLP professionals also indicated that they should:

- ❐ Assess education needs
- ❐ Design and develop course materials
- ❐ Select appropriate courses
- ❐ Conduct training programs
- ❐ Evaluate the effectiveness of all learning programs

We'll provide greater detail about the job descriptions when we treat each of the seven WLP roles in Chapters 2 through 8. But if, for whatever reason, you do not carry out the roles formalized in the job descriptions, you will create ambivalence about your professional roles. Perhaps of even greater concern was the notion that the current WLP professionals were not viewing themselves in the role of the WLP professional. Many continue to focus on carrying out the activity of training without focusing on desired results. That sometimes happens because they see training as their only role. It can also happen if they are asked to provide training but are not given the time to analyze the underlying problem they are supposed to address.

The accuracy of your job description is another issue that requires your careful attention. Many job descriptions we analyzed for this study were outdated. As mentioned above, most CEOs thought that either the seven WLP roles belonged to someone other than the WLP professional or that the roles were not exclusive to the WLP professional. Yet, the duties related to all seven WLP roles were found in the job descriptions. The fact that many job descriptions had not been updated regularly might have been an indication that they did not reflect the current situation of the WLP professionals in the organizations we reviewed. It might also indicate that WLP professionals are not always as proactive as they need to be to update their job descriptions or seize a new role.

Why Should You Care About Your CEO's Opinions and Perceptions?

We hope that, as you read this chapter, you began to see why it might be important to care about your CEO's opinions and perceptions about your work as a WLP professional. We summarize now for you some thoughts about the reasons why you should care about what your CEO thinks about WLP and the work you do. We also provide some suggestions about what you might do with this information now that it's been brought to light.

REASON #1: CARING ABOUT YOUR CEO'S PERCEPTIONS OF WLP MAKES GOOD BUSINESS SENSE

There is little doubt that CEOs are passionate about the financial success of their organizations. The tenets of WLP can assist an organization in addressing very real financial bottom-line results. However, as you and your organizational colleagues vie for additional financial resources to improve operations of the various disciplines in your organization, there is greater scrutiny of those requests for additional resources. Unless you are able to demonstrate in measurable terms how the additional resources will add value to the organization and its bottom-line, the likelihood of receiving those resources is weak at best. In fact, if you are unable to demonstrate how vital your role is, you may be considered expendable. We've presented a great deal of information in this chapter about globalization, technology, meeting customer expectations, new skill requirements for you and your stakeholders, and managing the knowledge capital of your organization. If you haven't partnered with your CEO and other key organizational players so that they know why and how resources will be used, your chances of obtaining future resources will be greatly diminished. Additional resources simply won't be a reality without your CEO's support.

REASON #2: NOT KNOWING WHAT YOUR CEO THINKS COULD BE DANGEROUS

In the opening of this chapter we asked you to think about how much time and effort you've put into discovering your CEO's perceptions about workplace learning and performance. If you are assuming that you are meeting his or her needs, assuming that all is right with the world of workplace learning in your organization, you've potentially placed yourself in a dangerous position. We were very surprised by some of the comments that the CEOs we interviewed made about our profession. One example is how much importance the CEOs placed on WLP playing a significant part in recruiting and retaining a competent workforce. We strongly suggest that you don't make any assumptions when it comes to what might be on the mind of your CEO about workplace learning and performance. With that thought in mind we recommend that you:

- ❏ Take proactive steps to advance the knowledge of your CEO and managers throughout your organization about your professional roles and the WLP field.

- ❏ Become a partner with the CEO, other leaders, and managers. The more they know about what you do and can do for the organization from a workplace learning and performance standpoint, the more credibility you will gain, leading to the retention of much needed resources to advance WLP practices in your organization.

❐ Reflect on contributions that the WLP function makes to your organization and tell CEOs and others about those contributions.

❐ Make a point of visiting your CEO regularly if at all possible. Your CEO might not be fully recognizing the many benefits you can provide to your organization while carrying out your professional roles.

REASON #3: CEOS' OPINIONS CAN BE CHANGED OVER TIME

The third reason why you should care about your CEO's opinions and perceptions is that his or her opinions can be changed! A great opportunity exists for you to play a major part in shaping opinions. The current thinking about WLP is that it is a fully strategic part of any organization. Unfortunately, simply "thinking" about WLP's place in your organization won't bring about any positive change. This is where you as the WLP professional need to step in and attempt to make some shifts in the culture of your organization. If you're immersed in a culture where your work is viewed as functional rather than strategic, one driven by "fire-fighting" rather than supporting achievement of strategic goals, limited to serving survival needs instead of viewing responsibilities in terms of the entire organization—then some changes are definitely in order. We suggest you go right to the top of the organization to begin the change process.

Remember the influence and power your CEO has to restrict, modify, or expand the scope of your responsibility. Remember also that your CEO can have a tremendous amount of influence in clearing the path for you to carry out your new WLP roles as well as helping you to instill a sense of shared responsibility for increased organizational performance with your stakeholders. Until you know clearly how your CEO perceives the work you do, you can't even begin to start working toward making the transition from training or HRD to WLP. This is one reason why it is vitally important to know your CEO's opinions and perceptions about the work that you do in your organization.

REASON #4: CEOS' PERCEPTIONS CAN BE CHANGED WITH INCREASED AWARENESS OF WLP

Your CEO may need to be informed and educated about what WLP is and how it can work in creating outstanding performance throughout your organization. CEOs may need to be attuned to the evolving nature of the WLP field. This is another opportunity for you to create meaningful dialogue with your CEO to help fully recognize just how important and necessary the work you perform is to your organization. Many CEOs said they had been involved and wanted to continue to be involved in their organization's performance improvement efforts. CEOs want personal interaction.

More importantly, your CEO is most likely talking and listening to other employees in the organization about WLP, thereby potentially shaping opinions based on other employees' perceptions. Is your voice as the WLP professional being heard at the highest level of your organization, or are others speaking on your behalf? Partnering with your CEO, other organizational leaders, and managers can have a powerful, positive influence on your future success. WLP professionals do not need to become corporate rebels to cause positive change, but they do need to stand by their principles, be tenacious, and creatively find ways to influence the decision makers in their organizations.[15]

Importance of Talking with CEOs

A future search conference held by thought leaders of the American Society for Training and Development in June 2001 underscored the importance of talking to CEOs about Workplace Learning and Performance and of finding ways to relate WLP to methods of increasing shareholder value. (A *future search conference* is a platform to bring together experts to talk about a topic and is fully described in Weisbord and Janoff's book, *Future Search*.[16]) Among the many topics explored by the thought leaders was "what's inside the head of the CEO." To answer that question, the thought leaders drew a picture of a CEO's head on a flipchart and identified what they believed would be four major areas of concern to CEOs—financial performance, operating excellence, employee focus, and customer satisfaction.[17] To that they contrasted topics they thought would be in the head of training or WLP professionals—which they listed on the flipchart as social responsibility, training programs, work/life balance, leveraging technology, and managing knowledge. The point of the exercise was to emphasize that real communication begins with common ground, and it is the responsibility of WLP professionals to establish that ground.

They also offered a list of sixteen action steps that WLP professionals could take to help establish that common ground. Among those action steps were:

1. Be proactive.
2. Demonstrate value-added in terms that relate to your CEO's agenda.
3. Develop your social intelligence.

Getting inside the CEO's (or anyone else's) head requires empathy and nonjudgmental posture. The article about that future search conference is significant because it underscores that thought leaders in the WLP field have been thinking hard about how to reach the CEO, a chief stakeholder in WLP efforts.

Self-Reflection

We've presented some insights from CEOs that, we hope, caused you to reflect on your own situation. Specifically, we addressed some competencies that CEOs perceived as important for WLP professionals to possess and the potential contributions you can make in helping to lead your organization to peak success. How does your opinion of the recommended competencies and contributions compare with the CEOs' opinions presented in this chapter? Exhibit 1-7 represents a worksheet for you to complete to compare your perceptions of your competencies and contributions to your organization to the CEO's views.

Reality Check

Why not schedule a visit with your CEO? Compare your perceptions of the suggested competencies from the CEO informa-

(*text continues on page 44*)

EXHIBIT 1-7. SELF-REFLECTION WORKSHEET: COMPARE YOUR PERCEPTIONS OF COMPETENCIES AND CONTRIBUTIONS TO CEOS' PERCEPTIONS

Directions: Use this worksheet to do some self-reflection. For each competency listed in the left column below, write your perceptions about what it means in the center column. Then write in the far right column your own perceptions about the contributions you make to your organization in that area. There are no "right" or "wrong" answers in any absolute sense.

Competencies	My Perceptions	My Contribution
Business Competencies		
Leadership Competencies		
Analytical Competencies		
Technological Competencies		
Technical Competencies		
Interpersonal Competencies		

EXHIBIT 1-8. REALITY CHECK

Directions: Using your completed self-reflection worksheet as your guide, make an appointment with your CEO and ask your CEO to comment about his or her perceptions of the six major competencies* appearing in the left column below. Use this blank worksheet to record your CEO's perceptions. Then compare the perceptions of other CEOs, offered in this chapter, to your CEO's perceptions about the competencies that he or she perceives to be important.

Ask your CEO what (business, leadership, analytical, technological, technical, and interpersonal) competencies he or she thinks you should possess to be most effective as a WLP professional. Record the responses on this worksheet. (*Note:* We've provided you with some examples of suggested competencies to prompt your CEO in the event he or she is unsure of what the competency areas might include.)

Business Competencies – Business knowledge, industry awareness, cost/benefit analysis, identifying critical business issues, and evaluation of results against organizational goals.

Leadership Competencies – Leading, coaching, and influencing others to achieve desired goals, visioning, ethical modeling, building ownership for workplace improvement initiatives.

Analytical Competencies – Analyzing performance data, competency identification, intervention selection, performance gap analysis, evaluating and improving interventions before and during implementation.

Technological Competencies – Distance education, electronic performance support systems, computer-mediated communication, understanding and applying existing, new, or emerging technology.

Technical Competencies – Understanding how adults learn, facilitation skills, feedback skills, designing and developing surveys, monitoring intervention.

SOURCE: Competencies are taken from William J. Rothwell, Ethan S. Sanders, and Jeffrey G. Soper. *ASTD Models for Workplace Learning and Performance: Roles, Competencies, and Outputs* (Alexandria, Va.: The American Society for Training and Development, 1999). Used by permission of ASTD. All rights reserved.

tion provided in this chapter with the comments you receive from your CEO. Exhibit 1-8 is a worksheet you can take to your meeting with your CEO to record his or her thoughts, opinions, and perceptions of competencies that an outstanding WLP professional needs.

Summary

The purpose of the chapter was to help you understand the importance of knowing your CEO's thoughts, opinions, and perceptions about the field of workplace learning and performance, and the work you perform as a workplace learning and performance professional. The distinguishing characteristics of training, human resource development (HRD), and workplace learning and performance (WLP) were presented for you to think about how you might begin making a transition from training or HRD to WLP. Key comparisons between the nature of learning in organizations and the relationships between the practitioner from the training, HRD, and WLP perspectives were presented. The key points of three research studies were discussed, highlighting the roles, competencies, and outputs of workplace learning and performance and CEO-perceived business competencies. Suggestions for how WLP professionals might contribute to meeting business challenges were also offered. Finally, reasons why WLP professionals should care about their CEO's thoughts, opinions, and perceptions were addressed.

CHAPTER 2

The Manager Role—The CEO Perspective

> I would think [WLP professionals] should be champions in unleashing the potential of our people as opposed to harnessing the potential of our people. There are plenty of management people in the company that will harness what's there. I think there are all too few that unleash the potential and I would think the learning officers are those that should be unleashing the potential of people.
>
> A CEO INTERVIEWED FOR THIS BOOK

Management in any form is undoubtedly a difficult realm. Managers are forced to struggle to please the people both above and below them on the organization chart, often simultaneously. The manager is typically the person responsible for activities associated with finding employees (recruitment, selection), encouraging employees to work (using pay raises, promotions, incentives, recognition), and moving employees out of structured, budgeted positions as necessary (through downsizing, firing, outplacement). The very mention of the word "manager" often conjures up a range of memories and associations—and, admittedly, some of those are negative. You can probably think of a manager in your past whose impact on your work and life was less than desirable just as you can probably think of managers whose impact was favorable.

While it is true that poor managers do exist in most organizations, excellent ones exist as well. So, what helps to form perceptions, in simple terms, about what makes a good manager or a bad manager? There are many schools of thought about management that have evolved. There are also various management styles suggested by researchers on the topic. We'll briefly discuss some of these issues a little later in this chapter. Although the focus of this chapter is on the WLP role of manager, it seems appropriate to begin by sharing some of the history of general management. Examining how prevailing views about managerial roles have evolved over time should help you make connections about how you fit into the overall organizational picture in enacting the WLP role as manager.

Personal opinions about managers are, of course, subjectively based on past experiences. You may experience a manager as "good" or "bad" because you hold certain attitudes that shape your opinions about what you *think* makes a good or bad manager. Your perceptions could have been formed by the way you have seen managers behave in certain situations, and whether that behavior matched your idea of what was right. It could have been something as simple as whether your personality matched the personality of your manager. The environment in which you were brought up may even have shaped your perceptions. In any case, the perceptions you possess about managers didn't just spontaneously generate—they were formed over time by your experiences. The same is true of CEO perceptions of the WLP role of manager. For example, here's a view expressed by one CEO who suggested that current perceptions of roles are formed from experience:

● "You've really described a traditional management role. I would say from my experience that in various locations throughout an organization like mine that there are people that fit that description, but that's typically where there's a larger cadre of people who are involved in training and development. I don't believe that my organization development leader plays that role particularly."

As mentioned in Chapter 1, our research indicated that the perceptions CEOs held about the WLP field did change over time. If these perceptions can change, how can we help to shape them, especially about the work that we perform in the WLP role as manager? We believe the first portion of the answer lies in correctly identifying the nature of the role or the duties inherent in the role.

How we can effect changes in others' perceptions of the work of WLP professionals enacting the role of manager lies in demonstrating competency in performing the expected duties. Possessing the ability to perform these duties effectively is by far the most critical component in the larger scheme of WLP professionals enacting the manager's role. It is through knowing, understanding, and practicing competent behavior that you can catch "the eye of the beholder"—including CEOs. Competence—like truth, beauty, and contact lenses—is in the eye of the beholder.[1] One CEO was not convinced that the definition of the WLP role of manager really fit, based on the CEO's past and current perceptions of the role. However, the following comment lends credence to the notion that if a WLP professional enacting the manager role competently carries out that role, there is a very good chance that perceptions can be changed:

- "I'm going to be real straight with you on this. The managing function [for WLP professionals] as described takes very high skills and is a very key position or it could be perceived as a key position because you're talking about strategic planning...it would be very hard to fill that role using that job description."

With this thought in mind, we will carefully present the competencies necessary for WLP professionals enacting the manager role, competencies that—if demonstrated appropriately—are sure to get you noticed by others so that their perceptions can be shaped in positive ways.

The final portion of the answer lies in arming yourself with the knowledge of how others perceive the WLP professional who enacts the manager role. This knowledge will allow you to focus on developing the competencies that may not be your strong suit and capitalize on those competencies in which you currently excel. We will highlight the perceptions of CEOs who shared their thoughts about the WLP field. Specifically, we'll focus throughout this chapter on the CEOs' perceptions about the WLP professional who enacts the manager role. For example, one CEO offered this opinion about the importance of appropriately managing your organization's resources:

● "In order to maximize utilization of resources, my perception is that you need someone that can manage whatever resources you have....In our case we have a multiperson training function that goes across all areas."

Although this is only one quote from one CEO, it still provides some clues as to what was on this CEO's mind when thinking about the WLP professional who enacts the manager role. There are many clues that are communicated to you regularly about your role as WLP professional when you enact the manager role. You need to zero in on the clues and cues. You need to listen carefully for them and reflect on how you might use the information to help you develop yourself.

Throughout this book, we encourage you to reflect on how competent you perceive yourself to be in performing WLP roles. Further, we will challenge you to seek the opinions of other organizational members about your work so that you can successfully meet your stakeholders' needs and expectations.

The WLP Role of Manager

Managers have changed the way they operate over the course of many centuries. Most, if not all, of the changes have been improvements over what existed before. The WLP role of manager has undergone similar changes. After all, someone had to teach the following generations how to continue with, and improve upon, tradition. But the WLP role of manager in modern times developed in a blink of an eye compared to the role of the general manager. Forty years is hardly a blip on the overall evolutionary timeline. Yet, in that very short period, much has changed for those WLP professionals who must enact the manager role. These changes have been, for the most part, in the scope of the competencies required to best enact the role.

First, let's look at a recent description of the functions that any manager should perform. They are:

- ❑ Planning (establishing goals)
- ❑ Organizing (determining what activities need to be completed to accomplish those goals)
- ❑ Leading (ensuring that the right people are on the job with appropriate skills, and motivating them to levels of high productivity)
- ❑ Controlling (monitoring activities to ensure that goals are met).[2]

This description of what managers do has not changed significantly in 150 years. One CEO's perception of the traditional manager role was very similar to the functions that any manager should perform:

- ● "[The manager] needs to set direction, enlist and motivate a support team, and to make it happen."

When Leonard Nadler completed his doctoral dissertation in 1962, the word "role" was not used. Nadler described what we now call roles as tasks. It wasn't until the late 1960s and early 1970s that the word "role" started to appear in the literature of the field. Still, there are surprising similarities to the training director tasks that Nadler described and the definition of what a typical manager is expected to do today. Let's compare a few definitions. Key terms related to the traditional duties of the manager are highlighted.

In 1962, Nadler suggested that training directors should perform five tasks:

1. Obtain and *control* a budget
2. Choose, purchase, and evaluate training equipment
3. Provide *leadership* and *supervision* to training staff
4. *Determine* needs, plan curriculum, conduct training, and evaluation
5. Obtain and share information concerning training planned and accomplished.[3]

In 1978, Pinto and Walker described the role of the manager of the training and development function as: preparing budgets, *organizing*, staffing, *making formal presentations of plans, maintaining information on costs, supervising the work of others,* and *projecting future needs.*[4] By 1983, McLagan had defined the manager of training and development role as *planning, organizing,* staffing, *controlling* training and development operations or training and development projects, and linking training and development operations with other organizational units.[5] The manager role became less specific with McLagan and Suhadolnick's *Models for HRD Practice* (1989). They defined the HRD manager role as supporting and leading a group's work and linking that work with the total organization.[6] The most recent definition, the definition of the WLP professional who enacts the manager role, includes all the key words from the traditional manager definition. The WLP manager *"plans, organizes,* schedules, *monitors,* and *leads* the work of individuals and groups to attain desired results; facilitates the strategic plan; ensures that WLP is aligned with organizational needs and plans; and ensures that the administrative requirements of the function are accomplished."[7]

Although in a few examples mentioned above the words used to describe the duties of a manager of the training, HRD, or WLP functions are not exact matches with the words used to describe typical manager duties, the intent is quite similar. For example, in the definition of the WLP role of manager, the word "monitor" is used in place of "control." It was not at all surprising that some CEOs had a difficult time distinguishing the duties of the WLP manager from the duties of the typical manager.

● "I mean the description you gave [of the WLP professional enacting the manager role] could be equally well applied to any manager and certainly that would be an expectation of a manager almost wherever that manager was, including in this [training] department."[8]

It is evident that the duties of most managers are similar. So, what sets the WLP professional who enacts the manager role apart from other managers? We believe that the answer lies in the competencies needed to enact the role.

Why Is the Manager Role Important?

According to *ASTD Models for Workplace Learning and Performance*,[9] the WLP professional enacting the manager role "plans, organizes, schedules, monitors, and leads the work of individuals and groups to attain desired results; facilitates the strategic plan; ensures that WLP is aligned with organizational needs and plans; and ensures that accomplishment of the administrative requirements of the function." Those who carry out the role sometimes bear job titles such as Training Director, Director of Human Resource Development, Chief Learning Officer, Chief Knowledge Officer, Vice President of Organizational Effectiveness, or President of the Corporate University. They may also bear such function-specific titles as Director of Technical Training, Vice President of Management Development, Manager of Leadership Development, or Sales Training Director.

The role is important for two major reasons:

1. WLP professionals who enact this role integrate all the other roles. Someone must manage, coordinate, and orchestrate the efforts of analysts, intervention selectors, intervention designers and developers, intervention implementors, change leaders, and evaluators. The manager role does that, overseeing that all roles work together effectively.

2. WLP professionals enacting the role ensure that WLP efforts (such as the operations of the training department, the organizational effectiveness or OD group, or interventions) are vertically aligned to the strategic objectives and business needs of the organization and that all WLP interventions are horizontally aligned with each other.

Of course, the manager role of WLP shares many activities and responsibilities in common with other management positions. For example, it is the manager who will be asked for a plan for the organization's WLP efforts, a budget for the department or interventions, and staffing decisions for WLP-related jobs. But the role is unique in that incumbents should possess much knowledge about how people learn in workplace settings and can integrate those learning approaches to achieve improvements in individual, group, and organizational performance. A strategic failure by the manager of WLP will lead to the elimination of the WLP function or to staffing reductions, just as a strategic failure by a CEO may lead an organization into bankruptcy or widespread downsizing.

The scope of this role can be enormous. If you think of what an orchestra conductor does, you begin to get the idea. The manager of WLP brings together and facilitates all the people, methods of learning, and objectives for learning to achieve a unified vision of how learning can contribute to enhanced organizational productivity and competitiveness. He or she examines the full scope of means by which people can learn in an organization and then works with others to craft a strategy to direct individual, group, and organizational learning to garner improvements in performance. He or she also focuses on two kinds of learning: one that has to do with passing down the lessons of organizational experience; a second that has to do with helping others generate new knowledge, new information, and creative new approaches to gain competitive advantage.

At this point, a word is in order about what is meant by the phrase *learning intervention*. After all, managers of WLP must possess keen awareness of all the ways by which people can learn and then help organizational decision makers use those methods effectively to gain competitive advantage and breakthrough improvements in productivity. Say the phrase *workplace learning*, and many traditionalists will immediately think you mean off-the-job training—and particularly classroom-based instruction, though increasing numbers will also think of e-learning.

But the reality is that workplace learning has much broader meaning. For one thing, most workplace learning occurs on the job. It can—and usually does—happen in real time. People face a problem, and they immediately set out to find a solution. They are learning in this process. Alternatively, they have a creative thought about a new way to do something and set out to collect information or experiment. As they do that, they also learn.

The point is that workplace learning occurs in many ways and contexts. People learn from those with whom (and for whom) they work. For instance, the personalities of their supervisors may differ and may, in turn, sensitize people to what they pay attention to. People learn from the customers they serve. They learn from the work they do and the projects to which they are assigned. They learn from the timeframes on which they work, such as long-term and short-term projects. They learn from the geographical locations with which they must deal and the different national or ethnic cultures with which they come into contact. Examples of that might include job rotations or international assignments. They learn from the assignments they do—such as starting up something new, shutting down something old, turning around failing efforts, or overcoming complacency with successful efforts. They learn from the working styles with which they come into contact. And, of course, the focus of such learning can be individuals, groups, the organization, and even the organization and such stakeholders as customers, suppliers, distributors, wholesalers, competitors, and other groups.

The phrase *learning intervention* refers broadly to all the means by which people can learn. While the word *intervention* implies that such learning is planned for a reason, the fact is that people can also learn in unplanned ways (*informal learning*) and as a byproduct of their work experiences (*incidental learning*). Indeed, experience itself is prized precisely because people learned something from it.

The point to all this is that the WLP professional enacting the manager role must think beyond single learning solutions (such as classroom training or even e-learning) to create a comprehensive plan for change through learning. That is not to diminish the value of training or e-learning. Instead, it speaks for a need to think in broader terms about who learns in organizations, what they learn, when they learn, where they learn, why they learn, how they learn, and how that learning can be turned to individual, group, and organizational advantage.

Learning efforts designed to solve human performance problems or seize human performance improvement opportunities are therefore called learning interventions. Classroom training is one example. But there are many others. A job rotation can be a learning intervention.

An internship can be a learning intervention. On-the-job training or coaching can be a learning intervention. In short, any venue by which people learn can be regarded as a learning intervention.

The challenge facing WLP professionals who enact the manager role is to work with the organization's decision makers to bring all these learning interventions together.

CEO-Identified Competencies for the Role of Manager

We all possess competencies. Most competencies developed through our life experiences and include knowledge, skills, values, personality traits, motivation levels, and attitudes. When you enact the WLP role as manager, you use your competencies to enact many behaviors in the workplace. These behaviors produce outputs that you provide to others. Simply possessing competencies, however, is not enough. You must possess the *correct* competencies to achieve results against the backdrop of corporate culture. It's the quality of outcomes, and the perceptions of those who receive them that lead to results. We firmly believe that competence is the key to future success, and a focus on managing and developing competencies offers an organization its only real sustainable competitive advantage.

So, how do you determine which competencies are essential for successful performance in the WLP role as manager? No one can claim to know with absolute certainty. It is impossible to foresee every circumstance related to WLP management. Predicting with certainty the outcomes related to the competencies essential for enacting the WLP role of manager would prove even more difficult. Still, numerous competency studies have helped to shape the current thinking about the necessary competencies most often associated with the WLP role of manager.

Competencies for all seven of the WLP roles can be arranged into six categories: analytical, business, interpersonal, leadership, technical, and technological competencies.[10]

Within the major competency groupings, there are competencies thought to be specific to the WLP role of manager.

It should come as no surprise that the manager role is by far one of the most important roles played by the WLP professional. This role is listed first for a very good reason—it encompasses most of the competencies related to the other six WLP roles. It is not only critical that WLP professionals enacting the manager role possess the competencies listed below; they must also understand how to integrate them with the people who perform WLP work under their leadership.

ANALYTICAL COMPETENCIES

Analytical competencies are comparable to the creation of new understandings or methods through the synthesis of multiple ideas, processes, and data. There are fourteen analytical competencies inherent in the WLP role of manager. According to *ASTD Models for Workplace Learning and Performance*, the fourteen analytical competencies associated with the manager role include analytical thinking, career development theory and application, competency identification, knowledge management, organization development theory and application, performance gap analysis, performance theory, process consultation, reward system theory and application, social awareness, staff selection theory and application, standards identification, systems thinking, and work environment analysis. For the full definitions of these competencies, see the ASTD study.[11]

The ability to think both logically and serially is important for those who enact the WLP role of manager. These abilities help those enacting the role to demonstrate a superior level of managerial competence. *Analytical competence* means thinking ahead about the logical steps in a process, anticipating obstacles, and analyzing what needs to be done before it happens. One CEO had a good sense for what was expected of the WLP professional in this regard:

● "What we need to do is anticipate change and to the extent that someone in the educational or developmental field has that dimension, their value would increase tremendously.... It's about understanding the mission of the business but it's a little broader than that. [The WLP professional who enacts the manager role] almost has to anticipate the change and position our organization to be there at the right time. So there's a bit of mysticism involved as well, but I think it's an important component."

WLP professionals who enact the manager role also need to think about the end results of their efforts to improve the performance of an organization. Obviously, CEOs don't want their organizations' resources to be used frivolously; their focus is sure to be on achievement-oriented learning. CEOs also realize that the transfer and retention of learning are critically important components. As one explained:

● "[WLP professionals who enact the role of manager] need to have a good feel on what I call the usefulness of the training. Is this something that can be used and applied immediately? So, I want somebody that understands that [training's usefulness] and gives [the learners] only what they can use. And you don't have to dilute the training with a lot of things that take time, cost money, and really get in the way of applying what's useful because you have to ask yourself—how much do you retain from a training session? They go to a two-week training session and retention is pretty high the first week, but in six months, how much of what you learned have you retained and can you use? I want somebody to have an appreciation of that and understand efficiency of training. That has to be front and center in the mind of [the WLP professional enacting the manager role]."

Analytical competence can also be demonstrated when workplace learning is prioritized according to the needs of the organization.

● "Understanding where we're going strategically, making sure we have the skills assessment, that we prioritize the ones that will best impact us, and, most important, making sure that we have an environment where [the training] can be utilized."

The concept of organizational culture remained prevalent throughout our research. The culture of an organization can be likened to its personality. It defines the way people in organizations behave, what motivates them, and helps to define the values within the organization and its people. It is safe to say that an organization's culture is positive if it helps to improve the organization, and negative if it hinders success. WLP professionals who enact the manager role should look beyond the surface of the organization and immerse themselves in the strategic direction of the organization. One CEO emphasized how important it is for WLP professionals enacting the manager role to possess an intimate knowledge of a company's culture:

- "[WLP managers have] got to understand the company's culture...what the company is really all about."

Many CEOs spoke about understanding what the company is all about in slightly different ways. As one noted:

- "Understanding what people *need* to be able to perform their jobs and that's different from what people *want*."

This comment is right on the mark. Those WLP professionals who successfully enact the manager role need to distinguish between "felt needs" and "real needs":

- "The ability that they have to have is to do an accurate and honest assessment of what the capabilities are of the organization they're a part of."

This CEO seems to be talking about lip service or the "yes-man" attitude. It is important to tell CEOs what they need to hear about the capabilities of the people in the organization rather than what you think they want to hear. WLP professionals who enact the manager role should do that with everyone. As one CEO remarked:

- "I think they have to be politicians to some extent so they can talk with different department heads and coordinate the training activities and make sure they're getting everything we want out of a training program...and somehow have whatever efficiencies we can have as far as cross-training."

Those who enact the WLP role of manager are forced to "be politicians"; part of their job entails earning the respect of others in the organization so that promises can be made about the improved performance of the organization. This book is, in part, based on the assertion that knowing what others think about the work you perform can contribute to organizational success and, subsequently, to your own success.

● "They've got to be good at developing systems that are easily understood by non-HR people."

This aspect of analytical competency sounds quite simple, but herein lies a complex and crucial part of successfully enacting the WLP role of manager. Regardless of the depth and breadth of learning interventions you might recommend, or the instructions you might provide as a manager to your staff, everyone involved must easily understand your words. If people don't understand how learning is related to their workplace practices, or don't understand the outcomes they need to produce, little to no transfer of learning can take place. WLP professionals who enact the manager role should possess and use their analytical abilities to lead the workplace learning and performance effort.

CEOs indicate that those who enact the WLP role of manager need to possess analytical competencies to be personally and organizationally successful. After re-examining the analytical competencies associated with the WLP role of manager, use Appendix C-1 to analyze your own analytical competencies. Find your areas of strength and those analytical competencies in which you think you can or should improve. This self-reflection can be vastly helpful in fine-tuning your strengths and in building your competencies where you are not so strong.

BUSINESS COMPETENCIES

Business competencies are associated with the understanding of organizations as systems, and of the processes, decision criteria, issues, and implications of the operational units of non-WLP aspects of the organization.[12] According to *ASTD Models for Workplace Learning and Performance*, the eleven business competencies associated with the manager role include ability to see the "big picture," business knowledge, cost/benefit analysis, evaluation of results against organizational goals, identification of critical business issues, industry awareness, knowledge capital, negotiating/contracting, outsourcing management, project management, and quality implications.[13]

Business competency goes far beyond the ability to read a balance sheet, an income statement, or a budget variance report. Those aspects of business knowledge are considered today to be almost fundamental management requirements. Some CEOs expressed that this type of knowledge is a basic WLP manager competency.

● "They have to have some general business skills where they need to understand what their budget is and how do I manage this budget.... They have to have a good sense of what it costs to actually do in-depth training programs."

CEOs want you, if you are enacting the WLP role of manager, to not only think strategically but become an active member of the strategic planning process as well. To be an active member of the strategic planning process, you must know the business your organization is in—and know it well.

● "I think the main ability is to align the training and development activities with the strategy of the organization."

● "Number one is to be an integral part of the strategic plan in the company, understanding what the business needs are, [and] understanding our business strategy and how training can affect it."

This CEO continued:

● "Number two, make sure there's a good skills analysis done, understanding where the priorities of where we're the weakest. A lot of times we have five programs and even if they match what we're doing, we don't always set them up or make sure that the weakest areas are hit with priority."

Other CEOs reinforced the notion that, without a solid understanding of the business, a WLP professional who enacts the manager role would be hard-pressed to determine the most appropriate and effective direction the workplace learning effort needs to take. As they explained:

● "Well, I think it's very important that [WLP managers] truly understand the requirements of business. It's hard to know what kind of training and people development you need to do without understanding the business."

- "[WLP managers] have to understand what we do, what our strategy is, what our core competencies are, [and] what makes a successful company. The person needs to understand the business."

- "They've got to understand the business that their specific company is in...they have to understand what makes that business tick, how it makes money, what's important, and what's not important."

- "Understanding how the organization works and how it currently transfers knowledge and information throughout the organization."

- "I think also if you're talking about working in a business environment, whether it be for profit or not-for-profit, the other issue is that [WLP] people need to have an appreciation for the business, an understanding of what drives the business, an understanding of what are the primary issues in the business—in order to be able to tailor something appropriate. I think to really be an effective contributor, [a WLP professional] needs to understand the business and be able to think through understanding the business's mission and objectives, and understand the systems that the business has in place to deliver its products or service, to really be able to have a feel for what's needed in the organization."

- "The first thing they really need to understand is the business that we're in and understand what the talent needs of the organization and business are."

Business competencies appear to be high on a CEO's list of important competencies needed by those enacting the WLP role of manager. Do you know how to measure the knowledge capital of your organization? What is its value? Are you able to perform a thorough cost/benefit analysis and place a financial or nonfinancial value on the efforts of your WLP staff members and their contributions? How well do you know the business of your organization and the business of your competitors? It is imperative to find out exactly what your CEO expects you to know about the business of your organization; this is most effectively achieved by *asking* your CEO. You need to be aware that your CEO could very well be thinking this: "I know that the WLP manager should be a part of strategic planning...but how can he or she be a part of the process if I'm not sure that this person really understands the business and the implications of business?"

Use Appendix C-2 to assess your own business competencies. If you possess most or all of the business competencies, it is important to make this evident to your CEO. If you believe you possess few business competencies, it is still important to be honest about your business competency level with your CEO. Frankly, it would be impractical not to be up-front and honest about your level of business competence. After all, business competencies can be learned. Ask your CEO what he or she expects from you from a business competency standpoint, and then build the competencies as best you can. There are, of course, many ways to do that. You can choose a mentor (or mentors) and ask advice. You can participate in short-term task force assignments and long-term job rotations. Indeed, knowing how to build competencies is something you should already know something about. So, "physician, heal thyself."

INTERPERSONAL COMPETENCIES

Interpersonal competencies are associated with the understanding and application of methods that produce effective interactions of people and groups.[14] According to *ASTD Models for Workplace Learning and Performance*, the five interpersonal competencies associated with the manager role include communication, communication networks, consulting, coping skills, and interpersonal relationship building.[15]

The importance of interpersonal competencies cannot be overstated. Those who enact the WLP role of manager spend about 80 percent of their time communicating with others. At the heart of managing interactions among people and groups is the ability to communicate effectively. Communication permeates virtually every management function. For example, when managers carry out the planning function, they must gather information, write plans and reports, and meet with other organizational members to explain the plan. When managers lead, they must communicate with staff members to motivate them to perform the work of the WLP function. Interpersonal skills are built into every managerial activity. CEOs were quite direct in communicating their thoughts about how important effective interpersonal skills were to those enacting the WLP role of manager in their organizations.

- "It begins with communication. Someone who doesn't possess or can't develop good communication skills in listening, speaking, and writing would not be effective in the [WLP manager] role."

- "The ability to effectively communicate I feel is the number one attribute that [WLP managers] have to have. You can have an individual who can't teach or communicate with an individual but who can be a very powerful technologist— [but] that doesn't get the job done."

- "The first trait that [WLP professionals enacting the manager role] need is the ability to be a team player, and to understand that they are here to support the organization.... I mean the person has got to have a disposition whereby they can get a charge or a thrill out of developing effective systems that somebody else will probably roll out and implement."

Some CEOs thought that interpersonal skills were very much about sharing, rather than about speaking or writing. These CEOs viewed interpersonal skills as part of a process in which information is exchanged and understood for the purpose of influencing behavior.

- "I think they've got be good teacher-communicators. They've got to be able to get the message across, tailor it to the specific audience, and be effective in that manner."

- "It's strong engagement skills so that the relationships with the business leaders and the mutual discovery of weaknesses—how those can be offset and augmented through learning experiences. So [you need] strong engagement skills and then someone who's very knowledgeable about their field."

It might be the desire on the part of WLP professionals enacting the manager role to share understanding that will motivate employees to perform optimally.

● "I think they need good communication skills. They need to be able to sit down and talk with people, understand what their problems are, [and] understand the best way to develop some type of training program to fit their needs."

Use Appendix C-3 to evaluate your own interpersonal competencies. Think about ways you might improve these competencies. Then write your plan in the space provided.

LEADERSHIP COMPETENCIES

Leadership competencies are associated with influencing, enabling, or inspiring others to act.[16] There are six competencies relevant to leadership. According to *ASTD Models for Workplace Learning and Performance*, the seven leadership competencies associated with the manager role include buy-in/advocacy, diversity awareness, ethics modeling, goal implementation, group dynamics, leadership, and visioning.[17]

The best WLP professionals who enact the manager role use influence to improve the functioning of their organizations. More than influencing is required, however. A good leader will not so much empower as *enable* the people in the organization to excel. Leadership occurs between people (it is a relationship), involves the use of positive influence, and is used to attain goals. The CEOs we spoke with had a keen sense of what they expected from their WLP professionals as leaders.

● "You need somebody who has general leadership skills, who is entrepreneurial in nature, who has a good business sense, particularly as to the company's needs, and then [who has] good interpersonal skills—and I would also say good administrative skills."

Influencing and enabling others to grow, develop, and produce effective results is not an easy task. It takes a great deal of energy, as one CEO very poignantly put it:

● "One of the most important attributes that a [WLP manager] has to have is energy. If you're growing fast as a company, you devote all of your time and energy to that, and because of that you'll find across any company of this size that supervisors will not put their people in training programs because they don't have time. The supervisors can't take [their employees] out of the mainstream or they won't make their numbers. So it's a matter of having energy and drive to develop the right programs that we need and then convincing the managers/supervisors across the company that they really do have to put their people in these courses. It's a key issue."

This CEO went a bit further to describe a "before and after" situation:

● "I think in this organization we have good training activity, but there wasn't a real drive previously to move people into programs. And it really gets down to the issues that everyone is really tied up with full energy to meet numbers, and it's a question of how do you take a person out for two weeks, four weeks, a week or whatever without being productive? So we're trying a major thrust here....We just completed a detailed employee survey, on which we were very fortunate to get a 65 percent return, which is very good. And a lot of the issues were tied to training activities—how we reward, how we tie [rewards] to training programs, what do they need, etc. And we're just analyzing the data, and we're looking to make adjustments to the training program. But it really made a difference when we brought in a new person with a lot of energy. The type of person we brought in had broad experiences at similar-type companies, where they tried different approaches in terms of whether training or other types of programs [can] help employees be more productive and contribute more to the bottom line. The person brought those experiences, which then allowed him to adapt to this company the programs he knew were good experiences and that had actually worked there."

WLP professionals who act as managers need to have the highest level of personal integrity and solid values. At the same time, they must never use their influence for personal gain; this is where ethical leadership figures in. Making the WLP function an important and vital part of an organization is necessary, but one must never hurt others along the way to gaining the prominence that the field deserves. CEOs are sensitive to this, but still want WLP managers who can win fairly.

- "Clearly [we want a WLP manager to be] someone who has a strong values orientation, is willing to be a model in values, and [who has] a strong desire to win."

One CEO spoke eloquently about the ability of those who enact the WLP role of manager to unleash the potential of others in the organization and shed light on how those enacting the WLP role as manager might be different from other managers:

- "[They must possess] sensitivity for people as a resource, as opposed to people as employees, the difference being that our people asset is the one asset that will do more or has the capability of doing more than what is outlined in an instruction manual. They can provide initiative. They can provide a wide range of thought and ideas. And I think the people in those roles should think of the technical training as being the base load, but the real value in their positions is unleashing the thinking potential of these people and the ability of these people to innovate, raise new ideas, and to solve problems in nontraditional ways. So, I think they have to be change-oriented people comfortable with new ideas, new thinking, and be comfortable with sponsoring approaches that give people more latitude as opposed to less latitude. I would think these types of people should be champions in unleashing the potential of our people as opposed to harnessing the potential of our people. There are plenty of management people in the company that will harness what's there. I think there are all too few that unleash the potential, and I would think the learning officers are those that should be unleashing the potential of people."

CEOs also expect those who manage WLP to dialogue regularly with them as a way of ensuring that they remain focused on meeting organizational needs:

- "The person has got to be approachable, and people have to feel comfortable communicating with him or her. He or she must be an advocate and a gatherer to gather the various constituencies in the company to consider these kinds of issues...and [have] the ability to dialogue with me, the CEO, so that we are on the same page."

Another area of competence in the leadership category deals with diversity awareness. Although diversity is often thought about as an understanding and acceptance of others' differences, one CEO used the word "empathy" to express some ideas about diversity awareness:

● "I think the number one most important skill is the ability to empathize with employees and their situation and likewise with managers and their situation. I think the most effective training and development directors are those individuals who are capable of putting themselves in the shoes of our employees and understanding their particular situation and issues and developing programs with that in mind. I think learning only works when people are motivated to learn, and so you really need to be able to put yourself in the shoes of those individuals that you are trying to get to learn to understand what their motivations are so that you can tailor something that meets their needs, that satisfies their issues. The second most important skill or attribute is an open mind. I think that's especially important in our multicultural society today. So the person has to have an appreciation for the different kinds of issues and motivations of different people."

Reflect on your own leadership competencies in Appendix C-4. In which areas could you improve your leadership competencies?

TECHNICAL COMPETENCIES

Technical competencies are associated with the understanding and application of existing knowledge or processes. Two major competencies are required from a technical standpoint: *facilitation* and *feedback*.

Technical competence alone will not make you a superior WLP professional when you enact the manager role. Many times it's the best worker (the most technically proficient employee) who gets promoted to a manager position. This is a common situation; the most technically competent employee becomes the manager because others can theoretically use him or her as a valuable resource for information. Of course, technical competence alone does not give a person "what it takes" to be the best manager. There is no question that one must possess appropriate knowledge, skills, and attitudes associated with the WLP field to be a competent practitioner, but one must also possess knowledge of management and the skills and attitudes associated with the process of managing. Further, it is the manager who needs to be able to help others to discover new insights and ensure that performance information gets to the right people in the organization. As one CEO noted:

● "Obviously, [WLP professionals who enact the manager role] would have to have knowledge in the practice of management and supervision. They would have to know how to manage people. If they're training, they would have to understand education and how to teach. They would have to have a real in-depth knowledge of the company's policies, procedures, and processes as well as of outside agencies. I believe they would have to have skills in planning and implementation of plans, good analytical skills, and be able to communicate both verbally and through the written word."

Another CEO hit the nail on the head with a comment about *facilitation skills*:

● "I also think that [WLP professionals who enact the manager role] would have to have a strong ability to facilitate the meetings and coordinate meetings and have an ability to look at and analyze problems and then solve them. They have to have the ability to handle all types of working situations, again having a knowledge about work and an understanding of the workplace."

CEOs clearly understand the importance of *feedback* to ensure that whatever is taught in a learning situation is used and appraised.

● "Maybe the most important of all is that [the training] is actually being implemented...you know, the follow-up to know that the skills we're enhancing and the techniques we're training weren't just somebody going away for a week, getting out of work to attend a training course, and just coming back to using the old techniques because they didn't really start to adapt [the training]."

How would you rate your own technical competencies? Use Appendix C-5 to reflect upon your strengths and potential areas for improvement in the technical competencies area.

TECHNOLOGICAL COMPETENCIES

Finally, *technological competencies* are those competencies associated with the understanding and appropriate application of current or emerging technology. According to *ASTD Models for Workplace Learning and Performance*, the two technological competencies associated with the manager role include computer-mediated communication and technological literacy. For the full definitions of these competencies, see the ASTD study.[18]

There is no doubt that technology has changed the way we work. In fact, technology redefines the way jobs are performed so that it's difficult to keep up with the changes. When you enact the manager role, you lead the way in ensuring that technological advancements related to the field are recognized, evaluated, and perhaps implemented depending upon the unique situation in the organization. CEOs recognize the value of technology in their businesses. To some extent, CEOs want their managers of WLP to help decide what technology would be most appropriate for their organizations.

"I think it's very important that [WLP managers] stay on top of all the new technologies and opportunities and ways that there are to deliver education. This is such a fast-changing field. It's important that [WLP managers] be able to judge the relevancy of [changing technology] and that they are knowledgeable about the different ways that education can be delivered."

Use Appendix C-6 to assess your technological competencies related to your role as a manager of WLP.

Developing into the Manager Who Matches CEO Expectations

If you are currently enacting the WLP role of manager, the competencies and self-reflection worksheets presented in this chapter have, we hope, helped you to assess your current level of competence. If you aspire to enact the role of manager of WLP, the competencies presented here will serve as a guide for the areas of competence that are important for you to develop. The CEOs were very precise in their descriptions of the competencies that they want their managers of WLP to possess. Their perceptions of the necessary competencies for managers of WLP paralleled the ideas researched and reported by Rothwell, Sanders, and Soper in *ASTD Models for Workplace Learning and Performance* (1999). Still, there were many CEOs who saw little difference between the WLP role of manager and the role of any other manager. Several CEOs believed that all managers need to enact the WLP role as manager:

● "All our managers have training and development responsibilities in our organization. I would say that every manager is responsible for the development of people in his or her work and so I think the perception that the management of training resides only within the department of education or only within training is false...the responsibility for on-going education of staff cuts across our entire organization."

Our research indicated that many CEOs thought the WLP role of manager really belonged to other managers. Although WLP as a field supports the active involvement of others (including other managers), the process of improving human performance can be compromised when role activities are not carefully monitored. Without an intimate knowledge of the entire WLP process, other managers might not be fully equipped to guide the WLP process in the most effective way. The likelihood for increased organizational performance may even be impeded if other managers are implementing a "hit or miss" approach to developing talent.

It is evident that your CEO needs to know your competencies in performing the WLP manager role. You, if you are the manager of WLP, should be the most competent, well-equipped member of the organization to lead the WLP process. Demonstrating that you have the competencies to perform the job will help others, including your CEO, to see why you should be the enabling agent, resource expert, and learning specialist facilitating the process of learning and performance improvement in your organization. Honestly assess your level of competence against those competencies necessary for successful performance in the WLP role as manager. Know what you have, where you excel, and where you need to improve. Then make it apparent to your CEO—along with others in your organization—that you are competent to perform the WLP role of manager.

Summary

This chapter focused on CEO perceptions of WLP professionals enacting the manager role. The chapter briefly reviewed the importance of management (generally) and its importance to WLP professionals who enact the manager role. Our research revealed that many CEOs think that all managers—not just WLP professionals acting in that role—should bear management responsibility for WLP. However, many managers probably do not possess sufficient competence in WLP to enact the role effectively.

CHAPTER 3

The Analyst Role—The CEO
Perspective

> [A key to success for the WLP professional is] understanding where we're going strategically, making sure we have the skills assessment, and then most importantly making sure that we have an environment where the new skills can be utilized.
>
> A CEO INTERVIEWED FOR THIS BOOK

What Is the Analyst Role?

According to *ASTD Models for Workplace Learning and Performance,*[1] the WLP professional enacting the analyst role "troubleshoots and isolates the causes of human performance gaps or identifies areas for improving human performance." Those who carry out the role sometimes bear job titles such as trainer, HR developer, performance consultant, or organizational effectiveness coordinator. Like many other roles in WLP, those who play the analyst role often do so as a result of a situation.

Imagine that you are sitting at your desk and an operating manager calls you. She may ask you to implement something specific, such as a training course or an attitude survey of her work team. In this situation, the solution (intervention) has been requested. What remains unknown is what problem prompts that request.

Alternatively, suppose that you get a call from a supervisor at a distant company worksite. She asks for your help in solving a problem. For instance, she might say "my work team has a morale problem, and we'd like your help to solve it." In this situation, the (presenting) problem is known, but its causes and the best solutions to address it remain unknown.

In either situation, it is at that point that WLP professionals put on the analyst hat and begin to act in the role. They start asking questions to troubleshoot the problem, explore the opportunity, or collect information. Typical questions may focus on the reason for the request, its timing, its scope, its cost, its impact on the organization, or many other things.

In many ways, the analyst role is comparable to that of a medical doctor playing the role of diagnostician. If you go to a physician, she will begin by asking you many questions. She might begin a visit with you by posing an open-ended question like "What seems to be the problem?" or "How are you feeling today?" If you tell her you have a headache, she will begin asking you questions about that. (Most doctors initially assume that you are telling the truth and are not just faking illness to get special attention and sympathy.) Few doctors assume that you know what is causing the headache. They know that is for them to discover through questioning, physical examination, and (if necessary) medical evaluation through tests. They also know that, before medicine can be prescribed or some therapy recommended, the root cause(s) must be identified.

The analogy is worth thinking about. WLP professionals enacting the analyst role function like physicians as diagnosticians. They receive requests for solutions (such as training) or for help with problems (such as poor morale, high turnover, or poor communication). At that point they need to begin asking many questions—and perhaps collecting detailed information—before they can get to the root of the issue. And, of course, they must get at the root cause(s) before choosing the appropriate approach to solve the problem.

The analyst role really involves multiple levels. WLP professionals enacting that role have traditionally focused primarily on training needs analysis and program evaluation, but changes in technologies, market conditions, customer expectations, and business operations have expanded the types and levels of analysis expected from WLP professionals. At its core, the analyst role involves breaking down problems and learning needs, and applying learning tools, to aid the organization to achieve its objectives. The analyst role is based on troubleshooting problems, finding performance improvement opportunities, and thinking, perceiving, and developing understanding of employee learning needs. An analyst watches how employees perform their jobs, assessing and recommending programs that will get results.

Why Is This Role Important?

The analyst role is essential to every aspect of WLP work. CEOs expect us to integrate content knowledge of workplace learning with business knowledge of the organization strategy and the business environment. To serve CEOs and organizations, WLP professionals must be analytical in developing learning programs that address business needs and showing the value of these learning programs in the organization's performance.

Throughout the evolution of WLP, the analyst role has been connected directly to learning needs analysis, individual skill assessment, employee development, and program evaluation. To connect workplace learning to organization performance, analysis must integrate an individual's ability to meet expectations for outcomes within a current backdrop of the organization's business challenges. This new definition of the analyst's role reflects a perception of the need to stay in constant touch with organization strategy and understand how learning programs can help to formulate or implement that strategy. CEOs indicate that effective analysis of human performance begins with a current view of the organization's business environment, strategy, competitors, and financial position. This facilitates a synthesis of learning needs assessment with the organization's business challenges and strategy to produce learning programs—and other interventions—that influence performance. As one CEO observed:

● "I think the main ability [of the people responsible for WLP] is to align the training and development activities with the strategy of the organization. They should not be trying to develop things on their own. They should go out and get the things that are out there in the world that will meet our needs at a specific time."

WLP professionals can use CEO opinions about the analyst role in several ways:

❒ To review current approaches to how learning programs are developed

❒ To assess learning programs currently provided, and how program content balances business needs with learning needs

❒ To reflect on how program teaching responsibilities leverage line management expertise and involvement

❒ To assess whether the WLP professional's enactment of the role meets CEO expectations

WLP roles and competencies have been, historically, developed by asking WLP professionals about what they do and what they believe they should do. Although competency models of this kind have helped to raise the level of professionalism in the field, and paralleled an increase in the level of learning programs throughout business and industry, they have unfortunately ignored external feedback from stakeholders. CEO input on the analyst role provides a reality-check for competency models based solely on the perceptions of WLP professionals, because their input describes a unique blend of competencies that have not been identified in previous treatments of the analyst role. These new findings emphasize the importance of synthesizing ideas and constructing learning programs that address business needs. As one CEO noted:

● "I think that [we have] to make sure that [WLP professionals] are an integral part of meeting the business challenges we face. Too many times we have [someone who says], 'Okay, I've got to go do training, and here are all these courses, and this is a great course on a certain function, and let's run everyone through it.' But it's not a priority for our business at this time. And so the first ability I look for is for someone to be an integral part of the strategic plan of the company, and understanding what our business needs are. I find a lot of companies don't integrate the Human Resources function into strategic planning and I always have. In my last couple positions, the HR leaders have said that [*laughs*] they find that refreshing. But they haven't always been involved because a lot of times it's a technical or product-oriented plan and they're not involved in developing those. But I like them to be involved in the two- or three-day strategic planning sessions to understand what the challenges are that are facing us. Because the training has to tie into that. So it's important for them to understand our business strategy and how training can affect it."

According to CEOs, WLP efforts need to be directly associated with a business challenge or with organization strategy. Research conducted with forty-four CEOs found that analytical skill ranked second in importance as a commonly identified ability and was regarded as equal in importance to communication and broad perspective abilities.[2] Demonstrating knowledge of the organization's business was the only ability more frequently identified as important by CEOs. See for yourself what our research revealed about the competencies CEOs felt were essential for WLP professionals (Exhibit 3-1), and note that the competencies are linked to comparable ones appearing in the ASTD competency study of WLP.

Business Challenges and the Analyst Role

Business operations have changed in fundamental ways since the origins of the WLP field and its predecessors, training and HRD. Businesses have undergone (and may currently be navigating) an energy crisis, the deconstruction of the steel industry, the rise of the Asian economy, restructuring and re-engineering, globalization, e-Economy, ethical challenges, and subsequent regrouping. History is not necessarily an indicator of future

EXHIBIT 3-1. COMPETENCY DIMENSIONS OBSERVED BY CEOS

Competency Category	Competency	Definition
Analytical	Competency Identification	Identifying the skills, knowledge, and attributes required to perform work.
Analytical	Performance Gap Analysis	Performing "front-end analysis" by comparing actual and ideal performance levels in the workplace; identifying opportunities and strategies for performance improvement.
Analytical	Performance Theory	Recognizing the implications, outcomes, and consequences of performance interventions to distinguish between activities and results.
Analytical	Social Awareness	Seeing organizations as dynamic political, economic, and social systems.
Analytical	Systems Thinking	Recognizing the interrelationships among events by determining the driving forces that connect seemingly isolated incidents within the organization; taking a holistic view of performance problems in order to find root causes.
Business	Ability to see the "Big Picture"	Identifying trends and patterns that are outside the normal paradigm of the organization.
Business	Business Knowledge	Demonstrating awareness of business functions and how business decisions affect financial and nonfinancial work results.
Interpersonal	Communication	Applying effective verbal, nonverbal, and written communication methods to achieve desired results.
Interpersonal	Relationship Building	Effectively interacting with others in order to produce meaningful outcomes.
Leadership	Buy-in/Advocacy	Building ownership and support for workplace initiatives.

SOURCE: William J. Rothwell, Ethan S. Sanders, and Jeffrey G. Soper. *ASTD Models for Workplace Learning and Performance: Roles, Competencies, and Outputs* (Alexandria, Va.: The American Society for Training and Development, 1999), pp. 53–56. Used by permission of ASTD. All rights reserved.

developments. Changes in the business world are not cyclical. The introduction of the World Wide Web to business processes and models has created a new organizational world within which to operate. In Rosabeth Moss Kanter's book *e-Volve!*

(2001), she characterizes the impact of the World Wide Web on change in the business environment as follows:

> Constant change is built into the very nature of the e-world. The Web and associated network technologies are both stimuli for e-culture (making it necessary) and facilitators of e-culture (making it possible). It is like a spiral of increasing force: The more the Web is used, the more uses are identified, and the more it must be used to do more things. Change produces the need for more and deeper change.[3]

Advances in technology and information movement are changing how businesses and people perform. The abundance of information and new forms of technology that allow businesses to analyze and interpret information offers the WLP professional a leading position for implementing organization strategy through integrated learning programs. This leading position really begins with the analyst role.

The rate of change in the business world requires analytical behaviors in every aspect and at every level of business. From director to front-line employee, the ability to analyze information, troubleshoot problems, and find opportunities for quantum leaps in productivity improvement are becoming as fundamental as the ability to read. The most important competencies required by an analyst are determined by the type of business change that an organization is experiencing.

The following five points highlight the importance of the analyst role in WLP and broaden the definition of this role beyond traditional understandings of it. To illustrate how the five levels of analysis are demonstrated, three different business change scenarios will be described and reflected on in the context of each of the five levels.

❏ *Point 1*. All manager positions require analytical thinking. Data-driven analysis is a core management competency.

❏ *Point 2*. Change is constant in business, and the discipline of working with analytical processes allows us to adapt to new environments quickly.

❏ *Point 3*. New technologies such as Enterprise Resource Programs (ERPs) allow for access to data and real-time assessment and analysis of performance-related training needs.

☐ *Point 4.* To fully integrate WLP programs throughout the organization, analysis allows associations between learning and performance to be made that increase the level of buy-in for WLP programs.

☐ *Point 5.* Consistent analysis of WLP programs fosters a common understanding of an organization's mission's critical success measures and supports performance management.

TRANSITION

The first scenario, described below, is about an organization in transition. The change taking place is occurring both within the organization and with the organization's customers. The CEO quotation below describes a business challenge that requires analysis on multiple work environments, and multiple learners' needs. Use this description to reflect on the five levels of analysis during business change.

● "We are in the process of *transitioning* our company's products and services, significantly. We are reengineering internally significantly. We are upgrading, enhancing our product line to serve the new economy more efficiently and particularly large corporations and customer relationship management and marketing programs. And it's going to require that, you know, *all our people gain new knowledge of the technologies that we have developed and figure out how to deploy them for their customers and in our channels.* We're going to have to educate not just people internally, but we're going to have to now begin to deploy these technologies directly into our customers' environments."

The transitioning change described here requires information on both the organization's products and services and the customer environments where services are being delivered. In some cases, WLP professionals will have to offer learning interventions to customers and other stakeholder groups as well as to employees of the organization. Effective analysis for WLP would involve data from both the clients' and host organizations' environments describing client objectives, critical performance measures, technology being used by organization and client, the type of change taking place (currently and in the future), and how learning interventions will provide people with appropriate knowledge to perform their work. The art of the analyst role rests in using business data to describe the type of change occurring, and then provide an environment that allows learners to teach each other how to deploy technologies for the customer's benefit.

FINANCIAL

The second scenario, described below, is about an organization facing financial challenges. The change taking place deals primarily with decreasing the level of debt the company supports and increasing the company's market share. The CEO's description of this business challenge focuses on the financial issues facing the organization, and meeting the challenge requires analysis to link the organization's WLP programs to the objective of decreasing debt. Use the description to reflect on the five levels of analysis during business change:

● "We really have four business challenges. The first one is *financial*, and that is *debt reduction*. We're a private company. We'll go public eventually and we're very highly leveraged, which means we have a debt to capitalization ratio somewhere around 75 percent. So one of our first challenges is to generate a lot of cash and pay down debt, and that means managing capital spending carefully, making our earning targets, etc. So it's purely financial. We want to de-leverage over the next couple of years. That would be number one on the list. Number two would be to *grow the business* in terms of more volume, more market share, and achieve in our business what we call 100 percent vertical integration. And we have two divisions. We have paper mills that make paper that is used to produce corrugated containers. And we supply our own box plants. We have seventy-seven of them and they use about 82 percent of our mill production. We sell about 18 percent obviously to the outside. We would like to be 100 percent integrated. In other words, we have a captive home for all of our product. So it's growth and integration. Third would be *to have the right people*. In other words *strengthen the management team,* what would be organizational development. And number four, which does get into the training area, is to *optimize our performance through improving employee skills.* And so only one of the four is training related."

The financial challenge described by the CEO requires an analyst to blend the organization's financial and strategic information with traditional learning needs and performance gap analysis information. Using financial data for debt reduction and increased performance (through improved skills) is an example of the association level of analysis. Financial and performance measures are constantly changing due to new levels of technology. Debt reduction and performance levels can be used as critical success measures, helping to develop buy-in for WLP programs. Although the CEO describes this business challenge as primarily financial, he also recognizes that optimizing human performance is part of the issue. The analyst role in this scenario is to integrate the two parts, debt reduction and human performance improvement, into an effective learning program.

STAFFING

The final scenario describes the challenge of recruiting, retaining, and developing staff. The change faced by this organization is growth. The CEO describes the challenge of recruiting managers who can help to identify and develop growth opportunities for the organization. Use the description to reflect on the five levels of analysis during business change.

● "The first one would be *attracting and retaining what I'm calling growth managers.* The kinds of people that I put in this category as growth managers would be any and all individuals within a company who may be involved in either research for new products and/or development of new products, project managers involved in product development and product research, and individuals within the company who may be involved in identifying technology opportunities for either licensing new technology, acquiring it, or creating joint ventures. So it involves the *whole category of growth, including individuals involved in selling and marketing.* So to me, the hot individuals that we need to continue to focus on trying to attract and retain would be *any and all people associated with the growth of the company.*"

The challenge of attracting and retaining key staff requires analysis of external business opportunities and innovation in creating work environments that foster organizational growth. Attracting and retaining a growth-oriented workforce requires data on future business opportunities and a current competency profile for the R&D, sales, and marketing departments. The analyst role would necessitate working with areas of the organization that need growth managers, becoming familiar with available market data, assessing the current workforce growth capabilities, and constructing a learning program designed to help achieve growth objectives. We see that this CEO's business challenge is to attract and retain growth managers. That challenge requires analysis beyond traditional training needs assessment, and requires data on markets, sales, growth competencies, and performance.

The business challenges facing an organization at any given time determine what role the analyst should play. The analyst role involves recognizing critical business information and collecting, organizing, synthesizing, and packaging this information so that employees can see how their learning relates to the business. Business challenges may involve transforming the organization through new strategies, applying new technologies to new customers, improving operational performance, or recruiting and developing a workforce. While the analyst role has broadened with changes in business, WLP professionals can take heart in the fact that the new roles are built upon the core analyst functions already in place. Core analyst roles—such as needs and task analyst, program evaluator, and strategist—are still required,[4] but it is important to understand that CEOs see these roles as working from, and relating back to, the organization's business context. The following section is a brief review of core analyst roles as defined by previous competency studies.

Traditional Analytical Competencies

Throughout the evolution of the field from training and HRD to WLP, analytical activities have been defined by two primary activities: skill assessment and program evaluation. The earliest competency studies of training developed by Pinto and Walker[5] and McLagan[6] defined the analyst role in terms of responsibilities that involved designing data collection tools, assembling data on skill level, identifying ideal and real performance, and developing training programs to improve performance. Early competency studies of training and HRD identified needs and gap assessment activities as one half of the analyst role.

Early definitions of analyst roles also included program evaluation responsibilities that highlighted concern for demonstrating program impact, but it was not until the most recent WLP study that program evaluation was defined in specific relation to increasing individual, group or team, and organizational performance. This study's definition of the evaluator includes a feedback loop between WLP professionals and stakeholders, which enables the realistic evaluation of training effectiveness. The feedback loop addresses the CEOs' desire for continuous dialogue between WLP professionals and managers on how learning programs (and other performance improvement interventions) are linked to business needs.

Skill assessment is another core activity of the analyst role. Skill assessment begins with job or competency analysis and an understanding of the major responsibilities and duties in each job. It is sometimes assumed that skill assessment takes place after a person is hired. Early definitions of needs analysis and diagnosis had the HRD practitioner developing questionnaires, assessing feedback, and developing programs to correct skill deficiencies in current employees. Ideally, however, the hiring interview would include questions aimed at assessing skills and competencies required for successful job performance.

CEO-Identified Competencies for the Role of Analyst

CEO perceptions of the analyst role enacted by WLP professionals reinforce earlier study findings but expand the need for organizational involvement. CEOs do not see the analyst role in a radically different way from how WLP professionals view it, but they do see the need for their analysts to supply the same type of analysis that the director of sales and marketing, director of finance, or any other senior level manager provides. For the analyst, this type of analysis involves:

❏ A current and focused skills assessment of the workforce

❏ Recognition of the organization's strategy and the skills training aligned with that strategy

❏ Knowledge of the areas of the organization most in need of training

❏ Knowledge of the costs of training for the area budgets receiving training

❏ Knowledge of managerial awareness of training needs and involvement with the training program

❏ Analysis that shows the level of support necessary for training to change behaviors at the work site

In a nutshell, the analyst role functions to provide proof of the necessity of training and shifts in employee behavior. Whereas CEO perceptions of the analyst role identified skill assessment functions (which are already a core competency for WLP professionals), their perceptions also included business, interpersonal, and leadership competencies. Each competency area essential to successful performance in the analyst role is discussed in the following pages.

ANALYTICAL COMPETENCIES

First and foremost, the analyst role requires competency in performance analysis. CEOs regard performance analysis as combining traditional skill assessment and an intuitive ability to recognize training needs within the organization. An effective analyst builds support by using both a quantitative analysis of the organization's learning needs and a qualitative vision of where the organization's people aspire to be in the future. Appropriate analytical behaviors involve using gap analysis and social awareness to create an organization's training needs map. (Of course, other learning interventions may also be used.) The analyst must be able to apply learning programs to operational and strategic performance issues. As one CEO observed:

● "[The WLP professional enacting the analyst role] must understand completely the cultural change we're trying to create. Then he must go out and find out where the deficiencies are in the organization by integrating himself with management and with our customers to create the training programs to get us to where we need to be."

Understanding performance theory, and the processes involved in performance gap analysis and competency identification, are key expectations of CEOs for WLP leaders. The analyst role begins with a focus on the work and the person performing the work, the subsequent creation of a development plan for the individual, and ends with the organization's performance measure(s). Interestingly, when CEOs were asked to identify the business challenges facing their organization, they were as concerned with recruiting and retaining key human resources as they were with organization profitability. This analytical flow illustrates CEOs' desires to put people first and develop human resources while maintaining a focus on their organization's development. In short, they want to build human capacity while making profits. Exhibit 3-2 presents four levels of analysis required by WLP professionals who enact the analyst role.

EXHIBIT 3-2. LEVELS OF ANALYST ROLES

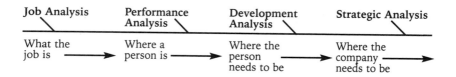

Job Analysis	Performance Analysis	Development Analysis	Strategic Analysis
What the job is →	Where a person is →	Where the person needs to be →	Where the company needs to be →

Competency identification and talent assessment can be utilized in many areas of the WLP function. Daily demands include helping managers recruit for open positions, creating hiring interview questions to writing performance assessment plans, formulating individual development plans, understanding skill requirements, and identifying competence. As one CEO noted:

- "I think [WLP professionals] would need to be able to spot and evaluate talent. They need to know where talent is and how to look for it and how to evaluate people with regard to that. The WLP person needs to do this for two reasons. One is so they can go out and get the right people to get the right jobs. In other words, matching the right talent with the organizational need. But also to look at needs and knowing what's there and what isn't there and what can be developed and strengthened and what can't."

The analytical ability to assess and target the organization's workforce capability—and the ability to effectively use resources to strengthen employees' competencies—are clearly recognized as important by CEOs. Recognizing strong and weak competencies, and identifying where key skill training is needed, are also important facets of the analyst role. The levels of analysis identified by CEOs include tracking individual training participation, job performance and development areas, and how individuals' core competencies can be leveraged in other areas of the organization. The following quotes from CEOs reveal how a well-documented competency profile allows the organization to target training to people and areas that are in the most need and thus provide the organization with the right people at the right time.

- "The person responsible for WLP needs to make sure there's a good skills analysis done. Understanding the priorities of where are the weakest areas of the organization. A lot of times, we can have five programs, and even if they match what we're doing, we don't always set them up or make sure that the weakest areas are [covered by] the training. The people that are aggressive will go ask for the training and get it, and that's great. It's some of our top performers, but they're adding on top of what they've already had over and over. And the average isn't really increased. And we need to make sure by using skills assessment that we have increased the whole capability."

- "I think that there's clearly a role for the WLP leader in understanding exactly what our needs are going to be going forward from the standpoint of succession, what the business direction will [require] in terms of specific skills and talents that we may or may not have within the business. So it goes back to understanding the mission of the business."

The final analytical competency area of the analyst role is connected to social awareness. CEOs know that their organizations involve complex webs of culture and personality. In the current environment of downsizing, new technology, and increased attention to performance, individuals are grappling with knowing—and owning—their positions. People struggle to differing degrees with knowing, understanding, and adapting to new expectations in their positions. Recognizing fear, anxiety, and apprehension during periods of business transition is a responsibility of WLP leaders. CEOs expect those WLP professionals who enact the analyst role to demonstrate empathy, compassion, and humanistic behaviors through the organization's learning programs.

● "I think probably the number one most important skill—and I'm not even quite sure it's a skill—is the ability to be able to empathize with employees and their situation and likewise with managers and their situation. I think the most effective training and development directors, human resource development managers, or whatever, are those individuals who are capable of putting themselves in the shoes of our employees and understanding their particular situation and issues and developing programs with that in mind."

BUSINESS COMPETENCIES

The second competency area tied to the analyst role is business related. Business competency reflects an ability to understand the organization as a system. CEOs identified business competencies as:

❒ Partnering with departments in the identification of learning needs

❒ Being able to integrate the organization's culture into the learning programs

❒ Understanding the business needs of the organization

Previous competency studies have included longer lists of business competencies required of WLP professionals, but at the highest level of an organization, CEOs recognize behaviors that reflect an ability to develop programs that integrate current business needs within the organization's culture and people.

Identifying learning needs is an organizational process. WLP professionals who enact the analyst role should partner with line managers, supervisors, and functional leaders to identify training and learning needs. Needs analysis programs should begin with a feedback loop between WLP professionals and departments using learning to achieve improved results. Needs analysis is no longer the sole domain of the WLP department; learning within the organization is a shared responsibility. As one CEO explained:

● "I'm not a believer in a top-down management system. I'm a believer in a bottoms-up management system. I believe learning programs should really go down into the organization to find *people who are most knowledgeable in terms of needs*. Then the next thing is to find an individual who's knowledgeable about delivery systems. And that's a different individual in my organization. So the person who's responsible for the delivery system and the administration of these education programs is not the same person who defines them. That is, multiple people are involved in providing education programs. The ability to identify the needs, the learning needs, training needs, and then the ability to identify how those training or learning systems are delivered—all these require a team of people."

Partnering with departments to identify training needs is one way to integrate learning into an organization's culture. Cultural integration of learning programs requires the ability to see "the big picture." This involves knowing how a learning program fits within an organization's strategic plan, how the program should be delivered, who the participants will be, what the participants will use the program for, and how the program fits within the overall WLP mission.

Along with these internal issues, CEOs expect the WLP professionals who enact the analyst role to include external big picture issues as well. These include customer profiles and customer culture issues. Inclusion of the organization's customer culture information in learning programs prepares participants for work within that culture. In both service and product companies, understanding how customers use products and services is value-added information that learning programs can provide. One CEO made the point emphatically:

- "[Our employees] must have a *sense of the culture* that we're working in with our customer base, whether it be a normally hierarchical, very rigid military structure, or a very flat organization that operates much differently. So the training of our people, our management, *has to be tuned to the customers*, and that means the people that are in the training program must come away with a *strong understanding of that customer culture.* [The trainer] has to let them understand what we are investing and how the investment that we are making fits the program that we're conducting for that person. How it's supportive of it. And [the trainer] has to be attentive to the customer. So my simple answer is that the WLP position has changed in recent years from a traditional internal look and sorts of conventional metrics to an orientation where knowing the customer, the product, and the culture is most important."

Workplace learning programs are anchored by work objectives. As learning professionals, we are focused on the learning program: its structure, content, participant involvement, and feedback. An intense attention to the program, and the "nuts and bolts" involved in program delivery, can interfere with aligning a program to meeting business needs. Put simply, learning programs must be based on the business issues the organization faces. An analyst must therefore be vigilant about reflecting on how programs have an impact on, and are impacted by, current business issues.

CEOs recognize business competence. Business competence includes organization-specific information, such as:

❐   The goods and/or services the organization produces
❐   The organization's customers
❐   Organization mission

- ❏ Organization history
- ❏ Organization size
- ❏ Competitors
- ❏ Organization strategy

Learning programs must include organization-specific business information. This information, whether current or historical, provides employees with a relevant business context to which their learning is applied. CEOs expect learning programs to have a business context with which participants can relate.

● "[WLP professionals] really need to understand the business that we're in and understand what the talent needs of the organization and the business are."

● "I think it's very important that these people [WLP professionals] truly understand the requirements of business. It's hard to understand what kind of training and people development programs we need without understanding the business. I think [WLP professionals] need to be good business people and understand the business."

As is evident in these comments, CEOs aren't looking for full mastery of the organization's strategic plan. But they do expect WLP professionals to link learning programs directly to the work of the organization.

INTERPERSONAL COMPETENCIES

Traditionally, we don't think of communication and relationship building as analyst roles. These competencies are often considered "soft" and outside the realm of true analytical activities. In the eyes of CEOs, however, the soft competencies of communication and organizational networking are crucial to effective analysis and WLP work. Effective learning programs begin with clearly defined goals and objectives. Clarity is created through organizing information on skills assessment, organization strategy, performance measures, departmental responsibilities, competition, and customer feedback, and then communicating how a learning program will address a specific business challenge. Effective communication within the complex work of learning is difficult and requires a keen analytical process to make it work effectively.

CEOs recognize that strong communication skills are a common competency in all higher-level management positions. When learning programs are used as performance improvement interventions, communication is a core competency for effective programming. Effective communications reflect effective thinking; strong communication competency fosters organizational networking and support. As one CEO observed:

● *"Well it begins with communication.* Someone who doesn't possess or can't develop good communication skills in listening and speaking and writing would not be effective in the role of [WLP analyst]. But when you get past that and drive more specificity into the job, the key ability is to understand the mission of the business. I mean that's absolutely key, and then developing programs, in an organized fashion, that facilitate accomplishment of that mission."

Relationship building is the second area of interpersonal competency required by WLP professionals. The importance of openly listening to ideas, networking, involving others, and building strong relationships cannot be understated. Creating an environment where people want to learn, and are willing to help others learn, is crucial for WLP.

● "The WLP leader has got to be approachable and people have to feel comfortable communicating with him. He has to be an advocate. He has to be a gatherer of various constituencies in the company to consider the learning needs and these training kinds of issues."

Informal networks created by people who recognize common goals (strategy), and work together to create learning environments to achieve organizational goals, are crucial in creating high performing organizations. Learning occurs in many different environments, and the analyst must use resources available throughout the organization to develop new learning programs. CEOs prize abilities in developing a learning network and building support for learning throughout an organization. As one CEO explained:

● "Clearly [a WLP professional needs to have] a willingness to explore new practices from all sources, whether it's academia, other companies, or from wherever globally. Also, *strong engagement skills* to help in establishing relationships with the various business leaders and in the mutual discovery of weaknesses and how those can be offset and augmented through learning experiences. In addition to having strong engagement skills with the businesses, someone needs to be very knowledgeable about their field. Do they have a good network? Do they know what the literature says? Are they in the loop as far as what's going on out there in their field? Do they have a strong willingness to try new things, to try new ideas, and to experiment quite a bit?"

LEADERSHIP COMPETENCIES

The final competency area identified by CEOs relates to the ability to create buy-in and advocacy for learning programs. This requires assessing departmental performance and designing programs that address learning needs within the scope of organization strategy and business goals. To create buy-in, the WLP professional uses results from needs analysis, and other sources of information, to prescribe a learning intervention. The learning program advocate walks a fine line between working toward meeting the needs of the department and furthering the use of learning programs in the organization. CEOs recognize this balance. One CEO had this to say:

- "I think they have to be team players. I think they have to be politicians to some extent so they can talk with the different department heads and coordinate the training activities and make sure that we're getting everything we want out of a training program and somehow have whatever efficiencies we can have as far as cross-training is concerned."

The complexity of addressing business challenges and performance goals through coordinated learning programs that involve diverse groups of people is undeniably daunting. WLP professionals enacting the analyst role are called upon to collect and assess all information relevant to proposing a learning intervention that addresses performance concerns. As an analyst, the WLP professional must demonstrate a high level of content expertise, feel comfortable communicating with people at any level of the organization, and develop support to move the organization forward. As one CEO put it:

● "[A WLP professional] really has grown into a very broad-based person, as I see it. And there are [workplace learning] jobs that I think are becoming increasingly difficult to fill because that person needs not only the traditional learning abilities, but also a much broader basis. For example, he must understand completely this cultural change to customer service that we're trying to create. He must understand and believe it!"

Developing into the Analyst Who Matches CEO Expectations

The analyst is the first person sought out by senior leaders for help in directing the strategy, content, and design of an organization's learning program. CEOs' views of the analyst role go much deeper than functional responsibility, however. CEOs believe that an effective analyst will tap into the pulse of an organization to determine its capabilities for change. The analyst will identify where an organization's capabilities can be found and where the organization's human resources need to be deployed to achieve a strategy. CEOs believe that WLP professionals enacting the analyst role need to engage key elements of the organization and build bridges leading to performance improvement. Although competency in the analyst role is crucial to all aspects of an organization's learning programs, the competencies required by the analyst go beyond merely identifying individual learning needs.

To briefly review, CEOs identified four competency clusters that support the analyst role:

- ❐ Analytical
- ❐ Business
- ❐ Interpersonal
- ❐ Leadership

Analytical competence includes abilities in identifying competency, performing gap analysis, applying performance theories to the workplace, being socially aware (within the organization), and thinking systemically. CEOs who referred to analytical competencies often placed them within the context of skill assessment and appreciation of employee challenges. *Business competence* includes an appreciation of "the big picture" and sound business sense. CEOs who identified business competencies referred to abilities for understanding the organization's culture and how business needs drive learning needs. *Interpersonal competence* reflects the ability to communicate effectively and build relationships throughout the organization that support company goals through learning interventions. Finally, *leadership competence* describes the ability to serve as a champion and advocate for learning and performance improvement programs.

The analyst role described by CEOs builds upon traditional needs assessment competence. Historically, the analyst role was defined solely within the bounds of training needs. But more recent competency studies in the field have included skills associated with business understanding and performance observation. CEO perspectives identified five analytical competencies similar to previous study findings. But unlike previous studies, CEOs associated competencies linked to business, interpersonal, and leadership skills with the analyst role. It is key to remember that the analyst role still requires focused attention to skill assessment and gap analysis. The information provided in this chapter is intended to help you understand what CEOs expect of the analyst and to emphasize that what CEOs expect go beyond traditional analytical skills.

Summary

This chapter focused on CEO perceptions of WLP professionals enacting the analyst role. The analyst plays a key role, since the diagnosis of human performance problems identified by the analyst becomes a starting point for performance improvement interventions selected to solve the problems. For CEOs, WLP programs need to be directly associated with a business challenge or with organization strategy.

The analyst role has its roots in a mindset focused on discovering the root causes of problems. This role can be compared to the role played by medical doctors who seek the cause(s) of illness without becoming distracted by symptoms. The chapter briefly reviewed the importance of analysis and summarized key CEO perceptions about WLP professionals who enact the analyst role.

CHAPTER 4

The Intervention Selector

Role—The CEO Perspective

> I think the main ability is to align the training and development activities with the strategy of the organization. [WLP professionals] should not be trying to develop things on their own. They should go out and get the things that are out there in the world that will meet our needs at a specific time.
>
> A CEO INTERVIEWED FOR THIS BOOK

We are bombarded every day by the media with suggestions about how we should improve our lives. To some, it seems that our culture is obsessed with continuous improvement, though sometimes that obsession is spun toward instant gratification and quick fixes. When thinking about how to solve workplace problems, too many people want interventions that will solve problems *quickly* rather than *effectively*. The intervention selector role is critical to the success of WLP professionals. But interventions often take time to work. Intervention selection is intimately connected to the analyst role explored in Chapter 3.

Before you can even begin to select an appropriate intervention, the problem you're facing needs to be thoroughly analyzed. Symptoms must be separated from root causes. Opportunities must be sorted into the possible and the feasible—as well as other categorizations.

Armed with specific competencies and knowledge, WLP professionals carry out or advise organizational members about interventions tailored to meet the needs of a specific audience in a specific situation. These interventions must be based on a thorough analysis of the situation. Further, WLP professionals can rely on sound research to act as the consumer testing ground for the wide variety of interventions available, assuming they know the differences among the various interventions, and are able to determine what will work best in a specific situation and corporate culture.

What Is the Intervention Selector Role?

ASTD Models for Workplace Learning and Performance defines the intervention selector as the "role that selects appropriate WLP and non-WLP interventions to address root causes of human performance gaps."[1] Before we go any further, it's important to define some key terms associated with this role. Several definitions of the term "intervention" can be found throughout the WLP literature, but they all share three common characteristics. First, interventions are typically long term in nature. Rarely does a "quick fix" get at the root causes of organizational performance issues. Addressing the root causes of human performance problems is almost always time-consuming. Second, interventions are evolutionary; they are planned courses of action aimed at helping an organization increase its effectiveness over time. Third, interventions are positive and progressive change efforts. Interventions purposely disrupt the status quo; they are deliberate attempts to push an organization toward a different, more effective state.[2]

An important part of the intervention selector role centers around choosing appropriate interventions. We can divide this portion of the definition into two distinct but intimately related concepts: (1) appropriate and (2) WLP and non-WLP. Part of your role as a WLP professional is to narrow down the choice of "appropriate" interventions through careful problem analysis (as presented in Chapter 3). Without careful analysis, the choice of interventions will more than likely not solve any performance improvement problem. Selecting interventions that are not based on careful, complete analysis can often make situations worse, just as a physician who prescribes the wrong medicine might only make a patient more ill. We'll present examples of this phenomenon in the next section of this chapter.

The difference between WLP and non-WLP interventions is also important to understand. WLP is concerned with improving human performance and addressing individual and organizational needs.[3] Thus, the focus of all interventions is on human performance improvement. Learning interventions are typically WLP related: training and development, career development, knowledge management, and organization development interventions—among others—fall under this category.

Nonlearning (management) interventions can also qualify as interventions. Management interventions, such as changing the design or structure of an organization or job, can be considered interventions, if the focus of the intervention is on enabling employees to perform their jobs more effectively. Other types of interventions include changing performance management systems, altering pay or incentive systems, maintaining sound employee relations programs, and matching individuals with appropriate jobs.

It can be challenging to clearly determine the difference between a WLP and non-WLP intervention; the distinction rests on the *primary intent* of the intervention. For example, improving the financial performance of an organization does not necessarily fall into the category of interventions. A bottom line can improve due to external forces such as lower interest rates or higher yields in investment dollars. If, however, the profit margins of an organization begin to decrease, and the decrease is determined to be due to poor human performance, then an intervention is most likely needed to improve human performance; this could in turn increase the financial performance of the organization. In this case, the *primary intent* of the intervention is to improve human performance.

The distinction between WLP and non-WLP interventions can become even more complex. For example, if a computer system upgrade simply makes the computer less expensive to maintain, the upgrade is a financial performance improvement. If, however, the upgrade provides employees with more efficient ways to do their jobs (ultimately improving their performance), it becomes human performance improvement.[4] Once again, the intent of the intervention is the real determinant of whether it is a WLP or a non-WLP intervention. See Exhibit 4-1 for an overview of the organizational areas where WLP and non-WLP interventions are most often implemented.

It is also important to understand the term "root causes" in this context. Medical examples are frequent in WLP literature, because they help to illustrate the important difference between the *root cause* of a problem as opposed to its *symptoms*. Physicians spend a great deal of time learning how to find the root causes of illnesses. They use diagnostic skills to narrow down the possible causes of a particular problem. They test, analyze, and often collaborate with colleagues to reach an educated decision on a therapeutic course of action. The intervention selector needs to possess similar skills. The importance of collaboration is a key point here. WLP professionals are not isolated in their responsibility for selecting interventions. The intervention selector should begin by speaking to the people who are affected by the problem. Remember that one hallmark of WLP is a collaborative effort with all organizational members to find solutions to improve individual, group, and organizational performance. Further, no one knows the problem better than the people who are experiencing it. Seeking their counsel is imperative, because few interventions will work if those who have the problem don't "own" the solution.

When a physician misdiagnoses the root cause of a patient's problem, the results can be deadly. This metaphor is adequate, as the intervention selector is dealing with organizational "health" issues. This role is a most serious one. Much time, effort, and money can go into selecting the most appropriate intervention. Choosing the incorrect intervention can be

EXHIBIT 4-1. AN OVERVIEW OF THE ORGANIZATIONAL AREAS WHERE WLP AND
NON-WLP INTERVENTIONS ARE USUALLY FOUND

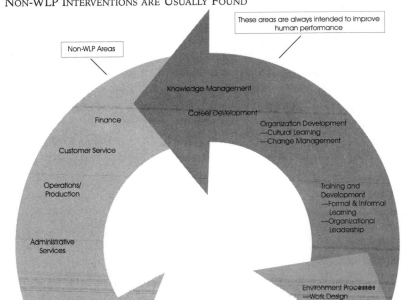

SOURCE: *Adapted from* William J. Rothwell, Ethan S. Sanders, and Jeffrey G. Soper. *ASTD Models for Workplace Learning and Performance: Roles, Competencies, and Outputs* (Alexandria, Va: The American Society for Training and Development, 1999).

extremely costly to an organization. People expect physicians to find the root cause(s) of their health problems, because they want the problems to be solved. This is no different in an organizational environment. If interventions are selected in a hurried manner, or are based merely on "gut instinct," you, as a WLP professional, run the risk of losing credibility with the members of your organization.

The many training programs designed to relieve the symptoms (rather than root causes) of organizational problems lend us an example of poorly analyzed intervention selection. For many years, training was the "quick fix" of the performance improvement profession. The problem with training was that it was often applied generically. Time, money, and effort were wasted because many organizational members were given the same dose of training whether they needed it or not. It is not our intention to unduly criticize training; at times a training intervention can and will get to the root causes of a problem. The point is that using "sheep dip" or "spray and pray" training as a generic fix will usually not gain the results you desire.

An uplifting training program, for example, rarely improves poor employee morale. The root causes of low employee morale tend to focus around low wages, poor leadership, weak organizational structure, or lack of employee knowledge and understanding of the organization's vision, mission, and goals. When the root causes of organizational problems are improperly determined, the blame is often placed on the WLP professional for selecting the incorrect intervention. Resources are wasted, and negative perceptions about WLP begin to surface in the organization. The lesson to be learned here is that trying to please the members of your organization with quick and easy solutions to problems is simply unwise. Spending the time to analyze a situation thoroughly and then selecting the appropriate intervention based on its root cause is the most productive course of action in the long run.

The final term in the definition that is worthy of discussion is "human performance gaps." A *gap* in human performance is the space between "what is" and "what should be." Appropriate interventions are aimed at narrowing or closing this gap. It is not difficult to perceive when an employee is not performing well. Selecting interventions that will bring a person's performance to a desired level, however, is more complex than it might sound. It is easier, after all, to see *what* is occurring than it is to determine *why* it is occurring.

The issue of employee safety is a pertinent example. Most employees know that they should follow safety procedures in the workplace. Obviously, employees don't need to be taught safety procedures if they already know them. So, why might they be performing a job in an unsafe manner? One possibility is that the procedures are so cumbersome that the average employee doesn't want to follow them. Another possibility is that those in leadership positions are not taking the safety procedures seriously, setting a poor example for employees. In either case, the root cause of the problem is not that the employees do not know the procedures. Closing the human performance gap here requires discovering *why* the employees are acting in an unsafe manner and then taking action to address that problem. This is an example of how time, money, and effort could be wasted on a safety-training program; training simply won't fix this problem. Once again, the ultimate goal of the intervention selector is to choose a solution that will address the root cause(s) of the problem.

Why Is the Role of the Intervention Selector Important?

Obviously, CEOs, managers, and other stakeholders want interventions that will close gaps in human performance. There are a number of reasons why the role of the intervention selector is important. The reasons deal primarily with:

1. The selection of the most appropriate intervention
2. The efficient use of money, time, and effort
3. Your own credibility
4. The credibility of WLP

REASON #1: THE SELECTION OF THE MOST APPROPRIATE INTERVENTION

This role is important because it affects all subsequent steps. The enactment of this role is the second major step in improving human performance, after a thorough analysis of the problem has been completed. Once an intervention is selected, the remainder of the process for solving the performance problem ensues. If an incorrect decision is made in choosing the intervention, the rest of the process can turn out to be a waste. As we have mentioned, all of the components needed to reach successful solutions to performance problems are interrelated. All of the steps are necessary and must be completed in order. An intervention cannot be selected without a thorough analysis of the problem. Designing and developing the intervention to meet the specific needs of the people and circumstances surrounding a problem cannot be done until the most appropriate intervention has been selected. Basically, the first reason that this role is important relates to the impact and consequences that the choice of intervention will have on the remainder of the process.

REASON #2: TIME, MONEY, AND EFFORT

Because most interventions to improve human performance are long term in nature, much is at stake when choosing an intervention. Choosing the most appropriate intervention will undoubtedly save time, money, and effort. Choosing the wrong intervention will have the opposite effect. Valuable time can be wasted, precious resources expended, and the effort of trying to fit "a square peg in a round hole" will frustrate both you and your stakeholders.

Organizations are living, breathing, interconnected entities. An intervention could stimulate a positive change in one area of the organization, but simultaneously create negative changes in other areas. Careful selection of the correct intervention needs to include an analysis of other areas of the organization that might also be affected. When dealing with serious human performance issues, "experimenting" with solutions is not always wise. Your approach to problem solving must be directly and logically aimed at the root causes of the problem.

REASON #3: YOUR OWN CREDIBILITY IS AT STAKE

Many eyes are watching, judging, and evaluating the WLP professional continuously. One sure way to lose credibility is by making intervention decisions without a thorough analysis of the problem. We found in Chapter 3 that making quick decisions, or arriving at conclusions before completing a thorough analysis of the problem, can be embarrassing at the very least, and at its worst, very costly to the organization. WLP professionals are human. You may be inclined to please your stakeholders by presenting immediate solutions to their performance improvement problems. It is difficult to avoid the temptation to make snap decisions to "prove just how competent you are." Stakeholders who want quick solutions can inadvertently cause a quick rush to judgment. Since you are the expert, they expect you to have ready-made answers to their questions. It is important to remain objective so that, whenever you are put to the test, you can demonstrate your abilities and prove your worth to the organization.

REASON #4: THE CREDIBILITY OF THE WLP FIELD IS AT STAKE

Many CEOs we spoke with didn't see the intervention selector role as a role just for WLPs. Often, they perceived that decisions related to selecting interventions for improved performance belonged to the managers responsible for problem areas. In fact, many CEOs didn't perceive the intervention selector role as a separate or distinct role at all; they viewed the role as an inherent part of any manager's job. When the CEOs were given the opportunity to reflect on the intervention selector role, however, many did mention that they could see how such a role could be played out collaboratively between the WLP professional and the manager. Some stated that they could see how the WLP professional could play a consultant role with managers to determine the most appropriate interventions for solving performance problems.

The point here is that, by demonstrating the competencies associated with the intervention selector role, you can not only increase your own credibility as a WLP professional but also elevate perceptions of the entire profession. We now turn to an examination of the competencies associated with the intervention selector role and why these competencies are essential to your credibility as a WLP professional.

Traditional Competencies of the Intervention Selector

The competencies associated with the intervention selector role fall under the general headings of: analytical, business, interpersonal, leadership, technical, and technological competencies.

Analytical competencies focus on understanding and applying six theoretical foundations. They include: career development theory, organization development theory, reward system theory, performance theory, staff selection theory, and training theory. The theoretical concepts are paired with the applications for a very straightforward reason. Teaching a person *how* to do something, assuming that he or she possesses skill in that area, is only half of the picture. Your understanding of the theories supporting the skills will also help others to see *why* a particular intervention is most appropriate. This combination of theory and application is essential for helping others to see the complete picture: how *and* why the intervention will improve performance.

Other analytical competencies include performance gap analysis and analyzing performance data. As previously stated, knowing what is involved in conducting a thorough front-end analysis is crucial to selecting the most appropriate intervention to solve the problem. The intervention selector needs to take that knowledge one step beyond conducting analysis, however. He or she must also be able to analyze the data in the context of seeking a near-perfect match between problem and solution. Building a sound approach for selecting and defending the chosen intervention begins with sifting through the important findings contained in the performance gap analysis.

The final three competencies associated with the intervention selector role are: knowledge management, systems thinking, and intervention selection. Once an intervention is selected to eliminate the root causes of a particular problem, managing the knowledge necessary to realistically carry out the intervention becomes vitally important. Systems thinking competency refers to an understanding of how problems and solutions are interrelated and how rarely a problem affects only an isolated organizational component. Systems thinking helps you to see, and share with others, how a proposed change in one part of the organization will likely affect other parts.

The business competencies associated with the intervention selector role are: cost/benefit analysis, identification of critical business issues, industry awareness, quality implications, and outsourcing management. Before an intervention can be "sold" to the organization, it is important to forecast the value of the intervention in terms of the costs and benefits associated with it. We suggest that you put this information in written (as well as oral) reports to your stakeholders. Your knowledge of critical business issues facing your organization, your demonstration of awareness of the trends associated with your industry, and how the recommended changes will impact the business aspects of the intervention, must be made clear to your stakeholders. This will help them focus their thinking on the link between the performance gap analysis and the selection of an appropriate intervention to close the performance gap.

Realistically, professionals from outside the organization are sometimes best equipped to handle some interventions. The competency of outsourcing management is important because 1) you need to recognize when the solution to a problem exceeds your organization's abilities, and 2) you need to be able to assist stakeholders in choosing the best resources from outside the organization to solve the problem.

The interpersonal competencies associated with the intervention selector role include: communication, communication networks, consulting, and interpersonal relationship building. Two important aspects of the intervention selector role include knowing how to effectively communicate the interventions needed to produce desired results and knowing what methods of communication will best get the message out to your stakeholders. Effectively applying the right combination of oral and written communication methods will help others gain insight into how the intervention will help and how your stakeholders might make the best use of their current resources. Relationship building with your stakeholders is key. Remember that the intervention selector cannot be expected to work alone to produce desired results; building relationships with others, and effectively communicating the plan to others, will increase the chances that the selected intervention will be successful.

The first competency in the leadership grouping is buy-in/advocacy. This refers to building ownership and support for workplace initiatives. Using interpersonal competencies to communicate goals with others involved in the performance improvement effort, and to keep all stakeholders informed of the goals and progress being made, will aid in their buying into the goals and keep them focused on end results. We urge you to reflect on ethical behavior as you work toward buy-in for the performance improvement effort. As it is often difficult to look beyond preconceived notions about what will be the best approach to solving a performance-related problem, it's important to stay focused on the results of the performance gap analysis.

The technical competency associated with the intervention selector role is adult learning. Perhaps the most important aspect of adult learning to remember is that adults need to know why they must change something before they will undertake the change. Simply telling adults that they must change or learn something new is not enough. They need to understand why change or learning is necessary. Adults want to take responsibility for their own decisions. This is why it's critically important to involve those in need of learning or change when selecting an intervention.

The final competency grouping deals with technological competencies. To select the most appropriate intervention, you need to know the various possible methods of delivering the intervention to the organization. You are not required to be an expert on all of the delivery methods available, but you do need to be aware of existing, new, and emerging technologies. Computer-mediated communication, distance education, and electronic performance support systems are useful for teaching new methods or procedures to large numbers of people in different locations simultaneously.

The competencies demonstrated while enacting the role of the intervention selector naturally lead to outputs. One main output is the provision of recommendations about selecting interventions to address or avert problems—or to seize opportunities. Another output of this role is the recommendation of how interventions can be combined. Often, a combination of two or more interventions may be needed to solve a performance problem. Forecasting how the intervention(s) will impact the organization is another output associated with this role.

One very important output deals with defining how the

intervention(s) will be aligned with desired business results. Remember that selecting interventions to solve problems is not enough; interventions must always be chosen with the organization's vision and goals in mind. Without keeping the organization's vision and goals at the forefront of the intervention selection process, interventions can actually do more harm than good to the organization and potentially waste precious organizational resources.

CEO-Identified Competencies for the Intervention Selector Role

As stated earlier in this chapter, many CEOs we interviewed perceived that the intervention selector role belonged to all managers. Some thought it might be a shared role between WLP professionals and managers. This perception of the intervention selector role as separate from the WLP professional was a bit troublesome; both the credibility of the WLP professional and the credibility of the WLP field seemed to be in question. As mentioned in Chapter 1, CEOs' perceptions of the WLP field have evolved over time based on their experiences in dealing with performance improvement issues. One reason why CEOs presented a less than positive view of the WLP professional's role in selecting appropriate interventions might be that their WLP professionals have not sufficiently met the challenges posed by the role in the past.

Another more critical reason for this perception is that you might not have understood how you fit into the scheme of the entire spectrum of roles as a WLP professional. In other words, if you view the work you perform as training, you will be viewed as the person who facilitates training programs, rather than as the person responsible for leading the WLP effort, the expert resource for determining the best interventions to meet your organization's performance improvement needs. The shared-role concept, however, is certainly not out of line with the overall tenets of WLP. Remember that WLP espouses shared responsibility for carrying out the seven WLP roles.

● "I can't really associate the words intervention selector with a trainer in this organization. The leaders and managers would select the interventions and then go back to the training structure that we have created to fill those voids."

We can gather from this comment that this CEO views the intervention selector role as part of the managers' responsibilities. Other CEOs supported that view:

● "I think that skill set should be held by managers in our organization....[The skill] can be improved through training, but the responsibility of that activity is the managers'."

● "This seems to me like a role or a function of, say, a manager....As part of their toolkit they might select interventions that make sense, depending on what the situation is."

Other CEOs made similar comments about who should handle the role of the intervention selector:

● "I don't see that as a separate role in our organization but a part of the leadership team's responsibility."

● "I would see the trainer working with managers where there's a problem with performance...being able to look at what the problem is, understand it, and then offer suggested modules or appropriate programs—specific interventions that would help that individual employee or manager do better."

● "The individual working in conjunction with the department would devise the best ways of conveying the message."

Some CEOs didn't hesitate to respond—but did not elaborate on their responses. For example:

● "Not at all by trainers."

● "[The role belongs to] human resources."

● "Done by managers."

● "I think that role is done by operational managers and somewhat by human resources."

Several comments were directly related to the competencies of the intervention selector role. For example, one CEO made it a point to mention the technological competencies necessary to enact this role:

- "There's no question that the Internet is radically changing our entire business model and the way we conduct business. Almost everything that we do has got to be reinvented over the next couple of years. And so we need to stay on top of all of the trends that are out there, and then figure out how it's going to change our organization and communicate that throughout the organization because it's going to change people's jobs."

Here we see an understanding of the competency of technological literacy: understanding and appropriately applying existing, new, and emerging technology. There is also a hint here that simply knowing the trends is not enough. The intervention selector must also communicate about these trends and their implications throughout the organization. The interpersonal competencies of communication, communication networks, and interpersonal relationship building need to be performed effectively.

One CEO recognized the value of a thorough analysis of performance problems, and related the analyst role to that of intervention selector.

- "In tangent with the analyst, the analyst has to have his or her bag of tricks, the tools for interventions....It's hard to identify a real problem if you don't know how to intervene and resolve the problem, so the trainer as interventionist needs to be a student of [how to] intervene because those tools change all the time....I think they need to know about the latest intervention methodology being applied to these problems. So I think that the [roles] of analyst and intervention selector have to be very closely aligned, capable of doing one or the other effectively."

The following CEO quote highlights the importance of the theoretical components of both the analytical competencies and the adult learning (technical) competency associated with the intervention selector role.

- "I think that the role [of intervention selector] is carried out between the organizational development person and the leader of the given department, and it gets into some educational theory on how best to transmit a given message. I would see it kind of like in a curriculum, having to be developed in conjunction with the department you're working with."

It is evident that this CEO sees the intervention selector role as a shared role within the organization:

● "I see [intervention selection] being done more from a recommendation standpoint...building on the analytical, then identifying interventions that could be made, and then recommending them to my management. I suppose this person could be the leader in carrying out or developing the intervention, but I don't see the training person basically doing that on their own."

Another CEO did not specifically address perceived competencies of the intervention selector but did focus on what the workforce might need in terms of learning in order for the organization to be successful:

● "[WLP professionals] need to understand our company's culture. [They also need to] enhance specific technical skills and job knowledge...to teach soft skills."

This CEO is drawing conclusions about the interventions his or her organization might need. This is a scenario in which the intervention selector could get trapped into assuming that these suggestions are commands that need to be carried out. It is important to consider that in a situation where a CEO expresses perceptions about the organization's learning needs, you, as the WLP professional, should gain more insight into the CEO's thought process. This demonstrates interest in the perceptions your CEO holds about the learning needs of your organization and also creates an opportunity for you to explain your role as a WLP analyst and intervention selector.

We have established that only by completing a thorough analysis of performance problems can a decision be made about intervention selection. The point here is that you need to embrace any opportunity to educate CEOs, albeit tactfully, about your roles and competencies as a WLP professional.

The following comment indicates a perspective that views training as just one possible intervention to improve human performance. This CEO also recognizes that interventions should not be generic solutions to problems, making it clear that interventions need to be selected to solve specific problems:

- "The word intervention implies to me that there's a problem....When we have an employee who is failing to meet our needs, we develop a workout plan for that employee that may or may not include additional training....The word intervention implies to me that there's an identified problem specific to an individual and that there's some planned effort to change that."

Another CEO mentioned other interventions that might be used to solve human performance issues:

- "Try to determine what the best course of action on a given problem that may or may not include training....It may be other techniques or modalities or other options to be pursued—it may be process redesign—so I think someone who [plays the intervention selector role] can discern what best fits this particular situation....I think this role would take a lot of creativity."

A few CEOs did see the WLP professional enacting the role of the intervention selector:

- "That may be the best description you've given so far of the education role. I think it might elevate the perception of the position and make it seem more practical."
- "I like the word intervention because it's proactive....I like the word selector because it's targeted, and so I think it's a positive role."

Two CEOs specifically invited discussion of performance improvement opportunities and possible interventions between WLP professionals and senior leaders:

- "Advising senior managers or advising me [the CEO] in a particular case of opportunities we can employ that would help the individual perform better."

● "I think they can serve as internal consultants to operational managers who are confronted with a problem on which they need assistance."

From the CEO comments above, it appears that there are broadly diverse opinions about the intervention selector role. Some CEOs expressed opinions about who should enact the role, while others expressed beliefs about the competencies necessary for carrying out the role. Of course, effective WLP professionals will take steps to discover the perceptions of their CEOs. The perceptions that require examination in greater detail are those that expressed that someone other than the WLP professional should be enacting the intervention selector role. In the next section, we discuss what you should do as an intervention selector, based upon the CEOs' comments in this section.

Developing into the Intervention Selector Who Matches CEO Expectations

There are four specific things you should do to enact the intervention selector role:

❏ Understand the role
❏ Understand the competencies associated with the role
❏ Evaluate your own level of competency to perform the role effectively
❏ Seek input from your CEO and other stakeholders in the organization about their perceptions and expectations of the role

The new paradigm of Workforce Learning and Performance (WLP)—as distinct from previous ones about training or HRD—supports your leadership in enacting the intervention selector role. But it also supports the involvement of other organizational stakeholders in determining the most appropriate interventions to address the root causes of human performance problems. Sharing the role can take many forms, and can provide numerous benefits to you and to the organization. By sharing the role with others, you will sensitize them to the complexity and importance of choosing the most appropriate interventions. Further, involving the people who will be affected by the change in making the selection of interventions typically produces a higher level of commitment to the solution. Adults want to take ownership of their problems; when they are included in the problem analysis and decision-making process for selecting the intervention, this ownership is much easier to gain.

Another benefit of including others in the intervention selection process is the opportunity to tap the wealth of knowledge others might have about the problem. Employees bring a vast array of life and work experiences to the job. Tapping their expertise can improve the quality of the intervention selection process and can conserve time, money, and effort.

It is also important to understand some of the challenges you might potentially encounter while performing the intervention selector role. The first challenge deals with selecting an intervention too quickly. The intervention must be soundly based on the performance gap analysis discussed in Chapter 3. On one hand, you don't want to make decisions hastily, but on the other hand, you don't want to prolong the process by making no decision at all. A second challenge is the temptation to overanalyze the problem. If you do that, stakeholders may wonder whether you have a proper sense of urgency and may become doubtful of your competence in selecting the most appropriate intervention. This could cause your stakeholders to become frustrated and lose the momentum to seize the opportunity to effectively solve the problem.

Become familiar with the many interventions currently available for finding the root causes of human performance problems. If you possess limited knowledge of interventions, and count on the few with which you are familiar to solve performance improvement issues, the most appropriate intervention to deal with a given situation may not be implemented.

Next, develop a communication plan that includes everyone in the intervention selection process. This will help to avoid unnecessary confusion about the details of the process. A solid communication plan will help you gain buy-in for interventions and develop advocates of the process, increasing commitment and support from stakeholders involved with the performance improvement effort.

Finally, don't experiment with new types of interventions until you know for certain that an intervention will have a positive impact on the situation at hand. Remember that many human performance problems are a result of poor communication, misunderstanding of goals, or lack of information to perform a job effectively. With a coherent understanding of the intervention selector role, you can turn to exploring the specific competencies associated with it.

Applying the Intervention Selector Competencies

There are a total of twenty-eight competencies associated with the intervention selector role, but only five of them do not overlap with competencies associated with the WLP roles of manager and analyst. We focus our attention on these five competencies. They are:

1. Intervention selection
2. Training theory and application
3. Adult learning
4. Distance education
5. Electronic performance support systems

The key issue in the intervention selection competency is selecting interventions that will address the *root causes* of a problem, as opposed to treating the *symptoms* of a problem. This competency develops over time as analytical competencies improve. For example, if a problem underwent a thorough performance gap analysis, then the selection of an intervention should be relatively simple. Intervention selection is limited, however, to the interventions with which you are familiar. Expanding your knowledge of the interventions currently available and keeping your eye on new and emerging interventions is crucial. A good place to start increasing your knowledge of the interventions available today is the *ASTD Reference Guide to Workplace Learning and Performance: Roles, Competencies, and Outputs.*[5] This two-volume set can help you identify, understand, and apply a wide variety of current interventions. The *ASTD Reference Guide* can also help to further your understanding of training theory and application. Additionally, several job aids are available to hone your skills and build your competencies in WLP.[6]

Adult learning principles have been published widely during the past thirty years or so. The best place to start for development in this area is with the writing of Malcolm Knowles, considered by many to be the first authority on how adults learn and how they use their knowledge, skills, and attitudes to perform their work. The technology-based competencies of distance education and electronic performance support systems deal with how knowledge can be delivered to learners. The *ASTD Reference Guide* can serve as an excellent resource on these technological competencies and their possible applications for interventions in your organization.

Reflect on your analytical, business, interpersonal, leadership, technical, and technological competencies for this role. Find your areas of strength and those competencies in which you think you could or should improve. Follow the directions included in Appendix C-7 to C-12.

The role of the intervention selector is not an easy one, but if you are armed with knowledge about the specific aspects of it, understand the contribution it can make to your organization, and build competence in enacting it, other organizational members are sure to take notice.

Summary

This chapter focused on CEO perceptions of WLP professionals enacting the intervention selector role. The intervention selector identifies possible solutions designed to address the root causes of a performance problem. The chapter reviewed the role and its required competencies, noting what CEOs had to say about them. Of special note is that CEOs generally believe that all managers, not just WLP professionals, have responsibility for identifying possible solutions to human performance problems.

CHAPTER 5

The Intervention Designer/Developer Role— The CEO Perspective

> **B**ecause our company is going through a very profound change, our ability to use the learning *systems*, training systems, and involvement systems will be a major part of making this culture shift to this new customer-orientation. And it will [have to] be [brought about] through both conventional and some nonconventional learning programs.
>
> A CEO INTERVIEWED FOR THIS BOOK

The intervention designer/developer role is at the front line of WLP programming. Because this role is responsible for designing interventions, it comes into direct contact with all stakeholders of a change effort and is crucial to the integration and use of learning as a performance improvement tool. Historically, the intervention designer/developer was one of the first WLP roles identified, since it involved preparing instruction for delivery.[1] But as computer technologies and other emerging instructional technologies continue to develop, and new forms of work evolve from new business technologies, it is one role that has changed more than any other.

Information technology has changed the way organizations operate, organize themselves, communicate (within and without) and, in a nutshell, how they stay viable. New business technologies have created Web-based companies, networks, systems, and training. The World Wide Web continues to redefine the role of the intervention designer/developer. This role has become very broad in scope, involves intensive collaboration with outside resources, but remains at the core of WLP functions.

The intervention designer/developer role has always contained inherent complexities. Although this role is most commonly understood as the one responsible for designing training interventions and curricula, it often requires services delivered through teamwork. Partnering with the learning needs analyst, the WLP manager, department line managers, and employees in order to create learning programs that address performance needs are core functions of this role. All jobs, to various degrees, involve working with others on a project-to-project basis, but the intervention designer/developer must work closely with many people on each learning intervention.

The outputs of the WLP intervention designer include: writing learning programs linked to an organization's business goals, involving line managers and department leaders in the program structure, and allowing for a program evaluation plan. Outputs of the WLP developer include: review of learning materials, recommendations about instructional strategies, the development of learning strategies, and research. This role can be regarded as combining many sub-roles.

CEOs perceive the complexity and rapidly changing nature of this role. From designing learning programs that address performance needs to creating hard-copy learning program supplies and delivering programs, the duties of this role are so diverse that it has often been regarded as one balanced between internally and externally housed positions. The availability of highly professional and ready-to-use training resources from vendors has increased and provides a broad source for materials. CEO comments on the role of the intervention designer/developer reveal the following three responsibilities:

1. Using the most current technologies to create innovative learning experiences
2. Integrating company learning programs across the organization
3. Changing employee behavior and impacting job performance

CEOs also understand that, in order to create cost-effective learning programs, some learning resources must be brought in from outside vendors. Knowing where to find appropriate and effective learning materials is very important to the intervention designer/developer.

Given the speed of change in today's workplace, it is good practice to continually assess how work is performed in each particular job. The information in this chapter is intended to ask the following questions of you as a WLP professional:

- Who is providing this role in your organization?
- How is the role being provided?
- Are the latest technologies being used in the role?
- How integrated is the role throughout the organization?
- How are WLP programs reflecting changes in employee behavior and at the job?
- Is this your role, and how do you match up with CEO perceptions of it?
- What are your strengths and weaknesses in the role?
- What does your role development plan look like?

This chapter will review the intervention designer/ developer role, and present CEO perspectives on the responsibilities related to it. The information provided here comes from research publications on WLP competencies, interviews with CEOs, and experiences working with WLP intervention designer/developers.

What Is the Intervention Designer/Developer Role?

The role of the intervention designer/developer has evolved

into a single function with deep requirements. Previous studies have identified as many as eight unique HRD roles now considered responsibilities of the designer/developer[2]:

☐ *Facilitator*: responsible for organizing and managing group processes so that individual and group learning occurs

☐ *Learning materials specialist*: responsible for structuring and preparing documented instructional materials

☐ *Instructor*: responsible for leading and presenting learning programs

☐ *Media specialist*: responsible for delivering learning programs in the most appropriate format (written, audio, computer, satellite, Web)

☐ *Program designer*: responsible for identifying learning objectives and the business need for the training

☐ *Strategist*: responsible for communicating how individual programs are connected to the organization's mission and vision

☐ *Task analyst*: responsible for identifying the sequence of activities required for learners to successfully perform their jobs

☐ *Theoretician*: responsible for applying adult learning theory to individual programs

The effective performance of each of these functions is crucial for the success of the instructional designer/developer. The combination of these roles into one increases the complexity of demands on the WLP professional.

The evolution of the intervention designer/developer role into what it is today reflects changes in the business world, which have broadened responsibilities and decreased divisions among many business functions. Changes in technology have allowed for (and forced) one-person positions to do the work previously done by many. Providing the outputs expected from this role requires partnering with others in the organization, outsourcing, and/or putting in extra hours to get the job done. The current definition of the intervention designer/developer includes the following activities[3]:

1.   Organize and lead group processes

2. Move throughout the organization and work with managers to design learning interventions
3. Identify and engage internal and external resources to use for training (experts and learning programs)
4. Identify learning objectives and customize learning programs to the needs of the participants
5. Instruct
6. Integrate the learning program into an organizational system for learning

These activities require WLP professionals to be thoroughly conversant with the business, its goals, strategies, and individual department functions. The designer/developer needs to be comfortable interviewing and communicating with experts, preparing task analysis, and writing, developing, and creating innovative learning interventions. And given the move toward increased globalization, many enacting the role must also be familiar with other cultures and other languages.

The competencies associated with the WLP role of intervention designer/developer have been categorized into the analytical, business, interpersonal, leadership, technical, and technological competencies:

❏ *Analytical Competencies*: According to *ASTD Models for Workplace Learning and Performance*, there are eleven analytical competencies associated with the intervention designer and developer role. They are analyzing performance data, career development theory and application, intervention selection, knowledge management, model building, organization development theory and application, performance theory, reward system theory and application, standards identification, systems thinking, and training theory and application.[4]

❏ *Business Competencies*: There are only two business competencies associated with the intervention designer/developer role. They are industry awareness and project management.

❏ *Interpersonal Competencies*: Only three interpersonal competencies are associated with the intervention designer/developer role: communication, communication networks, and interpersonal relationship building.

❐   *Leadership Competencies*: There are two leadership competencies for this role: diversity awareness and ethics modeling.

❐   *Technical Competencies*: Adult learning and survey design and development are the two technical competencies associated with this role.

❐   *Technological Competencies*: The four technological competencies include computer-mediated communication, distance education, electronic performance support systems, and technological literacy.

We have provided you with worksheets to think through how well you are prepared to demonstrate each competency category in Appendix C-13 to C-18.

Why Is This Role Important?

The intervention designer/developer role is important because it provides the content and the package for WLP services. The designer/developer uses the work of the analyst to focus on the skills to be improved, and to identify how participants' job performance fits within an organization's mission and strategy objectives. The working relationship between the intervention designer side of the role and the analyst role produces learning objectives and content for the program. The work between the developer side of the role and the intervention selector produce the packaging of the learning program, resulting in materials to reinforce learning objectives. The intervention designer/developer is responsible for structuring learning topics and producing learning materials. Ultimately, the retention and motivated application of learning content depends upon the planning skills of the designer/developer.

To boil it down, the intervention designer/developer is important for the following five reasons:

1.   *It is the point of stakeholder contact.* The role involves direct contact with all or many stakeholders of an intervention, and the immediate success or failure of learning interventions depends upon the interaction with stakeholders.

2.   *It translates performance needs into learning objectives.* The role involves interpreting results from performance gap analy-

sis into attainable program objectives so that problems can be solved.

3. *It provides a systematic approach for presenting company strategy.* The role is responsible for a "master plan" to use learning interventions that connect short- and long-range strategic goals to the learning needs of individuals.

4. *It reinforces organizational values and culture.* The role is responsible for designing learning programs that communicate organizational values and direct organizational culture.

5. *It links individual performance to company performance.* The role is responsible for increasing awareness of individuals' impact on the performance of the group and the company.

CEO Opinions About the Intervention Designer/Developer Role

CEO opinions on how WLP programs are used can shed light on the role of the intervention designer/developer. Interview data from twenty-eight CEOs in organizations with 1,000 or more employees revealed that they perceive the primary objective of workplace learning programs is to create new skills and behaviors.[5] Although most of us would expect management to agree that workplace learning programs should be geared toward meeting the business needs of the organization, we rarely hear about how learning is related to achieving strategic objectives. CEOs believe that WLP programs should be used in the following seven ways to meet business challenges and facilitate change.

1. PROVIDE COMPANY-SPECIFIC KNOWLEDGE

WLP programs provide a resource that results in the sharing of technical and business information about a company's products, services, customers, competitors, markets, and processes. Increased company-specific knowledge is the intellectual capital that supports an organization's core competency and leads to sustained strategic advantage. Whether this information involves technical aspects of goods and services, or business information on markets or competitors, CEOs believe that WLP programs should be used to transfer this knowledge throughout the organization. According to one CEO:

● "For us the biggest challenge is making sure that those managers can articulate the value-added technology that our company brings to our clients. And certainly, our in-house learning programs are a key component of increasing the ability of our technical managers to articulate the value-added technology that our company can bring to our clients. And once again, our chief technologists within our Advanced Technology Centers shoulder those. Because a lot of our technology is proprietary and patented to our company, the only place that we can develop this knowledge base and learning is within our own company through our learning programs."

In short, then, learning programs serve a dual purpose of communicating the fruits of experience while also providing a venue to generate new ideas.

2. TEACH TECHNICAL SKILLS

Another function of WLP programs is to build worker capacity to apply the technical skills necessary to particular jobs. Technical skills range from routine processes used within specific jobs to working with software applications, from the use of tools to fabricate products to the control of technological hardware in assembling systems. An example of these types of WLP programs is the ISO certification process. Teaching technical skills through WLP programs creates a broader market for company products. As one CEO explained:

● "Keeping the equipment up and performing close to perfection requires really smart technicians. So the first thing that learning programs have got to do is train these technicians, in terms of how to maintain the tools and, when tools go down to improve the mean time to repair. So clearly you got to have people that can train the people to do that. Second, your engineers have to be knowledgeable relative to new processes and new techniques."

3. PERSONALIZE COMPANY CULTURE

WLP programs are a means to transmitting the company's mission, values, and cultural topics, and to facilitate structural corporate change. Total alignment between an individual position and the company mission must be reinforced through formal and informal means. CEOs expect the company's WLP programs to reflect and reinforce existing company values, while also stimulating company change. As one CEO put it:

● "Workplace learning is used in our company in managing the transition to a specialized product market. Our learning programs are absolutely essential. It's got to be learning that meets the mission of the business and really drives the business to attain the mission or the vision that we've set forth."

4. RECRUIT, TRAIN, AND RETAIN HUMAN RESOURCES

In a tight labor market for skilled employees, WLP programs can attract and develop new employees, both strategically (for the company), and personally (for the individual). New employees are more likely to join a company that they believe will provide them with the training necessary for their success. Structured WLP programs are looked upon as a recruiting tool. Employees who use learning programs to develop skills that lead to better-paying jobs in other organizations can be a concern, but most CEOs we interviewed believe that effective WLP programs function as employee retention and development programs. One CEO emphasized that:

● "First of all, I think job fairs provide an opportunity for the people out in our communities, who may be prospective employees, to come and see us and learn what jobs we have available. Job fairs give us an opportunity to sell our organization and provide information concerning our mission and values as well as our vision, and they allow people to see that this is a good place to work. I also believe that learning programs provide an opportunity—once we get the employees—to educate the employees to our specific organization with orientation programs that would be more or less general orientation programs. Specific departmental orientation programs then…get right down to the job, and then contin-ue to check on the competencies of our employees, making sure that they are meeting the challenges through education, through in-service training, and the like."

5. SYSTEM

WLP programs provide an infrastructure that enables an organ-ization to teach, increasing employee awareness of individual jobs and the larger business issues concerning the company. WLP programs also provide an avenue for increasing involve-ment and excitement among people in the company:

● "One of the first things that new people do, other than ori-entation and things like that, is to come in contact with somebody who's going to train them, or teach them how to do their job. And from the standpoint of our stores we need to have effective systems in place so that the people that we do screen and hire are challenged and excited from day one."

6. GENERAL BUSINESS SKILLS

WLP programs are used to increase the workforce's basic busi-ness skills and cross-functional abilities. Learning programs provide a means by which general business skills can be built among all employees. According to one CEO we interviewed:

● "We use learning programs to build basic fundamental types of skills that you need to work, [teaching our employ-ees] how to make business decisions coupled with techni-cal decisions….We've been in fact training a lot of our employees in basic business concepts so they'll know how to make good business decisions. Essentially we try and cre-ate a whole bunch of business managers, [giving them busi-ness skills to go] with the technical skills that they obvious-ly have to have to succeed in this kind of environment."

7. COMMUNICATION

CEOs use WLP programs to broadcast organization information and develop new skills among individuals. One CEO we inter-viewed explained that:

● "There's no question that the Internet is changing—radically changing—our entire business model and the way that we conduct business. Almost everything that we do has got to be reinvented over the next couple of years. And so we need to, one, stay on top of all of the trends that are out there, and then two, figure out how it's going to change our organization and communicate that throughout the organization, because it is going to change people's jobs."

Shared Responsibility

Perhaps no other role in the WLP portfolio requires as much technical skill as the intervention designer/developer. To review, technical skills are defined as those competencies directly related to WLP products and services—that is, adult learning, facilitation, feedback, intervention monitoring, questioning, and survey design and development. CEOs do not believe that this role is exclusive to the trainer, and, given the broad nature of the position, it is fortunate that CEOs don't expect one person to carry out all aspects of the role. Upon review, we see that the role requires four core activities:

1. Organizing the logistics for the learning program
2. Designing learning interventions
3. Leading learning programs
4. Aligning learning programs to the organization's strategy

Input from CEOs reflects that they appreciate the complexity of this role, and expect some responsibilities to be delegated to others either inside or outside of the organization.

In a study of sixteen CEOs of health care providers throughout the United States, twelve believed that the intervention designer/developer role required partnering with others outside the organization's in-house training function.[6] Some CEOs did not believe the role of intervention designer/developer belonged exclusively to trainers; they viewed it as a management function. Others believed that the role *required* going outside the organization.

● "We'll look at the intervention that's necessary, then we'll go and get what we need to fill the void as best we can afford it."

This perspective sees the intervention designer/developer as someone who "would be an outside trainer who would design and develop interventions."

One CEO provided a "bird's-eye" view of the role, saying:

● "I think that when you start getting into creation stages for these programs you've got to deal outside your organization to get someone who's not so close to the forest they can't see the trees. On a day-to-day basis your trainers are very good at identifying problems that are repetitive, but when it comes to the creative aspect, I don't think they have the time or the resources to do R&D, but they do have the ability to call in a consultant from time to time."

The significant CEO insight here is that the intervention designer/developer role is too complex and time-consuming to be handled by one person. CEOs throughout the United States see the role as a joint responsibility between WLP professionals and operating managers. This partnership leverages the technical strength of the WLP professional with the operational knowledge of line mangers to produce learning interventions based on sound adult learning principles while directed at achieving company-specific objectives. As several CEOs explained:

● "I guess the responsibility for the [intervention designer/developer] resides with our line management, working with our department of education to see that the needs are met."

● "I see [the trainer] being consultative, advising me or top management to work hand-in-hand to create those interventions and evaluate the effectiveness of those interventions."

● "[The role of intervention designer/developer] doesn't belong specifically to a trainer, instead it belongs to whoever serves as a consultant to the organization to solve the problems....But I don't think I would hire someone to be the thinker for someone else."

● "[The intervention designer/developer role is] done by managers in consultation with those performing the training function."

The responsibility for learning intervention design and development is jointly shared by line management and the WLP department, and at times may involve using outside resources. CEOs articulated expectations that the role should provide planned learning programs that improve performance.

- "I think it's [the intervention designer/developer's role] to develop some pragmatic plan which deals with the problem where it occurs."

- "It would indicate somebody who analyzes the need [and then tries] to design a training program to meet that need....They might use pre-packaged programs that are on the market, they might develop it from scratch, or a combination of the two."

- "I think [the intervention designer/developer is] someone who can take the situation or problem and develop and design whatever the appropriate intervention may be, whether it's a program, educational, or process redesign....I see [this person] as someone who could actually conceive and create something as opposed to selecting from a pre-existing group of options."

- "You've determined the gap, you've assessed the alternative ways based on background experience or other connections to address that gap, and you've gone through a process of determining the most appropriate way to intervene...then you design that intervention."

- "I guess I see [the intervention designer/developer role] in this case as more of a specialist—someone who can be brought in on a particular type of problem...what comes to my mind is more of a specialist."

CEO-Identified Competencies for Intervention Designers/Developers

Effective learning programs begin with the end in mind. CEOs are interested in the design and development of learning programs that interest participants while involving the whole organization and solving business problems. CEOs expect their companies' learning programs to be engaging and interesting for the employees in the program, but more importantly, to involve other company resources in the design of program objectives. By recognizing the perceptions of the senior leader, and developing competencies that reflect those perceptions, a WLP professional can increase the relevance and efficacy of an organization's WLP programs. In the end, CEOs expect participants to be stimulated by new information presented in programs, and to be able to use this information in their jobs.

● "When somebody attends, for instance, a one-month training program in Dallas, Texas, that individual shows up there on day one, and on day thirty, he has a knowledge and practical basis to go back to his remote location and provide that technology or service or apply the knowledge...from this training program. So that's what I would call effective."

Providing company-specific knowledge and skills were two of the most common CEO-identified objectives of WLP programs, along with the need for learning programs to be creative, exciting, culturally aware, and company inclusive. In this chapter we have organized CEO input into three key competency elements for the intervention designer/developer. In this role, CEOs expect WLP professionals to:

1. Create innovative learning experiences.
2. Integrate learning programs across the organization.
3. Collaborate on changing job-specific employee behavior.

1. CREATING INNOVATIVE LEARNING EXPERIENCES THROUGH CURRENT TECHNOLOGIES

The first competency identified by CEOs for the intervention designer/developer role is the ability to apply current technologies to provide broad access to interactive and engaging learning programs. CEOs are aware of the new opportunities provided by the World Wide Web for delivering user-friendly, interactive, animated learning. The fact that virtually every employee has a Web-enabled computer on their desk, or has access to one in their company, reflects the necessity of technology-based learning.

● "I think it's very important that they stay on top of all the *new technologies and opportunities and ways that there are to deliver education.* This is such a fast changing field. [Take] the example I gave you of me taking a lecture course, a one-hour lecture on *active technologies delivered through the Web.* I mean that wasn't available a year ago, at least not for our company. And we have new technologies and ways to deliver courses. I think it's important that the person [in charge of designing learning interventions] have a good understanding of the business, in as many aspects of the business as possible, so they can understand what kind of training is necessary."

The theme of business competence permeates all aspects of CEO-based WLP competency perceptions, and ties into the efficient use of technology. Good business sense and the use of technology can be applied to two areas of concern for intervention designers/developers:

- ❐ Making sure the content of the program has direct business application
- ❐ Being aware of company budgets and the costs of technology.

Although CEO comments are directed more toward the concern for application of learning programs to the company's business needs, CEOs and other levels of management want to know what new technologies will cost the company.

- ● "I think these people need to be *good business people* and understand the business, and it's very important that they stay on top of all the *new technologies* and opportunities and ways that there are to deliver education. This is such a fast-changing field."

Our research indicated that many CEOs linked technology, creativity, and employee interest in learning. Several CEOs referred to WLP professionals as needing to demonstrate abilities to use technology in concert with interpersonal skills, facilitation skills, and research skills. For an intervention designer/developer, technology should not be separated from the total learning program, but instead be integrated throughout. Technology should be used to make employees aware of learning programs, prepare them for the learning program, deliver the program, and develop feedback on the program. CEOs see technology not only as a learning delivery vehicle, but also as a tool to encourage employee involvement:

- "[WLP professionals who successfully enact this role need] excellent people skills, facilitation skills, training skills, some *motivational skills*, [and] in today's technology-driven age, an appreciation of and understanding for how technology is used to increase interest in learning."

- "In many cases, that is not traditional classroom work. It is other types of learning environments, and so I expect those people to be *innovative* in those areas and be bringing the latest, most up-to-date kinds of things. And that requires them to get out into the world and see what's going on in terms of training and development with our competitors in comparable companies."

- "Someone who's very knowledgeable about his or her field. Do they have a good network? Do they know what the literature says? Are they in the loop as far as what's going on out there in their field? These people need *a strong willingness to try new things, to try new ideas, to experiment quite a bit*."

2. INTEGRATING COMPANY LEARNING PROGRAMS ACROSS THE ORGANIZATION

The second of the three competencies CEOs identified for the intervention designer/developer role is the ability to integrate the whole company into the learning process. CEOs insist that learning programs involve line management expertise and in-house knowledge resources. As we have seen in this chapter, providing company-specific knowledge is one responsibility of learning programs. By using line managers as instructors or design consultants, the intervention designer/developer builds an internal support system for learning programs, leveraging the organization's human resources and human capital to customize learning content design. CEOs expect WLP professionals to present content that improves individuals' abilities to perform their jobs and to deliver learning programs that can be supported by managers throughout the organization:

- "I think that the *ownership for this knowledge learning and the use of information belongs across an organization* and all the leadership positions, and not just HR. Frankly, the HR person can be a catalyst, but the people that manage the people drive the day-to-day behavior of an organization. So I think this has to be from the *top down a priority*—from the CEO all the way down through the organization—that this is important and that *everybody takes ownership.*"

● "Clearly, understanding what people need to be able to perform their jobs, and that's different than what people want. The second thing that I think is something that is just starting to emerge, and that's understanding...*how the organization works and how it currently transfers knowledge and information throughout the organization*—and then how to tailor programs to help facilitate that."

Along with the expectation for company support of learning programs, CEOs also expect learning programs to be applied in an effective systems approach. This expectation may seem to be outside of the traditional scope of the intervention designer/developer, but it is important, as the very nature of systems skills requires all stakeholders to take responsibility for their part in the system. CEOs expect the intervention designer/developer to create course content that is aligned with company goals and objectives. The content needs to be current, and the format developed in a way that leads to ease in delivery and use on the job. Appreciating the systemic nature of learning interventions, and how the design of learning programs fits with the other elements of the program, WLP professionals must demonstrate an ability to see the larger objectives of learning within the organization's mission:

● "I mean the person has got to have a disposition whereby they can get a charge or a thrill out of developing effective systems that somebody else will probably roll out and implement. We've got 6,300 employees, so you know [that when] you put somebody in this job, they're not actually going to be out in the field doing a whole lot. Their job is to develop and maintain effective systems. And of course, to improve them as the company changes and the needs of the organization change."

● "The next thing is to find an individual who's knowledgeable about delivery systems. And that's a different individual in my organization."

3. CHANGING EMPLOYEE BEHAVIOR AND IMPACTING JOB PERFORMANCE

The third competency identified by CEOs for the role of intervention designer/developer is the ability to change employee behavior and improve performance. The very nature of the WLP professional's role is summed up in this competency. CEOs expect intervention design to have a clear connection with employee behaviors, job performance, and possible solutions for improving results. Learning is expected to motivate and demonstrate ideal employee conduct. This designer/developer competency requires an ability to bring the life and soul of the company's products and services into each learning program objective. Each program should include current references to company strategy, goals, threats, and achievements. The intervention designer needs to be able to translate the company's business environment and performance needs into the instructional program. According to several CEOs we interviewed:

● "So he's got to have quite a library of experience relative to places to go for the training, compensation systems, incentive programs. The learning programs have got to work with other HR programs to *provide an incentive* for our people to undertake those things that will build them up for future assignments. So the HR person at our company is really a key spot. He's a very close associate of mine because the biggest and best asset we have across this corporation is the people we have."

● "They can have a very good feel for what I call the usefulness of the training. Is this something that can be used and applied immediately? *So somebody who understands what's needed and who gives them only what they'll use.* And don't dilute the training with a lot of things that take time, cost money, and really get in the way of applying what's useful, because you have to ask yourself—how much do you retain from a training session? You go to a two-week training session and your retention's probably pretty high the first week, but in six months, how much of what you learned have you retained and can you use? So it's really retention and the efficiency of training."

- "Let me just preface it by saying that I think the hardest two things to do in a company these days, one is training. And the second one is installing a new business system, like a new computer system. Those two things are very, very difficult in the hierarchy....Installing a computer system is more complicated than just training people how to use that system—it also involves getting them training while doing the work. The people who do the training kind of take it a little too much for granted and they don't understand how difficult a job it is to train well.... *They have to understand what we do, what our strategy is, what our core competencies are, what makes a successful company.* And again at our company, our motto is People Make the Difference. So, we want to have the best people in terms of skills."

Although training programs cannot be expected to provide a bridge over all performance gaps, the intervention designer/developer must be aware that each learning program needs to show how the skills or knowledge being taught will be demonstrated on the job, and how they will be directed to improve performance. Issues of compensation, up-to-date tools, and current business environment all impact employee performance. Although CEOs appreciate that learning programs do not provide a cure-all for the ills of company performance, WLP professionals should constantly work toward increasing employee awareness of how learning programs can be an investment for improving productivity.

Developing into the Intervention Designer/ Developer Who Matches CEO Expectations

The intervention designer/developer can be the voice of the company's WLP function. Employees may not know who was the manager, analyst, or intervention selector, but they will remember whether or not the course they took was worth their time, and how the material was presented to them. This role is important because it provides the human contact for the company's WLP function. The following six areas for review provide a guideline for personal and programmatic development for the intervention designer/developer.

1. UNDERSTAND THE ROLE

This role has evolved into a broad, deep function requiring collaboration and partnering skills. What previous competency studies of training and HRD identified as many separate roles, have now been combined into the single role of intervention designer/developer. The disparate roles supporting it require skills ranging from interpersonal to technological, and from a task-specific to a developmental focus.

There are many aspects of the role; your job is to find your areas of strength. After you have identified your competencies, identify with whom to partner to enact other aspects of the role. Remember, CEOs expect learning programs to be innovative and company-specific. When you consider your company's learning program content, how is it explicitly related to current business issues? Are your company's learning programs designed to be updated and kept relevant to company strategy? Are your programs developed with a cost-effective and efficient use of resources? How exciting are your programs? As we have learned, this role is very complex, and CEOs expect the intervention designer/developer to be innovative in impacting performance.

2. KNOW THE COMPANY'S BUSINESS

Obviously, the design of a learning program begins with its use in the business. What is your company's business? How has it changed? What is the current business environment for the company's products and services? Answers to these questions provide a context for you and your learners to understand how each learning program is linked to meeting the needs of the company. Each learning program should begin with an update about the business, and a brief statement of where the company stands in meeting its strategic goals and objectives.

3. KNOW THE COMPANY STRUCTURE AND THE JOBS SUPPORTING EACH UNIT

Understanding how organizations are structured and connected is vital for two reasons:

❐   It creates a mental map of how divisions and units are aligned and related.

◻ It provides the intervention designer/developer with a directory of where to go to involve people in program design, and how to integrate learning across the organization.

This "macro-map" of the organization leads to the deeper job level of the organization, where the WLP professional can connect performance measures to individuals. With job/unit level performance information, a WLP professional can create learning interventions to address performance targets. How well do you know the organizational structure of your company? What do your company's job descriptions look like?

4. KNOW WHERE YOUR ORGANIZATION'S KNOWLEDGE CAPITAL RESIDES

One way to increase buy-in for learning programs is to involve managers in training program design. A core question regarding competency-based compensation programs is whether to pay employees for competencies that are not utilized in their jobs. This concern has evolved from an awareness that people bring significant competencies to work that may not have direct applicability to their jobs. Intervention designers should try building all areas of employee competence, and involving those competencies in their design and development role. The immediate place to use untapped organizational competence, or knowledge capital, is in design or instruction roles. What is the knowledge capital of your organization? Is it documented?

5. BECOME YOUR COMPANY'S RESIDENT WORKPLACE LEARNING EXPERT

As explored throughout this chapter, the intervention designer/developer is at the front line of WLP practices. CEOs expect WLP professionals to be the leading resource to provide learning solutions to meet business challenges. Becoming a strong source of knowledge on workplace learning requires a solid understanding of learning theory, and ready access to sources of knowledge on learning. Throughout the evolution of this role, the core body of content knowledge has included: adult education, group processes, instruction, data gathering, and strategy for organizational learning. Currently, the role of designer/

developer also requires knowledge of distance education, multimedia learning environments, e-learning, and self-directed learning.

6. USE TECHNOLOGY

The importance of embracing new and emerging technologies cannot be overstated. Clearly, technology is the driving force behind many changes in the WLP field, and it is redesigning many of our processes. Keep in mind that CEOs are not technology experts. They are as amazed at what can be done with new technologies as we are. We don't necessarily need to know "how it works," but we do need to know how to use technology to achieve our goals. The sooner we begin using new technologies to support learning throughout our organizations, the sooner we will become full partners with our CEOs and other senior leaders in directing the organization toward its goals.

Summary

This chapter focused on CEO perceptions of WLP professionals enacting the intervention designer/developer role. The intervention designer/developer was one of the earliest roles associated with the work of professionals doing work in the field now called WLP. This role bears responsibility for preparing materials to support performance improvement interventions. This chapter reviewed the competencies that are essential to carry out the role effectively and noted what CEOs had to say about them. Of special importance is that the CEO comments gathered from our research indicated that CEOs feel that the role has three key responsibilities:

1. Using the most current technologies to create innovative learning experiences
2. Integrating company-learning programs across the organization
3. Changing employee behavior and impacting job performance.

CHAPTER 6

The Intervention Implementor Role—The CEO Perspective

> The person responsible for WLP is integral and part of the strategic plan in the company, understanding what our business needs are. Because the training has to tie into that. So [requirement] number one is to understand our business strategy and how training can affect it, asking those questions. Number two is to make sure there's a good skills analysis done, understanding the priorities of where we're the weakest. And number three, and maybe the most important of all of it, is [to make sure that this training] is actually being implemented."
>
> A CEO INTERVIEWED FOR THIS BOOK

Many WLP practices are commonly understood by what is involved in implementing interventions. Images are still rather commonplace of the traditional trainer frantically arranging times and dates to carry out teaching assignments, facilitating classroom instruction, and teaching multitudes of employees new methods of performing their work. These images are, in a sense, historical; the WLP field has evolved in significant ways in the last few decades. The notion of human resource development had become a firm part of our professional lives by the 1990s.

Human resource development was the major wave of expansion for the training and development field since Leonard Nadler coined that term while conducting a class at George Washington University in 1968.[1] *Human resource development* (HRD) is defined as "the integrated use of training and development, organization development, and career development to improve individual, group, and organizational effectiveness."[2] This definition expressed the need to expand the field from the application of isolated solutions (such as training) to facilitating organizational change and improving in the performance of the entire organization.[3] WLP professionals have had to work hard to eradicate outdated images of their function—such as the one above—in the minds of their customers.

One image that has plagued the field since its modern genesis is that our function is solely activity-based. This image reflects a perception that once we find the "right" activity for addressing a performance issue, and put that activity into action, we can confidently wipe the dust off our hands and walk away. Implementing an intervention undeniably plays a critical role in getting to results, but the implementation of activities alone cannot be considered the logical end of the process. Analyzing problems is as important as implementing solutions. It follows logically that the process ends with evaluating the solution. In developing and designing interventions, if we stop short at the implementation stage, or simply allow an activity to occur, we cannot know whether the time and effort expended were worthwhile.

It is important to clearly understand what the role of the intervention implementor includes. In the first section of this chapter, we discuss the role of the intervention implementor, and what it can—and should—do for your organization.

What Is the Intervention Implementor Role?

The intervention implementor "ensures the appropriate and

effective implementation of desired interventions that address the specific root causes of human performance gaps."[4] The term "appropriate" in this definition means the most fitting manner in which to implement selected interventions. Some common ways in which interventions are implemented position the WLP professional to serve as instructor, administrator, facilitator, organization development practitioner, or career development specialist. The instructor presents information and leads learning experiences. The administrator ensures that the facilities, equipment, materials, participants, technologies, and other components of the learning event are present, and that the logistics of the learning event run smoothly. The facilitator leads groups to learn in positive ways. Organization development practitioners focus on influencing, and supporting, changes in corporate culture to eliminate the root causes of performance problems. The career development specialist helps others assess their individual competencies, and then assists them in setting goals to attain necessary career objectives.

Most current WLP professionals have the skills to handle these responsibilities. The intervention implementor might also serve an organization appropriately as a compensation specialist, process re-design consultant, or workspace designer. Some WLP professionals might not have extensive experience in these areas; in that case, it's up to us to get help from others. Finding the most appropriate ways to implement interventions is critical to the success of the WLP effort.

In the context of the intervention implementor role, "effective" means producing a *desired* and *decisive* effect. This is achieved by carefully monitoring the implementation of interventions and helping others to understand the vital role they play in the overall strategy of the situation. These are two of the most important activities leading to the successful implementation of interventions, and ultimately, to the results desired by the organization's decision makers for improved performance. Once again, it is imperative to ensure that *desired results* are achieved through the activities involved in implementing interventions. An implementation cannot be considered complete unless it is both appropriate (utilizes the correct approaches) and effective (achieves desired results). In the next chapter, which deals with the role of the change leader, we'll see how this role ensures that results are sustained and become institutionalized.

Like the other WLP roles discussed thus far, the intervention implementor role has undergone—and will continue to undergo—an evolutionary process. It has changed primarily due to shifts in the expectations of our constituents. Following is a brief review of the history of the intervention implementor role.

One of the first major studies sponsored by the American Society for Training and Development (ASTD) was conducted by Patrick Pinto and James Walker.[5] The highlights of this study were published by ASTD in 1978. The article, "What Do Training and Development Professionals Really Do?," focused solely on training and activities associated with it. Pinto and Walker described at least five activities still considered inherent to the current intervention implementor role[6]:

1. Conducting classroom training
2. Group and organization development
3. Individual development planning and counseling
4. Managing internal resources
5. Managing external resources

Descriptions for each of these activities are presented in Exhibit 6-1.

As we can see from the descriptions in Exhibit 6-1, Pinto and Walker presented solidly researched activities for trainers at that time. None of the five activities, however, are results-oriented. All five are still important activities today, but none of them help trainers understand how the results of performing the activities are effective.

Other important studies sponsored by ASTD in subsequent years helped to refine the role of the intervention implementor. In *Models for Excellence*, Patricia McLagan (1983) conducted research aimed at defining the activities of training practitioners as roles. These roles became key to grouping competencies and outputs into distinct categories to help us understand their meanings.[7] Although the roles defined by McLagan in 1983

EXHIBIT 6-1. PINTO AND WALKER'S FIVE ACTIVITIES RELATED TO THE INTERVENTION IMPLEMENTOR ROLE

Conduct Classroom Training: Conduct programs, operate audio-visual equipment, lecture, lead discussions, revise materials based on feedback, arrange program logistics.

Group and Organization Development: Apply techniques such as team building, intergroup meetings, behavior modeling, role-playing, simulation, laboratory education, discussions, cases, issues.

Individual Development Planning and Counseling: Counsel individuals regarding career development needs and plans; arrange for and maintain records of participation in programs; administer tuition reimbursement; maintain training resources library; keep abreast of EEO.

Manage Internal Resources (Borrow): Obtain and evaluate internal instructors/program resource persons and other instructional materials.

Manage External Resources (Buy): Hire, supervise, and evaluate external instructors/resource persons; obtain and evaluate outside consultants and vendors.

SOURCE: Pat Pinto and James Walker. "What Do Training and Development Professionals Really Do?" *Training and Development Journal,* 1978, *32*(7): 58–64. Used by permission.

were only applicable to training and development, they opened the path for performance improvement practitioners to begin framing their activities in terms of competencies and desired outputs.

Models for HRD Practice was published by ASTD in 1989. This study was also led by Patricia McLagan, and served to expand the realm of competencies and outputs of training and development under the more encompassing heading of HRD. This expansion included training and development as well as career development and organization development. HRD helped organizations improve human performance through the use of a wider range of tools, providing more powerful approaches to affect individual, group, and organizational change. Exhibit 6-2 compares the role of the intervention implementor to similar roles in the 1983 and 1989 McLagan studies.

We no longer rate our success within the profession without simultaneously rating how effective the results of our work are to our organizations. This distinction is found in a compar-

EXHIBIT 6-2. A COMPARISON OF THE INTERVENTION IMPLEMENTOR ROLE TO SIMILAR ROLES IN THE *MODELS FOR EXCELLENCE* AND *MODELS FOR HRD PRACTICE* STUDIES

WLP	Models for HRD Practice	Models for Excellence
WLP Intervention Implementor: The role of ensuring the appropriate and effective implementation of desired interventions to address specific root causes of human performance gaps.	**Administrator:** The role of providing coordination and support services for the delivery of HRD programs and services.	**Program Administrator:** The role of ensuring that the facilities, equipment, materials, participants, and other components of a learning event are present and that program logistics run smoothly.
	Individual Career Development Advisor: The role of helping individuals to assess personal competencies, values, and goals and to identify, plan, and implement development and career actions.	**Individual Development Counselor:** The role of helping an individual to assess personal competencies, values, and goals and to identify and plan development and career actions.
	Instructor/Facilitator: The role of presenting information, directing structured learning experiences, and managing group discussion and group processes.	**Instructor:** The role of presenting information and directing structured learning experiences so that individuals learn.
	Instructor/Facilitator: The role of presenting information, directing structured learning experiences, and managing group discussion and group processes.	**Group Facilitator:** The role of managing group discussions and group processes so that individuals learn and group members feel the experience is positive.

SOURCE: William J. Rothwell, Ethan Sanders, and Jeffrey G. Soper. *ASTD Models for Workplace Learning and Performance: Roles, Competencies, and Outputs* (Alexandria, Va.: The American Society for Training and Development, 1999), p. 49. Used by permission of ASTD. All rights reserved.

ison of the major goals of training, HRD, and WLP. The major goal of training is improved knowledge, skills, and attitudes about the job. The focus here is on individual employees; obviously, employees need appropriate knowledge, skills, and attitudes to perform their jobs well. The major goal of HRD is the integration of training, organization development, and career development for the purpose of achieving improved performance through planned learning. This might be considered step two in the process toward thinking in terms of results. The focus of HRD is on the improved performance of the organization as well as the employee. The major goal of WLP is improving human performance by balancing individual and organizational needs, and building knowledge capital within the organization to improve financial return. Clearly, the intent of WLP is to find ways to realize results.

To realize improvements in financial performance, an organization must have a clear understanding of the human performance factors that accompany all work processes. Focusing on results, then, means devoting attention to business outcomes while addressing humanistic and ethical considerations.

So, how does the intervention implementor focus on business outcomes while continuing to address humanistic and ethical considerations? A particularly effective way to focus on results is to seek goal clarity. To do this, a WLP professional must gain agreement from the stakeholders on the results that are being sought from the change effort.[8]

In other words, one critical aspect of performing the intervention implementor role is ensuring that the goal is agreed upon before the implementation begins. This is often easier said than done. Stakeholders throughout an organization often have difficulties agreeing on shared goals. If the focus of the goal is to achieve results, however, it is incumbent upon the intervention implementor to help stakeholders choose goals that are specific, quantifiable, and measurable. A common goal is one that all stakeholders can share.

One problem with shared goals is that conflict can arise over the specifics of end results. When conflicts arise, our tendency is often to get to the end result we think most appropriate by any means possible. This can lead to breaches of ethical responsibilities. Ethical breaches occur when people fail to live up to their moral principles.[9]

The intervention implementor is responsible for ensuring that the appropriate and effective implementation of interventions occurs. Proper implementation can lead to eliminating gaps in human performance and to results-based outcomes. Following is an examination of why the intervention implementor role is important to organizations and to the field of WLP.

Why Is the Role of Intervention Implementor Important?

Obviously, WLP professionals, along with other stakeholders, want the implementation of interventions and subsequent results to be successful. Any intervention that causes change within an organization creates some stress; even small-scale change can make some people quite uncomfortable. The implementation stage is where "the rubber meets the road," so to speak; a certain amount of stress is unavoidable. After analysis of the problem is completed, and an intervention selected, designed, and developed, the time comes to implement the intervention. Assuming that correct decisions were made up to this point in the process, implementing the intervention(s) is the next critical step to be carried out effectively.

REASON #1: THIS IS "THE BEGINNING OF THE END"

The first reason the intervention implementor role is important is that the successful completion of this stage signals the beginning of the end. If this step is successfully implemented, signs will soon begin to surface indicating that the problem or gap in human performance has narrowed or closed. This stage can be quite exciting; we feel the intrinsic reward of seeing that the previous steps, as well as this one, were done well. It is important to refrain from becoming overly confident, however. Don't forget that implementation is only the beginning of the end of the problem. There is still much work to do. The next two chapters will provide information to help ensure that the implementation remains successful, and that positive results are actually realized.

REASON #2: MONITORING THE EFFORT IS ONE OF THE KEYS TO SUCCESSFUL IMPLEMENTATION

Equal in importance to the specific planning and execution of an intervention is the successful monitoring of the implementation schedule. Monitoring, from an intervention implementor perspective, means taking the lead role, or actively and fully supporting another leader, in ensuring that the implementation plan is followed and realized. When you are in the lead role, others look to you for guidance to ensure that the implementation schedule is on target. When another person in your organization is in the lead role for implementing an intervention, your role might be less overt, but ensuring successful implementation is still a part of your job as a WLP professional. You need to carefully monitor the implementation process as an informed observer. The most desirable way to monitor the intervention implementation process is in tandem with others in your organization. Whenever you and those affected by the intervention implementation can work together to lead the implementation process, you can realize shared ownership of success. In an optimal situation, both the WLP professional and the affected parties take an active role in seeking improved performance.

REASON #3: HELPING INDIVIDUALS TO UNDERSTAND THE CRITICAL ROLE THEY PLAY IS ANOTHER KEY TO SUCCESSFUL IMPLEMENTATION

Part of the intervention implementor role involves supporting and encouraging learning. Everyone in the organization plays a part in this effort. It is important to continuously reinforce the notion that everyone concerned in the implementation of an intervention must work together; their active participation and support is a major factor in successful implementation. It is the intervention implementor's responsibility to ensure that all affected organizational members discover their role, regardless of how "large" or "small" that role may be.

REASON #4: YOUR OWN CREDIBILITY IS AT STAKE

Just as in other WLP roles previously discussed, many eyes are watching the implementation process. When you clearly understand your own role in the implementation process, you are able to assist others in understanding the parts they need to play. This is one way of establishing and maintaining your credibility as an intervention implementor. The goal is to have others look to you for guidance. The WLP professional should function as the resource person, enabling agent, and learning specialist guiding the process in concert with others. When training was the intervention of choice, skilled trainers were easily distinguishable as leaders responsible for training functions. Interventions have become far more complex, however, requiring increasingly collaborative approaches to solving performance problems. We now focus less on individual performance improvement and more on the performance of the entire organization. This necessitates a different, more sophisticated approach to learning. Recognizing and demonstrating behaviors that encourage a partnership between you and your learners will enhance your credibility as a WLP professional.

REASON #5: THE CREDIBILITY OF THE WLP PROFESSION IS AT STAKE

Once again, many CEOs we spoke with didn't see the intervention implementor role as limited only to a WLP-related role. Most thought that department managers should be responsible for implementing interventions. A perception of intervention implementation as synonymous with training was evident in many CEO comments. WLP professionals are often still thought of as trainers, whereas managers are considered to be responsible for decision making about the types of training needed in their departments. Training interventions are, of course, necessary within the WLP field; the problem is that the field has evolved beyond training as the sole intervention for improved performance. CEO perceptions, however, often reflect a view of the field as it existed forty years ago. We believe the reason for this outdated thinking is that we haven't sufficiently educated our organizational leaders about the changing nature of the field.

CEOs clearly understand the systemic nature of organizational performance improvement. The majority of them simply don't see WLP professionals driving change efforts. It is apparent that WLP professionals continually need to prove the value of their profession to senior leaders. One way to prove our worth and value is by ensuring that interventions are implemented properly, effectively, and successfully. A few successful intervention implementations might be all that it takes to demonstrate our worth to senior leaders. This is why we strongly encourage regular dialogue between you and your CEO. CEOs need to be educated about WLP, and they need to see how successful a well-implemented intervention can be for their organizations. One way to ensure that CEOs get the results they desire is by knowing and demonstrating the competencies essential to performing the intervention implementor role.

Essential Competencies of the Intervention Implementor Role

The competencies associated with the intervention implementor role fall under the headings of analytical, interpersonal, leadership, technical, and technological competencies. Although these competencies have been discussed in previous chapters, it's important to examine relationships among competencies in the context of different roles. None of the competencies can be thought of as mutually exclusive; each one either builds upon, or supports, another.

ANALYTICAL COMPETENCIES

According to *ASTD Models for Workplace Learning and Performance*, analytical competencies of the intervention implementor role deal with process consultation, training theory and application, and workplace performance, learning strategies, and intervention evaluation.[10]

Process consultation refers to using, monitoring, and providing feedback to continually improve the productivity of work groups. In many organizations today, the trend is moving away from individuals as generators of results to groups of people who can synergistically achieve more meaningful results. Traditional boundaries that existed between various departments or divisions in many organizations are being rethought and redesigned. There is often greater interdepartmental and interdivisional collaboration in helping organizations reach their goals. More collaborative efforts are demonstrating that, when people work together toward common goals, end results are more quickly and accurately reached.

This type of thinking applies quite appropriately to WLP efforts. WLP is not one department or function. Everyone needs to share the responsibility for improved performance. The process consultation competency suggests that the WLP professional take the "helicoptering" part of the role. *Helicoptering* refers to the ability to scan the workplace from a stationary position above the scene. In this way, the WLP professional can monitor what's occurring and provide feedback to aid group process, helping to improve the productivity of work groups.

Training theory and application refers to an understanding of how and why training interventions can be implemented for performance improvement. Although training has been overused as a "cure-all" for organizational problems, it remains an effective intervention when utilized judiciously and properly. Perhaps more important than training itself at this point is the fact that the ways in which training is delivered will continue to change, as technological advances help to bring greater numbers of people together in more sophisticated ways.

The competency of workplace *performance, learning strategies, and intervention evaluation* refers to the continuous evaluation and improvement of interventions before and during implementation. Even with the best analysis, the correct choice of intervention, and the most appropriate intervention design, changes in an organization's internal and external environments can occur before and during the actual implementation of the intervention. Although most organizations attempt to anticipate environmental changes, unanticipated events can occur that cause shifts in an organization's behavior.

Part of your role as a WLP professional is to ensure that the completed intervention obtains desired performance improvement results, even if those desired results are altered before or during the implementation process. Further, new methods for implementing an intervention may arise that were not available when the intervention was first conceived. In this case, you must alter the approach to an implementation process, if such improvements will achieve better or faster results.

INTERPERSONAL COMPETENCIES

Many of the interpersonal competencies associated with the role of the intervention implementor interact with analytical competencies. The interpersonal competencies include communication, communication networks, consulting, coping skills, and interpersonal relationship building.[11]

A WLP professional might be astute at scanning an organization's internal and external environments in order to evaluate and improve interventions before or during the implementation process, but without adequate *communication skills*, it's not likely that these judgments about the environment will be taken to heart or implemented. You need to be a competent communicator so that you can explain your ideas for improvement to others. It's not always easy to convince stakeholders to modify a course of action for intervention implementation; chances are that a great deal of effort has already been expended in dealing with a problem before the WLP professional arrives on the scene. You need to be able to effectively use oral and written communication skills to help others understand why there is a need for changing a course of action, ultimately assisting everyone involved in achieving desired outcomes. What you say, how you say it, and how others receive your words can literally make or break your credibility as a WLP professional.

The other interpersonal competencies are also important, of course. WLP professionals must be able to establish communication networks with key stakeholders, apply consulting skills on an as-needed basis during implementation, demonstrate coping skills to deal with the stress that always comes along with making change happen, and work effectively with others through good interpersonal relationships as an intervention is implemented.

LEADERSHIP COMPETENCIES

The leadership competencies associated with the role of the

intervention implementor are also related to the analytical and interpersonal competencies noted above. These leadership competencies include buy-in/advocacy, diversity awareness, and group dynamics.[12] *Buy-in/advocacy* refers to building ownership and support for workplace initiatives. The WLP professional often needs to take the lead in instilling a sense of ownership among stakeholders for interventions. As the expert resource on workplace improvement strategies and practices, WLP professionals are called upon to use analytical skills to regularly evaluate and improve interventions, interpersonal skills to effectively communicate the improvements, and leadership skills to create ownership of the problem and the solution among stakeholders. Further, the competency of *diversity awareness* is utilized to assess and communicate the impact of interventions on stakeholders. The *group dynamics* competency is very important; a keen eye must be focused on how groups of stakeholders are behaving, interacting, and where their preferences appear to be heading.

TECHNICAL COMPETENCIES

The technical competencies associated with the intervention implementor role are adult learning, facilitation, and intervention monitoring.[13] These competencies are relatively specific to the actual implementation of interventions. *Adult learning* refers to understanding how adults learn and how they use their knowledge, skills, and attitudes. *Facilitation* is helping others to discover new insights. *Intervention monitoring* is tracking and coordinating interventions to ensure consistency in implementation and alignment with organizational strategies.

One thing to keep in mind with regard to these competencies is that a variety of stakeholders might be responsible for the actual implementation of an intervention. The persons closest to the problem are often the most logical facilitators of an intervention. As WLP is a collaborative process, everyone has a part to play in reaching desired results. When others must take the lead in facilitating the implementation of an intervention, your role as the WLP professional is to aid others in performing their roles as competently as possible. Regardless of who takes the lead facilitator role, it is still incumbent upon the WLP professional to track and coordinate all interventions related to performance improvement. We are responsible for ensuring that interventions are implemented consistently and remain aligned with the strategies of the organization.

TECHNOLOGICAL COMPETENCIES

The technological competencies associated with the intervention implementor are computer-mediated communication, electronic performance support systems, and technological literacy.[14] WLP professionals are not expected to be skilled in the operation of all technological media, but awareness of existing and emerging technologies is necessary. In other words, you must be technologically literate so that you can recommend the best and most appropriate methods for implementing interventions. As technologies develop, facilitators and learners alike will have new methods and tools to use in the intervention implementation process. Some of the technological trends currently on the horizon include[15]:

- ❐ Increased sophistication among stakeholders (policymakers and managers) and users (learners) about instructional, presentation, and distribution methods.

- ❐ Increased expectations that organizations will apply learning technology, often on short notice and in real time.

- ❐ Increased willingness on the part of learners to use technology and understand its advantages and disadvantages.

- ❐ Increased sensitivity to the need to manage the environment around users of learning technologies. This sensitivity will prompt an awareness of the importance of creating a total learning environment, combining technology-based learning systems with social support networks in order to encourage collaborative learning. Also, it will prompt an increased understanding of how technology must be "transparent" to learners so that they can focus on content. This transparency requires a deep commitment to masking the distance inherent in distance learning.

- ❐ Increased willingness to use technology to assess learners' progress and evaluate results.

- ❐ Increased need for learning practitioners to possess technological competencies, such as the ability to use, select, and manage the full array of learning technologies available.

After reviewing these trends, it is clear that WLP professionals will soon be required to demonstrate proficiency in a larger range of delivery methods than ever before.

The competencies necessary for the effective enactment of the intervention implementor role are critical to the success of virtually every implementation effort. Knowing and skillfully demonstrating these competencies is absolutely imperative. Next, we examine what CEOs said about the intervention implementor role and its competencies.

CEO-Identified Competencies for the Intervention Implementor Role

Looking at the types of learning CEOs expect can help us make connections about why the competencies of the intervention implementor are important. Many CEO perceptions of this role relate directly to interpersonal and technological competencies. First, we examine some of the interpersonal skill interventions. One CEO described the importance of consulting skills for cross-functional team building:

- "We also have cross-functional team systems that we're putting in, which we found require guidance and outside counseling. We have counselors who are really involved in this cross-functional effort, [and who] really lead and help these groups work together and understand how to form a team and make it work."

This particular comment also addresses the leadership competency of group dynamics. In speaking about a management development program that includes cross-functionality, one CEO spoke of the importance of interpersonal skills development.

- "We focus on a manager's strengths, but one we really hit on is interpersonal development, which is actually management of people. We have found in general that is the toughest skill to teach somebody."

Another CEO said:

- "Many of our courses are for management...things like conflict management, problem solving, and teamwork."
All three of these skill sets require interpersonal skills.

- "At its very base level, learning begins with communication—effective communication of the mission and the vision and the strategy to get from where we are today to where we need to be. So communication is a vital component that spans our entire company."

- "Development of soft [interpersonal] skills focuses on issues associated with how does a manager learn to build a positive, effective, and productive relationship with his employees. Those skills include mentoring, coaching, counseling, soliciting feedback, hosting and running meetings."

These examples demonstrate the importance of interpersonal skills from the CEO's perspective. If people throughout organizations need these skills, WLP professionals must possess these competencies to lead the effort to improve interpersonal skills in their organizations.

Many technological interventions for learning take place regularly in organizations today:

- "It involves computer-based training. It involves software that attempts to teach people, and then it also attempts to assess what they've learned through the process. It's somewhat interactive in that we have people sit at a computer terminal, read and understand, and then we give them real-life, on-the-job experience with the subject at hand. Then we bring them back to the computer and teach them a little more."

According to one CEO, other uses of technology include:

- "[We use] the World Wide Web, we use CD-ROM, video with workbooks, and we use the classroom."

One CEO described how dependent organizations are becoming upon technology:

- "What we basically do now is have a series of in-house seminars, technical gatherings, and hands-on learning that are carried out in advanced technology centers. The [learners] can run the gamut from being able to use in-house software that we have to design, all the way up through some new instrumentation that we may have invented, or hands-on [experience] on how that instrumentation works either in the laboratory or in a field application. As we go forward, our belief is that we will become more and more dependent on the computer and simulations, in using our data in simulations for how to best produce [our product]."

One CEO we interviewed talked about desktop-delivered instruction:

- "We have all of these self-paced learning programs. I actually took a desktop-delivered course recently. We have instructional modules that we deliver over our own intranet. I didn't fully understand active technologies and I decided it was probably good for me to try to understand it, so I went out and found a course that we were delivering on that topic. Now you can ask me questions and I may be able to answer a few of them about active components."

Many organizations today use technology to monitor the work and productivity of employees:

- "Today, virtually all of our plants have computer stations on the floor to monitor labor, increase productivity, and spread information to more people within the organization so they can do their jobs better. In the past you would have had salaried individuals responsible for computerization of the organization. That's no longer true. People throughout the organization are trained properly in the use of computers."

As with other WLP roles, many CEOs viewed the role of intervention implementor as a managerial one. One CEO, when asked how the role of the intervention implementor was currently being carried out, stated:

- "[The role is carried out] by the management team, the middle managers. I think that the implementation of the intervention should be done by managers."

Other CEOs held similar perceptions about who should play the intervention implementor role. As one noted:

● "I see this [intervention implementor role] being carried out by, say, managers and supervisors within the organization....It takes you back to the manager's role of planning, organizing, and carrying out the strategic plan, which takes you back to the manager's role."

Managerial roles appear to be firmly planted and established in CEO's minds. The roles of the WLP professional need to become just as firmly planted and established; we are undeniably at the beginning of an uphill battle.

● "[Intervention implementation is] a management responsibility."

● "I think you need to get the units themselves to implement....I think the individual groups have to make sure the implementation occurs, and the [intervention implementor] could probably assist by acting as a cheerleader...but I don't think I would have them act as the actual implementor."

One CEO viewed implementation as a senior level responsibility:

● "That role in my mind is a CEO role....I have regional CEOs [and] I hold them accountable for implementation."

A few CEOs took the position that implementing interventions was a shared role:

● "It would be the line manager's responsibility...not necessarily to implement the training but to see that it was implemented....So it would be a shared responsibility between the manager and our education department."

● "The [intervention implementor role] is done in a variety of ways but certainly the trainers have that role where it's appropriate....The ones who design [the intervention] also play the leadership role in carrying it out, and sometimes it's external agencies or experts we bring in...and sometimes it's our own management team."

The next quote demonstrates an unfortunate perspective of

the WLP professional as somewhat uncommitted to long-term goals:

- "The intervention implementor is the one who is ultimately responsible for the intervention being implemented over time....The trainer is someone who comes in at a moment in time, takes a snapshot at what's going on, and moves on to other things....The implementor is whoever is responsible for that task over time, who has to make sure that the process continues."

Of course, this view is true. Managers share responsibility with WLP professionals in follow-through to ensure that people apply what they learn.

Most CEOs didn't view the intervention implementor role in great depth. Instead, the traditional trainer image explored at the opening of this chapter seems to linger when CEOs think about what they should do in implementing interventions; the WLP professional is seen as the person who arranges times and dates, and who facilitates training:

- "[The intervention implementor is] the teacher or the individual who conveys the message in a knowledgeable way that has been determined to be most effective."

- "I see the implementor as that person that's actually teaching the course."

- "The roles would be much more nuts and bolts...putting together timetables, time frames, milestones, activation planning."

The image of WLP professionals as solely "trainers" lingers in the minds of CEOs. Although some CEOs do seem to recognize the need and value of collaborative working relationships between WLP professionals and other organizational stakeholders, there does not appear to be a firmly held belief that WLP professionals should serve as expert resources and enabling agents throughout the implementation of longer-term interventions than training. So, what should you do as an intervention implementor? In the next section, we provide some practical suggestions for enhancing and better defining this role.

Developing into the Intervention Implementor Who Matches CEO Expectations

First and foremost, it is important to understand the intervention implementor role, and what is involved in effectively enacting it. We begin by emphasizing some key points. This role can involve training activities, but activities alone do not necessarily lead to results. CEO comments leave little doubt that this role continues to carry with it some very outdated ideas. The point to be made to CEOs is that learning can occur in many ways—some on-the-job and some off-the-job—and WLP professionals have an important role to play in the follow-through. Enacting this role must lead to results: the results that leaders and other stakeholders seek in terms of improved organizational performance.

Changing the perceptions that others hold regarding the intervention implementor role is a daunting task, and perceptions won't change overnight, but we have to start somewhere. We suggest that you begin by speaking with close colleagues in your organization; explain your concern that the image of the WLP field might be outdated. Express that you are keenly interested in participating in the follow-through stage of any intervention that is implemented. Ask your colleagues what their perceptions are about the WLP field in general, and specifically about the role of the intervention implementor. Then explain what the role is and what the role is intended to do. Invite recommendations for changing perceptions about the role in your organization. This is one way of establishing that WLP is collaborative in nature. Your colleagues may be impressed to know that the goal of WLP is to help with the follow-through.

Second, always follow the ethical principles inherent in the WLP profession. Ethical issues arise in the enactment of virtually every WLP role. WLP professionals might be called upon to analyze the general ethical behavior of an organization and then select, design, develop, and implement organizational codes of ethics or codes of conduct.

One very important part of your role is to set a model example of ethical behavior. Remember that your organization's reputation is very important to its long-term success. Ensuring that ethical behavior is practiced regularly within the WLP field will carry over into other areas of the organization.

Third, strive to form the habit of finding root causes of problems; the focus must always remain on end results. By keeping desired results at the forefront of your thinking, you will be able to encourage others to do the same. When you ask a stakeholder, "What do you think might be causing the performance problem?" insist on focusing on process, not personalities. Quite often, something is wrong with the process, and people typically follow whatever processes are in place.

Fourth, whether you find yourself in the lead implementor role, or in a role supporting another leader of the process, don't forget how important it is to monitor implementation. Persuade your stakeholders to recognize the crucial part you play in developing collaborative relationships before and during the implementation process. Shared ownership of the problem and solution is the ideal situation; make it clear that everyone has a part to play in improving organizational performance.

Fifth, carefully study each intervention implementor competency included in Appendix C-19 to C-23. Determine which competencies you currently possess, those competencies that you do possess but can improve upon, and those competencies that you do not possess. Use the exhibits as worksheets to assess each of the five competency areas associated with the intervention implementor role and set reasonable timeframes to reach goals to build the competencies you have and develop the competencies that you do not have.

Sixth, learn the perceptions your CEO holds about your role as an intervention implementor. Find out why your CEO holds those perceptions so that you can begin to work toward changing them in a positive way. This dialogue will provide an excellent opportunity to educate your CEO about the changing nature of the WLP field. Demonstrate why WLP intervention implementation is about getting to results. Share with your CEO the various competencies inherent in the intervention implementor role. If you need an opportunity to demonstrate your competencies in enacting the implementor role, ask your

CEO for that opportunity. The bottom line is that your CEO wants results when it comes to improving organizational performance. Knowing and enacting the intervention implementor role will surely help you achieve results, and ultimately, success.

Summary

This chapter focused on CEO perceptions of WLP professionals who enact the intervention implementor role. The intervention implementor actually follows through on the change effort as it is implemented. This chapter reviewed the competencies that are essential to carry out the role effectively and noted what CEOs had to say about them.

CHAPTER 7

The Change Leader Role—The
CEO Perspective

> So I think [WLP professionals] have to be change-
> oriented people comfortable with new ideas, new
> thinking, and be comfortable with sponsoring
> approaches that give people more latitude, as opposed
> to less latitude. I would think that they should be
> champions in unleashing the potential of our people as
> opposed to harnessing the potential of our people.
>
> A CEO INTERVIEWED FOR THIS BOOK

Change is often said to be the only constant today. The change
leader facilitates how people adapt to change and how change is
accepted and integrated into an organization. As a WLP professional, your expertise in workplace learning places you in the
uniquely valuable and potentially strategic position of directing
change through your programs and through the behaviors you
model. You are trained to use learning tools to build individual
competence as the business environment changes or in antici-
pation of its changes. When the tools you use, the products
your company produces, the services your company provides, or

your customers' needs change, your job is to figure out how to change the skills, behaviors and routines of individuals to meet or exceed business expectations. *Living* change is what change leaders do.

What Is Change?

The change leader role is unique among WLP roles. To understand fully what change is, and how the change leader role is executed, you need to understand what change means, and how the WLP field is involved in facilitating change within organizations. "Learning" is a form of change, and learning is defined by Rothwell and Sredl as[1]:

> A change in perceptions, attitude, and behaviors of an individual, group or organization. The term also refers to the second level of Kirkpatrick's hierarchy of evaluation, which addresses this question: *How much did participants learn by the end of a planned learning experience?*

It is clear from this definition that, as a WLP professional, you deal with change in everything you do, and you are concerned not only with changing individual, group, and organizational perceptions, attitudes, and behaviors but also with measuring the impact of those changes on individual, group, and organizational performance. The change leader role is unique because the role outputs include how WLP programs are presented throughout the organization and how learning programs influence the organization's performance. A change leader models change through program content and leader behaviors, constantly observing and assessing what needs to change and how well change has been adopted by the organization's corporate culture. As a change leader, you must continually monitor individual behavior and program outcomes.

The change leader role follows through on performance improvement interventions intended to help people in an organization adapt to change—or even anticipate change—in the business environment and in the results obtained from learning and nonlearning interventions. The role first emerged in a competency study conducted by Patricia McLagan and

ASTD in 1989,[2] which examined the essential competencies of HRD practitioners. At that point, economic and technological concerns had created new business assumptions for HRD that emphasized the need for the profession to address "increasing rates of change," "concern for quality and customer service," and "globalization."[3] The change leader role in the 1989 study replaced the strategist role from the 1983 study of training competencies, and it marked a shift away from a focus on internal concerns (such as defining training activities) to external concerns (such as improving individual or organizational performance through any intervention).[4]

CEO Perceptions of Change

CEOs sometimes see organizational change from a different perspective than do other members of their organizations. The change leader must gain an understanding of the CEO's view of change and help to translate that vision into a reality with others in the organization. In that process, it is essential to build an impetus not just for the change but also for enthusiasm for the change. In our interviews with CEOs, four primary types of change were identified (see Exhibit 7-1).

EXHIBIT 7-1. CEO-DEFINED CHANGE

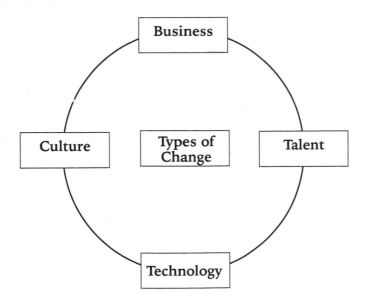

1. *Business change*: describes change in operating processes to increase efficiencies and bottom-line results, and addressing competition, deregulation, and increased pricing pressures

2. *Talent change*: describes change labor pools and ensuring a viable source of talent

3. *Technology change*: describes change in operational, product, and service technology used by employees and offered to customers, including the change that is created by the World Wide Web

4. *Culture change*: describes change in operational processes and mindsets away from the status quo

Understanding these four CEO perspectives of change can help change leaders to customize learning programs—and initiate other interventions—to direct behaviors in ways that will support business changes. In addressing increasing rates of change and the growing stress levels that accompany it, managers too often neglect to furnish people with the perspectives that can help them navigate through the change process. One responsibility of the change leader is to provide perspectives that reveal opportunities available in current changes and provide employees with reasons to embrace change.

One benefit of organizing change into meaningful categories for a workforce is that it allows people to identify clusters of change, and how change areas are related. As a change leader, you must understand how the CEO sees this process. You can organize yourself and your departmental resources to create understanding, and by doing that you can help the people in your organization successfully make transitions.

CEOs recognized five clusters of competency in the change leader role (see Exhibit 7-2; also see Exhibit 7-3 for an overview of the 10 competencies that make up the five clusters). CEOs mentioned business and interpersonal competencies of the change leader with about the same frequency. The single technical competency identified describes an ability to monitor the effectiveness of the change process throughout the organization. It is important to appreciate how these five competency clusters blend into the single role of change leader. CEOs see the five competency clusters (Business, Analytical,

Interpersonal, Leadership, and Technical) as facets of a single behavior. That means that, to fully embrace and drive change throughout an organization, you as a WLP professional must mesh all five change leader competency clusters into a seamless demonstration of professional conduct.

EXHIBIT 7-2. CEO-IDENTIFIED CHANGE LEADER COMPETENCY CLUSTERS

Change Leader Competency Profile

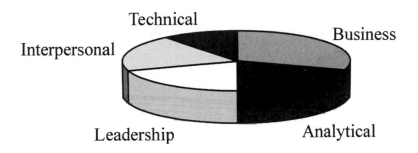

SOURCE: William J. Rothwell, Ethan Sanders, and Jeffrey G. Soper. *ASTD Models for Workplace Learning and Performance: Roles, Competencies, and Outputs* (Alexandria, Va.: The American Society for Training and Development, 1999). Used by permission of ASTD. All rights reserved.

The change leader is concerned with integrating and leading change throughout an organization. For change to be successful, the message of change must be linked to the organization's mission, vision, and values. The heart of the change leader's role rests in the ability to embrace change through an internal awareness of the company's business, strategy, and culture. This chapter provides information on CEO perspectives of the change leader role and is intended to enhance the effectiveness of your personal and programmatic work in the change leader role. Following is a brief review of the change leader's role.

EXHIBIT 7-3. CEO-IDENTIFIED CHANGE LEADER COMPETENCIES

Competency Category	Competency	Definition
Analytical	Process Consulting	Using a monitoring and feedback method to continually improve the productivity of work groups.
Analytical	Systems Thinking	Recognizing the interrelationships among events by determining the driving forces that connect seemingly isolated incidents within the organization; taking a holistic view of performance problems in order to find root causes.
Business	Ability to see the "big picture"	Identifying trends and patterns that are outside the normal paradigm of the organization.
Business	Evaluation of results against organizational goals	Assessing how well workplace performance, learning strategies, and applying the knowledge to performance improvement strategies.
Business	Identification of Critical Business Issues	Determining key business issues and forces for change and applying that knowledge to performance improvement strategies.
Interpersonal	Communication Network	Understanding the various methods through which communication is achieved.
Interpersonal	Relationship Building	Effectively interacting with others in order to produce meaningful outcomes.
Leadership	Group Dynamics	Assessing how groups of people function and evolve as they seek to meet the needs of their members and of the organization.
Leadership	Visioning	Seeing the possibilities of "what can be" and inspiring a shared sense of purpose within the organization.
Technical	Intervention Monitoring	Tracking and coordinating interventions to ensure consistency in implementation and alignment with organizational strategies.

SOURCE: William J. Rothwell, Ethan S. Sanders, and Jeffrey G. Soper. *ASTD Models for Workplace Learning and Performance: Roles, Competencies, and Outputs* (Alexandria, Va.: The American Society for Training and Development, 1999), pp. 53–56. Used by permission of ASTD. All rights reserved.

What Is the Change Leader's Role?

Continuous change is an element in all high performance organizations. Those organizations that succeed invariably display the ability to adapt to changes, or even anticipate it, as a routine part of their culture. In the past five years alone, we have seen quantum leap changes in computer technologies, manufacturing processes, B2B markets, materials technologies, customer–business involvement, ethical issues affecting business, and inter/intra-business partnerships. Among business strategists, issues involving collaboration and cooperation are discussed as frequently as those regarding competition. Inside organizations, new operations technologies are driving process redesign plans and fostering new ways to get work done. How change efforts get organized, implemented, communicated, accepted, and evaluated is the change leader's responsibility.

Put simply, the way that we think about change needs to change. Robert Reich, former Secretary of Labor, suggests that the old change agent role (a person who brings change into an organization to help the organization do things faster, cheaper, or better through new ways of operating, and getting closer to. the customer) is too mechanical. It reflects a limited, linear mindset. Reich believes that, as a result of developments in Web technologies, change efforts need to be supported within an organization by a group he calls *change insurgents*. These change insurgents are most effective when they enlist others in the organization, build support for their ideas upward and outward throughout the organization, and work within the system.[5]

The notion of the change insurgent directly relates to the change leader role. The change leader inspires the workforce to embrace change, creates direction for the change effort, helps the organization's workforce adapt, and ensures that interventions are continuously monitored and guided in ways consistent with stakeholders' desired results. The change leader, working through a team of change insurgents, provides a powerful model for driving organizational change. Because change management shares common objectives with the Organization Development (OD) field, it is important to establish common definitions of important terms:

- ❑ *OD intervention*: A planned change effort.
- ❑ *Organization change agent*: The role of influencing and supporting changes in organization behavior.[6]
- ❑ *Organization Development*: A long-term change effort direct-

ed to an entire organization or some part of it, using techniques from applied behavioral science. It focuses on ensuring healthy inter- and intra-unit relationships and helping groups initiate and manage change.[7]

❏ *Change*: A shift from one condition to another.

❏ *Change agent*: In Organization Development, the term refers to a consultant or third-party consultant-facilitator who assists in a change process or OD intervention.

❏ *Learning*: A change in perceptions, attitudes, and behaviors of an individual, group, or organization.

In 1989, the first outputs for the role of the change agent were defined by Patricia McLagan.[8] These outputs ranged from building effective teams to measuring the impact of change initiatives (see Exhibit 7-4). The results of a more recent competency modeling effort centered around OD can be found at www.execusurv.com/odc2/.

The role of the change agent has evolved and is now widely associated with what all managers are expected to do. The change leader profile has become associated more with helping to manage attitudes and expectations about change, and involving people in change processes, than with a static list of outputs expected from the role. The role is expected to produce defined outputs, but those outputs depend upon what type of change is occurring. In an interview with a former McKinsey & Co. director, R. Katzenbach, three change leader competencies were described that shed light on the dynamic, complex nature of the role[9]:

❏ *Flexible contributor*: Effective change leaders are productive in many working relationships. They move easily from a team-based project to a command and control hierarchy. They do what needs to be done to complete the assignment.

❏ *Comfort with collaboration*: Effective change leaders seek out in-house expertise to help create solutions. They go to the front-line employees, the people doing the work, for input on how to solve performance problems.

❏ *Current data/information driven*: Effective change leaders get facts from sources outside the organization. They bypass internal systems and gather current data from customers and competitors to create new information and a fresh perspective on change.

EXHIBIT 7-4. CHANGE AGENT OUTPUTS

Output	Quality Requirement
Teams	• Individuals have a shared vision of the task. • The group is aligned with organizational goals. • There is clarity of roles, capacity, and limitations. • The task is accomplished.
Resolved Conflicts for an Organization or Group	• Real conflicts are addressed. • Solutions are implemented and monitored. • All affected parties are willing to work toward a resolution. • Group performance is enhanced.
Changes in Group Norms, Values, Culture	• There is shared vision of the end result of the change. • Leaders advocate and model the change. • Developmental support is provided for internalizing new norms, values, or culture. • The change is operationalized. • The change reflects sensitivity to the impact of the change on individuals and on organizational relationships.
Designs for Change	• Key users are involved in the design process. • Individuals are committed to and support the changes. • Design anticipates the direct and indirect impact on individuals and the organization. • The change can be implanted.
Client Awareness of Relationships Within and Around the Organization	• The client's own ability to anticipate and plan for changes in environmental conditions and relationships is enhanced. • The client has an increased ability to make decisions based on an awareness of organizational relationships.
Plans to Implement Organizational Change	• They are congruent with the organization's mission, strategy, and vision. • They are workable. • Specific ways to measure effectiveness of the change are included and accepted. • Affected individuals support the plan.
Implementation of Change Strategies	• The client supports the implementation process. • Communication among all affected parties occurs on a frequent basis. • Adjustments to the plan are made as needed. • Disruptions that are part of the change process are anticipated and managed.
Recommendations to Management Regarding HRD Systems	• They are tied to the business strategy and organizational goals. • They are made from the users' perspectives.

SOURCE: Patricia A. McLagan and David Suhadolnik. *The Models for HRD Practice: The Research Report* (Alexandria, Va.: The American Society for Training and Development, 1989), pp. 23–24. Used by permission of ASTD. All rights reserved.

In our interviews, one half of the CEOs described the change leader role in a dynamic, insightful, and inspirational tone. Some key words and phrases used by CEOs to describe their perceptions of the role were these: *culture, moving to a different level, inspirational, sense of urgency, a vision,* and *an ideal.* CEOs perceive the role as one linked to communicating change throughout an organization and using appropriate tools and methods to incorporate change into daily operations. Note the key themes in the following CEO comments:

- "[The WLP professional enacting the role of change leader is] to be an inspiration for those in the leadership roles...to provide them with the knowledge base, the expanse, the tools to be able to accomplish needed change in the most successful way, and that's what I view a senior level trainer/consultant to be able to do."

- "[WLP professionals must be successful in] establishing a vision, a sense of urgency, developing a case for change...informing and educating various constituencies and building some momentum for whatever the change happens to be."

- "[A successful change leader is] somebody who understands the dynamics of change and can help coach an executive management-type person on the predictable reactions to change and ways of making the change process as effective as possible."

- "When you talk about change, that's really a kind of a cultural intervention and one that falls into this area of training that I described before as being more subjective....[The change leader role] is really [about] introducing the culture...working with the culture."

- "[The change leader] would bring the basic knowledge to the line managers...motivate them to see the advantage of moving to a different level and how you would do that...presenting [change] in a positive light."

- "[This role amounts to] recognizing where we need to be and helping facilitate those who are in place today or will be in place...helping them to become capable of addressing what will be."

The change leader plays a vital role in WLP. This role is now less linear than it used to be, taking into account complexity theory. Change leaders do not regard change as they once did— as having a "before" and "after"—but instead view change as continuous. It is context-driven. Change leaders not only deliver results but also embody and model change attributes, involving others in the change process and exciting members of the organization with the opportunities for involvement in change.

The type of change occurring within an organization determines how change leaders enact their role. How CEOs regard change is critically important to how change leaders design, execute, and evaluate change efforts. The next section presents CEO perspectives on the types of change occurring in business today.

CEO Perspectives on the Types of Change Facing Businesses

We asked CEOs: *"In the next two to three years, what are the business challenges facing your organization?"* Our assumption was that organizational change is driven by business change and that how change is recognized is key to how organizations adapt to it. Routinely asking organizational leaders: "What are the challenges your department, unit, or organization face?" increases awareness about how an organization must continually meet new demands. Appreciating how senior leaders recognize change and business challenges helps change leaders map plans to direct the change process. Awareness of the company's business challenges, and where the company is in implementing its strategic plan are change leader responsibilities.

In this section, we present four clusters of change as perceived by CEOs. These clusters were developed based on CEO responses to the business challenge question above. Exhibit 7-5 presents a complete list of CEO-perceived business challenges.

BUSINESS CHANGE

The first cluster of change recognized by CEOs deals with business challenges facing organizations. The business challenges

Exhibit 7-5. CEO-Described Business Challenges

Business Challenge	Definition
Financial	Driven by the need for increased operating efficiency, company growth, increased profitability, or increased shareholder value.
Recruiting	Concerned with attracting, developing, and retaining high quality talent.
Technology	Fully utilizing company technology to improve operational and financial performance.
Corporate Knowledge	Challenge of organizing and operationalzing the company's collective knowledge, and re-training the workforce, as a form of competitive advantage.
Internet	Development and implementation of an e-business plan.
Market	Responding to, and maintaining as an enterprise, with increased competition, deregulation, and increased pricing pressures.
Customer	Increased concern for customer perspectives, and stronger connections between employee behaviors and awareness of the company's customer.
Culture	Recreating a new company culture.

they described included changing the organization's mindset on business, raising employee awareness of the increased speed of company growth, and increased competitive pressures on the organization. Business challenges are constantly changing, sometimes on a daily basis; the change leader must routinely survey senior leadership on the challenges facing the organization. As three CEOs noted:

● "There are probably a number of [business challenges]. Number one, making a transition from how people have done business for many, many years to the way people are *doing business* now. I think our business probably has changed more in the last three or four years than it had in the previous fifteen, and I don't think that's just as a result of e-commerce. I think business has become truly worldwide. And I think [that there are] new skills that people have had to acquire and new ways of doing business. And I think that some of the older ways of doing business may or may not need to employ more people, but I think *the change has taken place. I think the biggest challenge is how to grow earnings.*"

- "Our biggest challenge is that we've stepped into a high-growth curve in terms of 25 to 32 percent growth curve per year in revenue and earnings. And with that in mind, we have taken over a company that two years ago was on a very parallel, flat curve in terms of revenue earnings. So we moved into a high-growth curve such that the biggest challenge is to *motivate and change the culture of the people to work to a high-growth capability. I think that's one of our biggest challenges.*"

- "In our business, there's rapid consolidation going on. We're in a very competitive field. It continues to get more and more competitive relative to the pricing and positioning of products in the competitive services that we have to offer relative to our competition. At the same time, our industry—the energy industry—is deregulating and that's creating new opportunities for us to compete. And while all that's going on, the biggest challenge is to keep up with that. And to [do] that, we need *talented people* who are always on top of the leading edge and *continually learning to change*—what we do and how we do it—to keep up and compete in that kind of an environment."

Obviously, a change leader needs to know the company's business and industry fundamentals. In this role, one should be asking questions such as:

- ❐ What are the company's short- and long-range plans?
- ❐ How is the company doing financially and strategically?
- ❐ Who are the company's competitors, where are they, and what are they doing?
- ❐ What is the company's current cash position?

Knowing the business challenges facing an organization will allow change leaders to participate in senior-level discussions, and contribute the expertise of WLP to meeting immediate business challenges.

RECRUITING FOR CHANGE

The second change cluster identified by CEOs reflects challenges in recruiting competent and qualified people. In high-growth and low-growth cycles, every organization seeks a pool of capable talent to take responsibility for operations and management. This challenge was described by CEOs as three-fold: recruiting self-starters, attracting and keeping qualified people, and attracting and retaining growth managers.

CEOs who identified recruiting challenges related them to changing how a company identifies and retains key, mission-critical people, as well as competent staff to carry out daily operations. Issues surrounding national, regional, and local supplies of labor are changing the nature of companies' operational environments, and are a major component of change in business. As four CEOs noted:

- "Without a doubt, *recruiting high quality people who are self-starters is the biggest business challenge facing our organization.* People who have initiative and, obviously, people who have the ability to grow and learn with the organization."

- "I don't think there's any question in our industry that the greatest challenge right now is the *ability to attract and keep qualified people,* without question. And it's probably come to play more in the last two years than at any other time in my experience, which is about forty some years now."

- "First, I think it's attracting and maintaining the appropriate number *of qualified and competent staff,* both from a technical, professional, and support perspective."

- "The number one business challenge would be attracting and retaining what I'm calling *growth managers.* The kinds of people that I put in this category of growth managers would be any and all individuals within a company that may be involved in either research for new products and/or development of new products, project managers, or individuals within the company who may be involved in either identifying technology opportunities for licensing new technology, acquiring it, or creating joint ventures."

Understanding a company's labor supply, and more importantly, a company's skill capacity, is another element of change discussed by CEOs. As a change leader, you are responsible for knowing the knowledge/skill/attribute requirements of your company's jobs. As a WLP professional, documenting the competencies of your company's key positions is the first step in leading change associated with recruiting challenges. The change leader should work with the analyst to develop a plan that assesses the skill pool within the organization, and changes the capabilities of people to meet the company's present and future business needs.

TECHNOLOGY CHANGE

The third change cluster identified in CEO comments describes challenges related to technology. Technology came into play in describing two types of change and the business challenges they create. The first challenge is that technology is rapidly changing how companies design and develop new products and services. Often, CEOs discussed change in their company's products and/or services as a *"change in our technology"* or a *"a change in how our technology is used by our customers."*[10] As WLP change leaders, we must know our company's technology, and we must stay closely attuned to our company's products and services, so that we know what the company's technology does for its customers and what differentiates it from our competitors.

The second type of technology change discussed by CEOs relates to the use of new technologies in business processes. Business process technologies use computers, the Internet, and enterprise system technologies to change how business operations are performed. A few examples include new software applications that allow work formerly performed by outside printers to be done in-house, use of the Internet to develop business-to-business and business-to-consumer markets, and organization-wide systems such as SAP or Peoplesoft that allow entire functions—such as finance and human resources—to use a single system architecture to organize data. As three CEOs noted:

● "For us, [the business challenge is] to make sure that we're staying aligned with an integration of our rapidly changing customer requirements and also the *quickly changing technology,* and making sure that we've matched the latest technology with the new customer requirements into an effective business model. That might sound generic, but it's very true in our telecommunications marketplace. We experience new things coming out every few months, and the customer always wants the latest, but again you have to match that. But you have to do it so you make some money, because you can always be investing in a new product and never, never get a return on it. And it's a nice kind of triangle that we have to balance effectively."

● "We [are] a large specialty steel producer in the United States. Our product forms are sold for applications inside jet engines, orthopedic implants, all kinds of electronic and corrosion applications. We're about a billion-dollar company and sell the product globally. Probably the biggest issue that will be on the minds of our people running this business will be the *changes necessary in the structure and the process of the business in order to stay viable and competitive operating from the United States in this global economy.* The insertion of the Internet and business-to-business dialogue is a borderless, *timeless technology* and will expose not only us but our customers to a much broader availability of information and capability around the globe than ever before. And I think the major strategic question ahead of us is how must we structure this old line company, which was founded in 1889 in the United States, in such a way that it can function effectively globally and, with this new technology, in such a way as a public corporation to generate the kind of returns that are appropriate to compete for capital."

● "Our company must change its *use of technology,* and technology will be our challenge in two respects. Specifically, number one would be our decision as to how to take advantage of the emerging *Internet capabilities* that are generally available to all of us in business. And number two is to capitalize on *emerging technologies* that are...coming to the market to allow our customers to become more successful practitioners."

Technology may be the ultimate change driver and business challenge facing organizations today. How and why a company changes with new technology depends upon the business environment and resources available to support the change. The business challenges of marketing new technologies to customers (in profitable ways), and using them efficiently in our organizations, are core areas of focus for the change leader. Change leaders need to discuss their company's technology, and how that technology is utilized in daily processes, with other senior-level leaders. The company's WLP programming must address current and future technological developments to help people keep pace with the change.

CULTURE CHANGE

The fourth change cluster identified by CEOs describes the challenge of changing company culture. Leading a change in culture begins with assessing how change is impacting a company's business environment, its financial, human, supply, production, and marketing resources, and demand for the company's products and services. Business culture is a mindset shared by all members of an organization, demonstrated by behaviors and work processes. As dominance in our economy has shifted from heavy industry, commodity, and manufacturing to customized, specialized manufacturing and services, customer feedback, higher quality standards, on-time delivery, seamless work processes, and technology-enabled marketing have increased in importance.

CEOs expect the change leader to integrate WLP programs into a comprehensive learning plan to change the mindset of the company. OD competencies and processes come into play here. Of the four business challenges identified, cultural change is one area in which OD practices and methods apply. Specifically, changing a culture requires an integrated, long-term (eighteen to sixty months) change effort. As two CEOs noted:

- "We must change our ability to not only satisfy our customers, but also bring them in as a partner in the businesses that we run. We must try to understand what does the customer want—quality, delivery, price, technical assistance, etc.—[and] we must change our culture from a manufacturing or business orientation to a customer orientation, bringing in underneath that all the business quotients

that you need to still have a satisfactory return to our share-
holders, growth to the company, all those kinds of things.
But first and foremost, I believe it's the culture shift that's
going to be the most important business challenge that
we've seen."

● "Our most important business challenges fall into two
broad categories. The first category is team building and the
creation of one team with a common goal and common purpose at our company, being that over the course of the last
two years we have expanded out of the merger and acquisi-
tion of three very large organizations in the United States
that operated their businesses in different ways, had different cultures, and competed very aggressively with each
other. So over the course of the next couple of years, it will
be critical for us to build a very clear identity for our single
company and for its team members."

Change is company-specific. The impact of change on
organizations is uniquely defined by each company's business,
leadership approach to company involvement, and capacity of
its workforce to accept change. How change leaders operate is
determined by their knowledge of effective characteristics of
change processes and how these characteristics operate within
the organization's existing culture.

CEOs therefore perceive change to be focused around four
general areas: business, talent, technology, and culture.

CEO–Identified Competencies for the Change Leader

Our interviews with CEOs revealed that CEOs tend to associate
two key characteristics with the change leader role. The first is
that the role belongs to the highest leadership level of the
organization. The second is that, for the change leader's work
to be effective, it needs to be championed by all managers
throughout the organization. CEOs see the change leader role
as belonging to themselves and other senior leaders but implemented by managers at all organizational levels.

These two characteristics provide the WLP role of change

leader with very important directives for developing a change plan. Examples of CEO responses to the question: *"How do you see this role being carried out in your organization?"* included the following:

- "[The change leader role is] a *function of leadership as far as I'm concerned, and I would not delegate that to anyone really other than myself."*
- "[The change leader role] sounds like *the CEO's job."*
- *"The leader of the organization* is the change agent, the change leader."
- "I see [the change leader role] at *the executive level*…it's been my experience that training and learning cannot sustain a change effort by themselves without executive management."

If your WLP function does not have a champion at the senior level of the organization, then the WLP professional enacting the change leader role must go the extra step to secure and nurture senior-level support for all change initiatives.

The second characteristic describes how change leaders successfully carry out their duties. CEOs believe that, for change to take hold, it must be supported and reinforced by management throughout an organization. CEOs perceive the change leader role to be part of a team effort in driving change, as the following quotations from the interviews seem to indicate:

- "I think [the change leader role is] the responsibility of all managers."
- "The senior management team as a whole…"
- "The primary responsibility resides with me [the CEO], and the secondary responsibility with each one of my executive managers."

Most CEOs we interviewed described perceptions about the role in terms of how it might be carried out. Some did not believe the role belonged to those who once held the title of "trainers" but belonged, instead, to others in the organization.

The first thing a change leader needs to know is that CEOs

perceive themselves to bear primary responsibility for leading change. Given this perception, all change programs, no matter how small or large, must involve the CEO. CEOs have great interest in why change is occurring and how it is connected to the strategic objectives of the organization.

In our interviews, change was consistently discussed as a major business challenge. The level of change—and the scope of involvement from senior-level leaders—may vary according to the magnitude of each change initiative, but competencies needed by change leaders will not. Our findings suggest that CEOs perceive four core change leader competencies: *drive, communication, broad perspective,* and *business knowledge* (see Exhibit 7-6). These four competencies surround all aspects of the change process. It should be noted that these competencies, while discussed separately, are regarded by CEOs as seamlessly integrated in fulfilling the change leader role. It is helpful to remember that a competency is defined as any characteristic that contributes to superior performance. As a change leader, you should be able to demonstrate these four competencies.

EXHIBIT 7-6. CHANGE LEADER COMPETENCIES

Ability	Definition
Business Knowledge	To align training to company strategy, keep abreast of the industry trends and the company's performance, and demonstrate the transfer learning to individual performance.
Communication	To communicate effectively throughout the organization, advocate on behalf of the organization and the individual, and facilitate group processes.
Broad Perspective	To assimilate numerous experiences into learning approaches, demonstrate open-mindedness, view employees as assets and able to empathize, and is aware of an organization's culture.
Drive	To demonstrate energy and enthusiasm for programs, and the capability of building bridges across barriers for learning program acceptance.

SOURCE: John E. Lindholm. *A Study of CEO Perceptions of the Competencies of Workplace Learning and Performance Professionals.* Unpublished doctoral dissertation (University Park, Pa.: The Pennsylvania State University, 2000). Copyright 2000 by *Dissertation Abstracts International.* All rights reserved.

DRIVE AND COMMUNICATION

The first two areas describe interpersonal competencies: the ability to drive change throughout the organization, and the ability to communicate the change message to all stakeholders. These two are linked because they require strong interpersonal relationships throughout the organization. The ability to drive change requires energy to work with all areas of the company in their change processes, knowledge of the jobs and roles provided by units, and awareness of how each organizational part fits with others. The ability to communicate change messages (to create learning programs that facilitate change) requires organizing and implementing a change communication plan and getting the word out to critical stakeholders for the change initiative. The core competencies of drive and communication work in tandem at the foundation of the change leader's role.

For the sake of clarity, these two key terms are defined as follows:

❐   *Drive*: Possessing energy and enthusiasm. An ability to recognize barriers to change and the ability to build bridges for change throughout the organization.

❐   *Communicate*: Ability to communicate effectively throughout the organization, articulate views and feelings, and facilitate meetings.

CEOs discussed the competencies of drive and communication in many contexts. Some presented the need for communication abilities based on a strong science and engineering background. Others discussed communication abilities in the context of one-on-one meetings, individual development, and training needs. One participant summarized drive and communication competencies quite adequately as the need for a change leader to possess the energy needed to win support throughout the organization for change programs. The CEO quotations below emphasize the importance of the change leader's ability to create meaningful, performance-related discussions throughout an organization, and to create interest, support, and participation for change programs.

●   "This might be a little bit of a different answer than you get from some of the other companies you're talking to, but I believe the number one ability that somebody in that role has—and if you look around our company, there are probably six individuals in our company, globally, that are responsible for this in-house training—but *the ability to effectively communicate I feel is the number one attribute* that they have to have. Of course, they've got to have a very strong technical background either in engineering or physics or geology—that is important, but the overwhelming, number one priority is that they are a good communicator. You can have an individual who can't teach or communicate, but he can be a very powerful technologist—[but] that doesn't get the job done. By getting the job done I mean making sure the people being trained know what to do when they get back to the work site. So communication, I think, is the most important attribute, followed by having experience and technical ability in our field. Again, those are related to engineering, physics, geology, geophysics, and geochemistry."

● "You need somebody who has general leadership skills, who *is entrepreneurial in nature,* and who has a good business sense, particularly as to the company's needs. It means also having very good interpersonal skills, knowing what the business needs are, and being [able] to communicate those effectively to the employees."

● "I think they need good *communication skills.* They need the ability to sit down and talk with people, understand what their problems are, understand the best way to develop some type of training programs to fit their needs. I think they have to be team players. I think they have to be politicians to some extent so they can talk with the different department heads and coordinate the training activities and make sure that we're getting everything we want out of a training program."

● "One of the most important things or attributes that person has to have is called *energy.* If you're growing very fast as a company, you devote all of your time and energy to that, and because of that you'll find across any company that people will not put their people into training programs because they don't have time. It's a key issue. I think in this compa-

ny we've had good training activity, but in the past there
wasn't a real drive to move people into the programs. And
it really comes down to the issue that everybody's really
tied up with full energy on trying to meet numbers, and it's
a question of how [you can afford to have] a person out for
two weeks, or four weeks, without being productive. It's
really made a difference when you brought a new person in
with a lot of energy."

BROAD EXPERIENCES/OPEN MIND

The third competency area described by CEOs for the role of
change leader relates to broad experience and open-mindedness. CEOs recognize that outside perspectives can help to reju-
venate a static work environment, and bring new energy into
existing programs. CEO input helped define the broad perspective competency this way:

> *Broad Perspective*: To assimilate numerous experiences into
> learning approaches, to demonstrate open-mindedness.
> Bringing numerous experiences into learning approaches,
> knowing the future issues facing the organization, the compa-
> ny's strategy, and how learning can be used to create change.

CEOs value experience that is related to their company's
business. Competence in demonstrating breadth of experience
and openness to exploring new possibilities were identified as
essential for change leaders by a significant number of CEOs.
Broad experience and open-mindedness are viewed as a macro-
level competency. A broad experiential viewpoint can help WLP
professionals translate approaches to change (and to learning)
from outside the company, presenting them in a way that facilitates the use of new ideas inside the company. The basic idea
is that experiences gained in similar external work environments, or in working with other similar business objectives,
can help WLP professionals facilitate effective organizational
change. As several CEOs noted in our interviews:

● "I think what we're looking for, the type of people we
  brought in, were people that had *broad experience* at similar
  companies where they had tried *different types of approaches* in
  terms of whether training or other types of programs would

help employees to be more productive and to contribute more to the bottom line. The person responsible for leading the change brought those experiences, which then allowed him to help the company adapt."

- "From my perspective, he and I have to come to an agreement about what the *future issues* are that our people are going to have to deal with in the corporation. And then he has to develop, either personally or through his people, the capability and the *knowledge to know where the right courses are*, where the right institutions are, where the right assignments are that will fulfill the training needs. So he's got to have *quite a library of experience* relative to the places to go for training, compensation systems, incentive programs. All of those things that will not only provide the learning needed for change, but motivate our people to undertake those things that will build them up for future assignments."

- "Well, the number one most important skill—and I'm not even quite sure it's a skill—is the ability to have an *open mind*. Historically, many in the training and education field have had a very limited view of what training and education was. I'm sure some of that comes from our process of educating people. People seem to think that this is how you do it and any deviation from it is inappropriate, and if it isn't working then there's something wrong with the people versus something wrong with the educational process. And so I think there's a lot of *open-mindedness needed*. I think that's especially important in our multicultural society today. Realistically, as I look at our organization, I [see that] a large hospital that is like a small city, with employees that range from unskilled labor all the way up to the most educated segments of our society, crossing all racial and ethnic and religious boundaries. So a person has to have an appreciation for the different kinds of issues and motivations of different people."

BUSINESS UNDERSTANDING OF CUSTOMERS/CULTURE/WORLD

The fourth and last area of CEO-perceived change leader competency centers around the ability to understand a company's business. Implicit here is the know-how to work within the company's culture. CEOs believe that in order for change to take place, a change leader needs to know how to discuss the company's products and services, the company's mission, the systems the company uses to deliver goods and services, the company's standards for quality, and the business environment in which the company operates. CEOs expect change leaders to know the nuts and bolts that hold the business together.

As a change leader, you need to know as much about the business as any other senior-level leader in the organization. This will allow you to apply principles of workplace learning and performance to change initiatives in a way that fits the company's approach to doing business. Business knowledge as perceived by CEOs is defined as:

> *Business Understanding*: To align training to company strategy, keep abreast of the industry trends and the company's performance, demonstrate the transfer of learning to individual performance.

Understanding the company's business and working within the company's culture are influenced by changes in the business environment. As the demands of the business change, so do the business competencies necessary to be effective as a change leader. As change leaders, we must appreciate the adaptive nature of competencies and the importance of stepping in and out of roles. Demonstrating business-understanding competency requires a senior-level, company-specific business acumen, and the ability to apply workplace-learning content that fits the work environment.

An example from a dot.com business is valuable in showing how organizational change is redesigned by changes in the business environment. During the heyday of dot.com investments, when organizations were moving at light speed to learn how to create a Web presence and integrate online technologies, change leaders were busy mastering e-learning, how their company's strategy was changing to meet new technology-based expectations of customers, and how to facilitate change in the new cyberspace workplace. Fast-paced, technology-based change seemed to be everywhere.

The business environment has changed, however. So has the business understanding of the change leader. Leading change in the post-dot.com business environment requires business understanding for managing decreased budgets, managing a downsized workforce, attracting and retaining skilled workers, and linking change programs to specific business needs.

Clearly, CEOs perceive business understanding to be a core competency for senior managers. As a change leader, your role requires you to discuss issues concerning company change and how it can be accomplished within current business environments. Issues involving change require fluency in the company's mission, customers, products, and culture, and knowledge of how human resources are prepared for adapting to new business requirements. In the words of several CEOs:

- "I think that if you're talking about working in a business environment, whether it be for profit or not for profit, the other issue is that the change leader needs to have an appreciation for the business, an understanding of what drives the business, and an understanding of what are the primary issues in the business in order to be able to tailor something appropriate. I think long gone are the days when you had people who simply took their marching orders and went off to develop a change program. I think to really be an effective contributor, a human resource development person *needs to understand the business, be able to think through the business's mission and objectives, and understand the systems in place* that the business has to deliver its product or service, *to really be able to have a feel for what's needed in the organization.*"

- "I think number one—they've got to *understand the business* that their specific company is in, okay? And they've got to understand what makes that business tick, how it makes money, what's important, and what's not important. Number two—and almost equally important—they got to understand the *company's culture*, what from a softer side is important and what's not important—I always say what the company's really all about. And then number three, they've got to be good teacher-communicators. They've got to be able to get the message across, tailor it to the specific audience, and be effective in that manner."

- "It's critically important for all of the individuals that are involved in those types of responsibilities that, number one, they have spent time *understanding our customers* and understanding the market that we participate in, because their unique skills that they bring to the table—their technical skills—need to be put in context of *the business environment* that we're operating in and that our customers are operating in....It is also very important for the workplace learning team to understand very specifically the articulated goals of the business unit that they're working with and that they are very competent in their own *unique skills that they bring to the intervention*, whether it be the human development interventions or technology interventions table....But they [also need to] bring some very, very sensitive listening skills to the table to make sure that what they have brought from a technical point of view is applied very effectively from a practical point of view."

- "The HR director or whatever title you may choose to use has to go a lot further than developing employee handbooks. They are responsible for training different people... like training people in *teamwork*. In many of our shop floors, for example, we talk about working together, team management, sell management...things that require expertise in production control, expertise in product quality. These have to be brought more and more into the forefront because—and I'm speaking a little bit from a manufacturing perspective—productivity increase, quality assurance, and things like this are becoming...an absolute given. *You're not going to do business in a world-wide economy unless that's there. And you need change leaders to be able to heighten the awareness of all the people throughout the organization,* and not only the people on the floor, but the people who have been with the company for a fairly long period of time that have to move into the [present] century, if you will."

- "The most important credential for any organizational leader is to have a decent understanding of what the company is delivering. In the past, HR traditionalists have worried about how many people I need, how do I hire, what's the cost of hiring, and dealing with personnel issues that always come up, but that really is far from the mark [today]. What the [WLP professional] in our company has to do is *understand the product we're delivering* and be able to make the many programs that they conduct fit within that environment. They must also have a sense of the culture that we're working with in our customer base, whether it be a normally hierarchical, rigid military-type structure or a very flat organization that operates much differently."

Overall, CEOs presented an image of the change leader as someone who is fully involved in the company's business, fitting change programs within the company's culture, demonstrating an open mind to new ideas, and possessing a passion for communicating and connecting with people throughout the organization. One CEO's comment on the most important ability of a change leader seems to capture the essence of the role:

● "Well I think [change leaders] have to have a sensitivity for *people as a resource*, as opposed to people as employees—the difference being that our people asset is the one asset that will do more or has the capability of doing more than a simple program that you dictate or outline in an instruction manual. They can provide initiative. They can provide a *wide range of thoughts and ideas*. And I think that [change leaders] should think of the technical training as being the base load, but the real value in their positions is unleashing the thinking potential of people and their *ability to innovate, raise new ideas, and to solve problems in nontraditional ways*. So [change leaders] have to be *change-oriented people, comfortable with new ideas, new thinking*, and be comfortable with sponsoring approaches that give people more latitude as opposed to less latitude. I would think that these types of people should be champions in unleashing the potential of our people as opposed to harnessing the potential of our people. There are plenty of management people in the company that will harness what's there. I think there are all too few that unleash the potential and I would think the learning officers, change leaders, and human resource people are those that should be unleashing the potential of people."

Developing into the Change Leader Who Matches CEO Expectations

In the change leader role, you as a WLP professional should support the CEO, working in concert to direct change efforts throughout the organization. People at the top are charged with many responsibilities and are not always in the best position to be working in the trenches on a daily basis as change agents or insurgents. But they are crucial in creating a climate where change is embraced and where people can perform within a dynamic work environment.

In our new economy, fundamental assumptions are changing—and even paradoxically, so are our assumptions about the change leader. Robert Reich suggests that to enable a company to excel and perform in the twenty-first century economy, a better term for the change agent is "change insurgent." Reich's change insurgent model is directed at impacting four areas for organization development[11]:

1. *Organizational capacity*: The change insurgent focuses on the workforce's capacity to produce/service newly emerging technologies or markets and increases awareness of this capacity.

2. *Organizational flexibility*: The change insurgent focuses on the workforce's ability to adapt to, and apply, new technologies and processes. The change insurgent tries to flatten the learning curve.

3. *Organizational technology*: The change insurgent focuses on moving everything he or she can online and Web-enabling the entire organization. The company should move from "old-line" to "online."

4. *Organizational hierarchy*: The change insurgent focuses on great ideas, insightful visions, and challenging examples rather than giving special deference to title, authority, or organizational level.

Reich's four areas of change provide topics for thinking about change and the results desired from change. As advocates and implementers of change, we as WLP professionals use methods and processes to change how our companies conduct business. By assessing our organization's capacity and flexibility, we not only prepare our workforce's future ability for change, but also track the results of the change initative.

How does your position match against the competency profile of the change leader as viewed by CEOs? We encourage you to reflect on the following suggestions and document your perceived abilities in this role.

1. *Understand the business reasons for the change affecting your organization.* Enacting the change leader role begins with knowing where you are and where you want to be. CEOs begin planning for change by looking at the business, remembering the company's mission and vision, and assessing change occurring in the business environment.

   ❏ In what current business environment is your company operating?

   ❏ What are the critical measures your senior-level leaders track in measuring your company's performance?

   ❏ What are the new systems being used in your company (process or technology)?

   ❏ How is the change that is taking place affect the capability of your workforce to perform?

2. *Review your learning programs' characteristics against four domains of change as perceived by CEOs.* CEOs perceive the four areas where change is occurring as primary focal points and objectives for learning programs. By objectively linking learning programs to CEO perceptions of change, you should use WLP programming to help people adapt to that change.

   ❏ How are your learning programs integrating business change into the learning content?

   ❏ How are your learning programs addressing retention and development of your company's mission-critical people?

   ❏ How are your learning programs using Internet technology?

   ❏ How are your learning programs creating a new work culture in your organization?

3. *Understand your personal strengths and weaknesses in the four competency areas for the change leader.* A final product of all

competency models is the development of a self-improve-
ment plan. As a change leader, consider:

❐ How do your competencies match against CEO-identified change competencies of drive, communication,
   broad perspective, and business knowledge?

❐ How do you demonstrate these four abilities in your
   daily conduct?

❐ How do you increase awareness of the change occurring in your organization through your organizational contact and discussions with others?

❐ Of the four competencies, what are your strong and
   weak points?

❐ What can you do today to improve in each area?

Because CEOs tend to view themselves as change leaders, it
may serve us well to reposition our thinking about this role as
more of a change driver or navigator position. We need to recognize the importance of workplace learning as a tool that
enables the workforce to adapt to change, and the role of learning as a means of creating an adaptable, creative workforce.

Summary

This chapter focused on CEO perceptions of WLP professionals
enacting the change leader role. Change leaders build enthusiasm for interventions. In our interviews, one half of CEOs
described the change leader role in a dynamic, insightful, and
inspirational tone. This chapter reviewed the competencies that
are essential to carry out the role effectively and noted what
CEOs had to say about them.

CHAPTER 8

The Evaluator Role—The CEO

Perspective

> I think to really be an effective contributor, a [WPL professional] needs to understand the business and be able to think through that business's mission and objectives, and understand the systems that the business has in place to deliver its product or service, to really have a feel for what's needed in the organization."
>
> A CEO INTERVIEWED FOR THIS BOOK

The evaluation of WLP practices requires a conscious effort and is increasingly key to your success as a WLP professional. Often the WLP intervention process will take months (or even years) to complete; documentation throughout the process is critically important. Regular reports showing that each step of the process was completed and evaluated are commonplace in WLP.

In this final chapter on the roles of the WLP professional, we explore the evaluator role, what enacting the role entails, and why this role is important. We will also describe the competencies associated with the evaluator role and share CEO perceptions of this role.

What Is the Evaluator Role?

According to *ASTD Models for Workplace Learning and Performance*, the evaluator "assesses the impact of interventions and follows up on changes made, actions taken, and results achieved to provide participants and stakeholders with information about the effectiveness of intervention implementation."[1] The first portion of the definition—"assesses the impact of interventions and follows up on changes made, actions taken, and results achieved"—provides us with insight into the holistic nature of the WLP evaluation process. The words "assessment of the impact of interventions" refer not only to the impact of interventions upon the completion of their implementation but also with assessment throughout the process. Many people think of "evaluation" as something that is done at the end of a process. For example, when we make a business decision, we evaluate the appropriateness and effectiveness of the decision to determine whether its results met our needs or the needs of others. In WLP, evaluation is an integral, continuous part of the process—not a single summative event.

Summative evaluation is used in WLP to justify an intervention, and should answer the question: "Did the implementation of the intervention result in a positive impact on the organization?" Summative evaluation is conducted immediately after the completion of an intervention. *Formative evaluation*, on the other hand, ensures that efforts at each step of the WLP process are on target—or perhaps that they need to be improved before widespread implementation. *Longitudinal evaluation* is conducted at a specified time after the intervention is completed to ensure that the intervention is still relevant, is still being carried out, and is still meeting the original established objectives. Evaluation in WLP must be formative, summative, and longitudinal; evaluation is necessary throughout the process.

As we analyze a problem, we must evaluate whether the analysis is thorough and accurate. In selecting interventions, evaluation ensures that the intervention selected is indeed the most appropriate one for the situation. As interventions are designed and developed, they need to be evaluated before implementation can take place. This formative approach helps to increase the likelihood that the end result of the WLP effort will be successful, and that the needs of the organization will be satisfied. The summative approach ensures that an intervention was immediately successful. The longitudinal approach ensures that the intervention continues to be successful.

These concepts are further evident in the last portion of the definition: "to provide participants and stakeholders with information about the effectiveness of intervention implementation." The information—you might call it feedback—that we provide to participants and stakeholders must be ongoing, regular, and complete. Focusing on results during every step of the WLP process is key; focusing on results means focusing on outcomes within each and every step to improve organizational performance.

The notion of continual evaluation is not a new concept, nor is it related solely to WLP. Even when training was the most popular intervention for improving individual performance, we can see how the suggestion of continual evaluation played out.

Nadler and Nadler suggested that evaluation and feedback should be a part of every step of the training process.[2] The evaluation and feedback step is centrally depicted, with continual communication from training practitioners to stakeholders and vice versa. This regular communication flow is critical to the success of the entire process. WLP professionals must determine not only what happened during each step but also how outcomes are tied to other steps in the model. Keep in mind that evaluation is used to examine the processes used to achieve outcomes as well as the outcomes themselves.

Another essential aspect of WLP evaluation is its focus on not only *what* happened but also *why* it happened. One way to gather information about the what and why of the WLP process is through *feedback*. Feedback is a mechanism that affords WLP professionals and their stakeholders with an opportunity to share experiences of the learning process. Keeping track of all the players in the WLP process is a daunting task and requires much attention. Regular feedback among all involved stakeholders throughout the process will provide you with greater dividends in the form of successful outcomes. Feedback can take various forms, such as meetings and oral or written reports. Facilitation skills—and verbal and written communication skills—are often particularly important in the feedback and evaluation process.

There have also been variations on the Instructional Systems Design (ISD) over the years. The ISD model is a systematic approach that provides a logical and detailed "road map" for developing and implementing results-oriented instruction. All variations on the model have had five stages in common: analysis, design, development, implementation, and evaluation. One representative example of the ISD model is called the ADDIE model. Like the Critical Events Model, the ADDIE model depicted in Exhibit 8-1 shows a strong emphasis on results or outcomes. According to Rothwell and Cookson, "Evaluation is a thread running throughout all phases of the ADDIE model. It is thus important to regard the evaluation phase in the ADDIE model not as a linear process in which each phase follows the previous phase in order, ending in evaluation, but as a cyclical process in which evaluation is linked to every phase to accountability and quality."[3] Evaluation criteria are based on the key issues addressed in each stage of the model.

The evaluation process inherent to WLP is quite similar. Evaluation in WLP means taking stock of results, comparing how close the new level of performance is to the ideal levels. WLP evaluation is designed to answer at least the following six questions:

1. How well did the intervention narrow the gap between *what is* and *what should be?*
2. How well did the intervention clarify the performance improvement objectives?
3. How well did the intervention serve to meet identified needs and achieve desired objectives?
4. What improvements in performance, if any, resulted from the intervention?

EXHIBIT 8-1. THE ADDIE MODEL AND THE EVALUATION CRITERIA

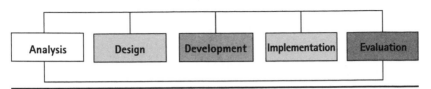

Analysis Phase Evaluation Criteria:

- Are all data accurate and complete?
- Have all the data been interpreted accurately?
- Can performance requirements realistically be achieved through training?
- Is the proposed course content complete?

Design Phase Evaluation Criteria:

- Are the instructional objectives related to the performance requirements?
- Do the tests follow from the objective?
- Do the materials facilitate the attainment of the objective?
- Is the instructional strategy selected appropriate for the desired training outcome?

Development Phase Evaluation Criteria:

- Are the tests valid and reliable?
- Do all media, etc. communicate effectively?
- Are student materials complete and facilitative of learning and performance?
- Do the instructor materials transmit the intent of how the training is to be delivered?

Implementation Phase Evaluation Criteria:

- Is the instructor qualified and able to instruct? [For instructor-led courses only]
- Are the training facilities and environment adequate?
- Where and how can the training be improved?

SOURCE: William J. Rothwell and Peter S. Cookson. *Beyond Instruction: Program Planning for Business and Education* (San Francisco: Jossey-Bass, 1998). Copyright © 1988. This material is used by permission of John Wiley & Sons, Inc.

5. What subsequent needs—that is, gaps between *what is* and *what should be*—did the implementation process uncover?

6. How well did the workforce accept the intervention?

The human performance improvement process model in the context of workplace learning is presented in Exhibit 8-2.

On the surface, this model appears deceptively similar to the model depicted in Exhibit 8-1. Each model begins with an analysis of a problem. Then, decisions are made about what is to be done to solve the problem. These decisions are subsequently implemented and evaluated to determine the success of the discovery (was the right problem identified?) and the implementation (was the gap between what is and what should be narrowed or closed?). The model shown in Exhibit 8-2 is actually only one part of a larger model for WLP. Exhibit 8-3 shows the complete process model used in WLP.

EXHIBIT 8-2. THE HUMAN PERFORMANCE IMPROVEMENT PROCESS MODEL

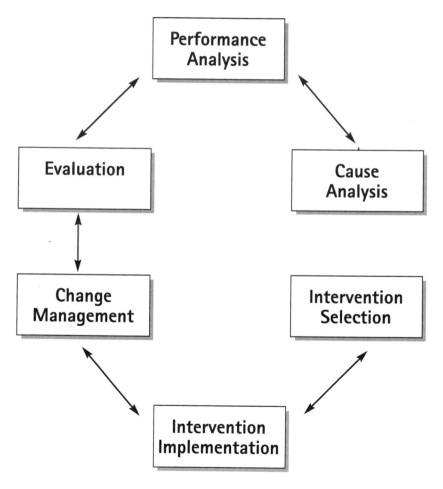

The WLP process takes into consideration the six steps in the human performance improvement model, but also shows the action research process, high performance workplace process, and external environment factors that must be considered in the evaluation process. The Critical Events Model and the ADDIE model focus on a single issue. Each is designed to find a problem and solve it, typically to improve workers' current performance levels; both models are well designed for that purpose.

WLP does not focus exclusively on learning interventions, however. Remember that WLP is the integrated use of learning and other interventions for the purpose of improving individual and organizational performance; the model used for WLP is both individually and organizationally focused. The action research model is incorporated into the WLP model because of this dual focus. Action research is often used to facilitate performance improvement in small or large groups—or throughout entire organizations.[4] The evaluation portion of the action research model stimulates a new push for change, promoting continual change toward increased group and organizational learning with performance improvement always in mind.

As we pursue ways to improve individual and organizational performance through the principles and processes of WLP, we need to consider organizational conditions that might help or hinder the process. Several conditions should be considered in the evaluation process that relate directly to how well an organization might support new learning and improved performance. The following need to be evaluated[5]:

1. How much and how well does your organization support training and continuous learning?
2. How much and how well does your organization share information?
3. How much participation do employees have in the decisions affecting them?
4. How well does your organizational structure support continuous learning?
5. How well do employees and managers work together in achieving organizational goals through effective partnerships?

EXHIBIT 8-3. A MODEL FOR WLP

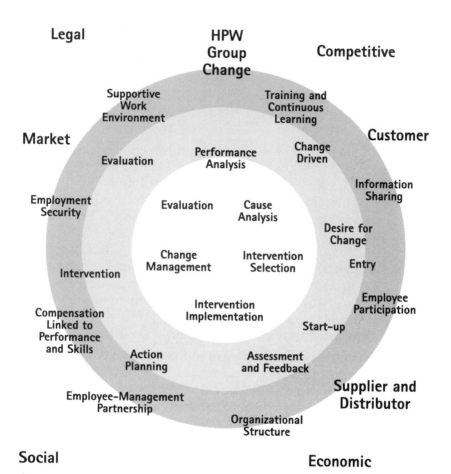

6. How well do the incentives, if any, provided to employees and managers match the effort needed to achieve desired results?

7. How secure do employees and managers feel when faced with changes that will affect their work?

8. How do employees and managers come to understand the reasons for change, how the change might affect their jobs, and how the changes are opportunities for improved performance?

9. How supportive of change and learning is the overall workforce, and how much prominence is placed on innovation, change, and risk taking?

The bottom line for this portion of the evaluation process is that learning and performance improvement is not likely to occur if organizational conditions do not support it. Although it is the responsibility of all organizational members to produce a high performance workplace, the evaluator role guides the process of determining how much organizational conditions support learning efforts.

The last portion of the model deals with the external environment. Any change within an organization is bound to have corresponding external forces that can affect the push toward improved organizational performance. Although most of the following environmental factors are typically considered during organizations' strategic planning processes, regular follow-up, feedback, and evaluation must be conducted to ensure that environmental factors will not interfere with interventions. Some environmental factors to be considered are[6]:

☐ *The Competitive Sector*: Who are your competitors now? Who are likely to become competitors in the future? What changing competitive conditions stimulate learning needs or change requirements at present and in the future? What is the influence of the competitive environment on performance expectations?

☐ *The Customer Sector*: Who are the customers served by your organization now? What customers might your organization serve in the future? How satisfied are your customers with your organization's products and services? What changes in customer preferences will affect the ability of your organization, groups, and individuals to perform effectively? What changes in the customer sector might affect present and future learning needs?

❐ *The Supplier and Distributor Sector*: What is the environment for suppliers and distributors at present? How does the performance of your suppliers and distributors affect your organization's performance? What learning needs are evident from interactions with your suppliers and distributors?

❐ *The Economic Sector*: What economic issues affect learning and performance? What changes in the economic sector might affect the ability of your organization, groups, and individuals to perform effectively? What changes in the economic sector might affect present and future learning needs in your organization?

❐ *The Social Sector*: What social conditions or trends affect the way your organization performs now, and the way it might need to perform in the future to be effective? What learning needs do these social conditions or trends stimulate?

❐ *The Market Sector*: What markets does your organization serve now? What markets will your organization serve in the future? How do changing market conditions create learning needs and affect performance expectations at present and in the future?

❐ *The Legal Sector*: What laws, rules, and regulations affect learning and performance? What changes in the legal sector will affect the ability of your organization, groups, and individuals to perform effectively? What changes in the legal sector will affect present and future learning needs?

Continual monitoring of the external environment will assist you, your organization's decision makers, and employees in identifying needs for learning, change, and performance improvement. Properly scanning the external environment for potential learning needs is a responsibility of the WLP professional among others.

Why Is the Evaluator Role Important?

Why the evaluator role is important is already somewhat evident from the previous section. Following are specific reasons intended to help you reflect on this key role.

REASON #1: EVALUATION LEADS TO PROCESS IMPROVEMENT

Perhaps the most obvious reason why the evaluator role is important is that each time the role is performed successfully, opportunities arise to improve the WLP process with each subsequent intervention implementation. When a new concept, such as WLP, is introduced into an environment, a period of adjustment is common as people become familiar with it. A thorough evaluation process is an excellent way to ensure that WLP becomes institutionalized in your organization.

REASON #2: EVALUATION LEADS TO INCREASED CREDIBILITY

Credibility is important to the success of the WLP field and to your own success as a WLP professional.[7] One challenge for the WLP profession is assessing the competencies that WLP professionals will need in the unpredictable future. Although it is tempting to retreat from this challenge, the very survival of the WLP profession requires that we continually retool ourselves to meet future challenges.[8] Correct and thorough evaluation of interventions will help you rise to the challenge of building the competencies that you will need in the future.

REASON #3: EVALUATION LEADS TO POSITIVE ATTITUDES ABOUT WLP

WLP is not designed, nor intended, to be performed solo. We clearly need the support and backing of our stakeholders. When they see the process work, when they see how their improved performance is making a positive difference for them and for the organization, they will want to do more to continue in a positive direction. Increased credibility with senior-level decision makers and CEOs is also important. Interventions to improve organizational, group, and individual performance have very real costs attached to them in time, effort, and actual dollars. CEOs will not hand out unbridled resources for efforts and interventions that don't work. When resources are needed in the future, CEO and other senior decision makers will be more apt to offer resources to continue the WLP work when they have proof that these efforts are indeed worth their costs.

Essential Competencies for the Evaluator Role

In the early days of training, evaluation was used to identify the impact of a program, service, or product. As the field progressed into HRD, the focus of evaluation shifted to identifying the impact of interventions on individual or organizational effectiveness.[9] With the advent of WLP, evaluation grew to assess the impact of interventions as well as follow up on resulting changes. This assessment of the impact of results allows us to provide participants and stakeholders with information about how well interventions were implemented, and determine how future interventions might be made even more effective.

The competencies necessary for this advanced level of evaluation follow closely with the competencies previously discussed. Competencies associated with the evaluator role come under the headings of analytical, business, interpersonal, technical, and technological. Once again, all of these competencies have been discussed in previous chapters, but it's important to examine the relationships between competencies in the context of different roles. Remember that these competencies are not mutually exclusive; they support and build on one another.

ANALYTICAL COMPETENCIES

Analytical competencies in this role deal with analytical thinking, analyzing performance data, performance gap analysis, performance theory, standards identification, systems thinking, work environment analysis, and workplace learning, learning strategies, and intervention evaluation.[10]

Analytical thinking refers to the ability to clarify complex issues by breaking them down into meaningful components and synthesizing related items. Evaluation in WLP is a very complex process; many factors need to be evaluated simultaneously. For example, each step within the WLP process needs to be continuously monitored to ensure that the process is on track, but one must also remain aware of external factors that could serve as barriers or as opportunities upon which to capitalize. Demonstrating how all the factors relate in a meaningful way by breaking the issues into easily "digestible" pieces for your stakeholders is critically important to the overall success of an intervention.

One way to accomplish this is by demonstrating competence in analyzing performance data. Analyzing performance data refers to interpreting data and determining the effects of interventions on employees, suppliers, and customers. This is one of the best ways to examine and demonstrate how performance has changed because of intervention implementation. Another way is through the competency of performance gap analysis, which refers to performing "front-end analysis" by comparing actual and ideal performance levels in the workplace and identifying opportunities and strategies for performance improvement. Performance gap analysis meshes with analytical thinking and performance data analysis to serve as a triumvirate of competencies that help stakeholders and employees see how interventions can make a positive difference for the organization.[11]

Another important analytical competency is performance theory, which involves recognizing the implications, outcomes, and consequences of performance interventions to distinguish between activities and results. As we have stated, WLP focuses on results. While it is true that results emerge from activities, and that the way in which results are achieved is important, we need to think ahead as to what activities will lead to the most successful results.

To determine what constitutes success for a WLP intervention, the competency of standards identification is necessary. What standards will meet the test for superior performance, compared with the standards currently in place in your organization? A common error is thinking of the problem at hand as an isolated issue. The competency of systems thinking helps us recognize interrelationships among events by determining the driving forces that connect seemingly isolated incidents. This allows us to take a more holistic view of performance problems to find root causes. Once the root causes have been discovered, the competency of work environment analysis comes into play.

This entails examining the work environment for issues or characteristics affecting human performance to better understand the characteristics of what would constitute a high-performance workplace within an organization.[12]

The final analytical competency is workplace learning, learning strategies, and intervention evaluation. This competency helps to ensure that WLP professionals and their stakeholders and employees are continually evaluating and improving interventions before and during implementation. At the beginning of this chapter, we discussed how evaluation and feedback have been utilized since the earliest performance improvement models to maintain focus on final results. Continuously monitoring, evaluating, and improving the process, if necessary, are fundamental tenets of WLP. The analytical competencies are tightly knitted together so that the possibility for errors and the chance of important issues slipping through the cracks are reduced.

BUSINESS COMPETENCIES

Business competencies are associated with the understanding of organizations as systems, and of the processes, decision criteria, issues, and implications of operational units of non-WLP aspects of the organization. The business competencies inherent to the evaluator role include: the ability to see the "big picture," cost/benefit analysis, evaluation of results against organizational goals, knowledge capital, and quality implications.[13]

The ability to see the big picture relates very closely with the eight analytical competencies above. This competency refers to identifying trends and patterns outside the normal paradigm of the organization. It is important to see beyond the "four walls" of your organization to determine how the external environment will affect, and be affected by, the results of an intervention.

The two business competencies of cost/benefit analysis, and evaluation of results against organizational goals, can be difficult to master. Depending on your level of financial expertise, it may be wise to partner with finance people in your organization to calculate accurate ratios of the costs of performance improvement interventions to their actual bottom-line benefits. The results of an intervention can then be evaluated in two distinct ways. The first is a strictly financial evaluation (accurate cost/benefit numbers), and the second is an evaluation of how well WLP strategies and results match with organizational goals and strategic intent.[14]

With both sets of data (hard and soft) in hand, the value of the overall knowledge capital of your organization can be determined. Further, this process will point out gaps in the knowledge capital of the organization, giving you a place to begin planning the next iteration of learning to further improve organizational performance.

INTERPERSONAL COMPETENCIES

Interpersonal competencies are associated with the understanding and application of methods that produce effective interactions among people and groups. The interpersonal competencies associated with the evaluator role are communication, communication networks, and interpersonal relationship building.[15] Obviously, communication is important; interaction with stakeholders is necessary on a regular basis. A WLP professional must constantly evaluate the forms and modes of communication he or she is involved in. For example, stakeholders may have different interpretations of the same message. Another communication issue involves listening; how you listen will affect the way others interact with you. In fact, if the goal of communication is mutual understanding of an issue, listening is essential. We urge you to reflect on your interpersonal competencies. The importance of communication skills cannot be overstated.

TECHNICAL COMPETENCIES

Some interpersonal competencies listed above are closely aligned with the technical competencies of the evaluator. To review, technical competencies are associated with the understanding and application of existing knowledge or processes. The three technical competencies directly related to the evaluator role are feedback, intervention monitoring, and questioning. Feedback, in this context, means providing performance information to the appropriate people, and also dealing effectively with the feedback you receive from others.[16] How you provide and accept feedback can help to make the evaluation process successful. A great deal of feedback is necessary as interventions are monitored throughout the WLP process. As we track and coordinate interventions to ensure consistency in implementation (and alignment with organizational strategies), the "give and take" interaction of the feedback process becomes critically important to the success of the overall intervention. We need to be prepared to question, and be questioned about, the process.

TECHNOLOGICAL COMPETENCY

The technological competency required for the evaluator is that of technological literacy. Part of the evaluation process might be to find new or better ways to assist learners in improving their performance.[17]

CEO-Identified Competencies for the Evaluator Role

CEOs are quite clearly paying attention to the evaluation process in their organizations:

- "I think it's a very important part of the training role to determine whether what you've done has been effective or not...so I see that as being carried out within the training function and something that's very important."

Your CEO is faced every day with investment decisions and other decisions about products or services that must be offered to remain competitive. CEOs are becoming increasingly aware that investments that occur *within* their organizations are equally important as (and in some instances even more important than) investments that occur at the industry level. CEOs are committed to ensuring that innovative learning processes become a regular part of doing business. At the same time, they recognize that dollars cannot be spent frivolously on learning interventions that don't improve performance. Evaluation is the surest way for a CEO to witness the results of dollars spent to improve the performance of an organization. As one CEO explained to us:

● "Maybe the most important [aspect of the evaluator role] is showing that this intervention is actually being implemented...the follow-up to know that the skills we're enhancing and the techniques we're training weren't somebody going away for a week or two...getting out of work to attend a training course for two hours a day for three weeks and then back to using the old techniques because they didn't really start to adapt them. Mostly people are anxious too. A lot of times our processes don't encourage it. You know, our managers say, 'Yeah, I know I've been trained on that and HR set it up, but here's how I really do it.' You know, the way we've always done it. And so we don't let people take advantage of what we're investing in. So many times it falls on deaf ears because when someone comes back [from a learning experience] we just don't endorse what they've been learning."

As we can see, there is clearly recognition that a thorough evaluation process is necessary. This CEO's comment lends credence to the fact that evaluation cannot begin (or end) when the intervention has been implemented. Evaluation must take place during the process to keep the intervention on track, and after the intervention is complete, an evaluation helps to avoid a pattern of "creeping backward." This refers to old patterns of behavior "creeping back" into the work environment due to the absence of a follow-up evaluation to ensure that new patterns of behavior have become institutionalized.

The following CEO comment references the technological competency of awareness of innovative new approaches to learning for improved performance. Also, the final portion of this comment deals with the interpersonal competency of communication. This CEO wants regular dialogue to occur between the CEO and the WLP professional as well as with other members of management.

● "[The WLP professional is] kind of the quarterback of this whole process...the knowledge of what's available out there and what the right things are is important....And then I think the ability to dialogue with me, the CEO, so that he and I are on the same page...that we attach the same level of importance to these things actually happening...that he is a driver, not just a receptor…that he sits in on succession planning sessions….He's got to be—I don't want to say a 'politician'—but he's got to be able to communicate effectively with the other officers and with management at all levels so that he's seen as a facilitator."

Next, we find references to both the business and analytical competencies of the WLP professional. The following CEO recognizes the importance of keeping in touch with the customer base to ensure that interventions will meet business goals. Further, this CEO mentions the interpersonal competency of listening.

● "I guess what is critically important is for all the individuals involved in those types of responsibilities is that number one, they have to spend time understanding our customers and understanding the market that we participate in because …their technical skills need to be put into the context of the business environment that our customers are operating in….It's important for them to understand the business goals of the business unit they're working with and it's important for them to be competent in the specific skill areas that they are using in the intervention….They [need] to bring some very sensitive listening skills to the table to make sure that what they have brought from a technical point of view is applied very effectively from a practical point of view."

The following quote highlights interpersonal skills as critical to effective evaluation. Communication is a key competency for ensuring that the results of WLP efforts meet all stakeholders' needs.

● "I think [WLP professionals] need good communication skills. They need the ability to sit down and talk with people, understand what their problems are, understand the best way to develop some type of training programs to fit their needs. I think they have to be a team player. I think they have to be a politician to some extent so they can talk with different department heads and coordinate the training activities and make sure that we're getting everything we want out of a training program and whatever efficiencies we can have as far as cross-training is concerned."

One CEO viewed evaluation as something one should do without thinking, as an inherent and natural part of the evaluator role. Evaluation can be thought of as a "silent partner," helping the agreed-upon intervention reach its intended results.

- "I almost see it as ingrained...you know, routine activities that whenever you do anything you always have a feedback loop that gives you the reaction as to whether it's working or not working....You start out with an objective and end the session with an evaluation as to whether the objective was achieved."

Another CEO highlighted the business and analytical competencies discussed earlier, expressing a belief that measurement is key to successful interventions. This CEO also stressed the need to establish a baseline before the intervention process begins (a parallel concept to the "front-end" analysis discussed in the analytical competencies) so that a reasonable and accurate comparison can be made between before and after. Before/after comparisons lend credibility to learning and performance efforts.

- "I see [evaluation] more as a measurement role...before you start the intervention process I think you need to establish a base line, and then after the intervention is complete, the measurement role can be done either by the manager of the area responsible or by the training department, whoever has the tools and the skills to do it."

Another CEO saw evaluation in terms of financial reporting with a customer-focused twist. Although calculating the cost-to-benefit ratio is important for the organization to see so that a determination can be made as to how well resources were spent, the bottom line is still *results*. If the customer (stakeholder) is not satisfied, then the intervention didn't produce the desired results. Even if the learning that took place was appropriate to the circumstances, the most important evaluations are still those based on customer satisfaction.

- "I think evaluation is largely done in terms of financial reporting, in terms of customer satisfaction...because ultimately the only evaluation that makes any difference are those evaluations that show up in terms of the customer view."

The following comments from two CEOs we interviewed reiterate that evaluation should be a part of everything we do as WLP professionals:

- "I see [evaluation] being carried out in multiple ways. One of the things that we do is to try to evaluate the impact of everything we do...from literally every meeting to the impact of the interventions—what did we gain, what did we lose—so [evaluation] is a standard part of everything we do."

- "In our organization the training department does [evaluation] with everything we do...they get evaluations of programs, they share those evaluations, they modify programs based on those evaluations."

As we see from the comments above, many CEOs focus on the measurement aspects of the evaluator role. We cannot stress enough how important the business competencies associated with the evaluator are to your own success and the success of our profession. In other words, CEOs want measurable results.

- "The structure that we've built is measurable and benchmarkable...if it's a specific issue or item we're evaluating then it would be designed so that it has measurable outcomes."

This comment describes why it is critical to adopt a holistic, strategic view of how learning contributes to improved organizational performance. It refers to the analytical competency of systems thinking. Two other CEOs added these remarks:

- "The [evaluator] would be someone who evaluates the overall training in the organization by taking a snapshot of everything that is going on in training. That snapshot [would give you] measurements that have been set up and hopefully carried out, which would become part of the training department's evaluation on a semi-annual basis."

- "The evaluation process is orchestrated by the person we're describing as our senior trainer....[Evaluation] is absolutely key and critical to the outcome."

Many CEOs do not view the WLP professional as the primary evaluator for performance improvement interventions. Some believe that the role should be carried out by the leadership team, some by the managers responsible for their areas, and one CEO saw the role as a CEO responsibility. Regardless of who bears the responsibility for conducting the evaluation process, your role as a WLP professional is to guide the process. As your competency level improves, you should demonstrate your value to your organization as the facilitator of the evaluation process.

- "In our organization [the evaluator role is] being carried out by our leadership team."

- "Unless the person was on the vice presidential level, I don't think that [the evaluator role] could be carried out effectively....When you're doing an evaluation, you're addressing issues that cross departments and that cross disciplines and you need to have clout to make that happen....I would not look at it as a trainer position."

- "I think that the role [of evaluator] is one of the responsibilities of managers in the organization, to constantly, continually, be evaluating the effectiveness of an effort within the organization...so I see [evaluation] as a role of virtually all manager positions."

- "I think that [the evaluator role] belongs on a higher level...it would belong on the executive level."

- "I [as CEO] would be the key agent working with senior management in implementing needed organizational change and would be the agent that not only guides the process but evaluates the process."

The final two CEO comments provide insight into the fundamental way that all of the WLP roles should be handled.

Everyone in the organization shares responsibility for ensuring that the evaluation process is conducted well.

- "The evaluator role is a multiple responsibility...it does not reside with one person."
- "It's not a single individual's job...it's got to be done by a group of people and they've got to hold themselves accountable for it."

CEOs' opinions of the evaluator role are varied, but here are a few main points to remember:

1. The focus of the evaluator role should be on results, not just activities.
2. Results must be measurable, both in actual improved performance as well as bottom-line dollar results.
3. Interpersonal competencies of communication (oral, written, and listening skills) are a must for success in the role.
4. We need to look for new and innovative ways to meet all stakeholder needs while scanning the environment (both internal and external) for clues about present and future learning needs.

Developing into the Evaluator Who Matches CEO Expectations

First and foremost, think of evaluation as continuous. The evaluation process begins before the WLP intervention process begins. The end result must be clearly articulated so that stakeholders and participants have a path to follow as intervention implementation begins. Every step of the process needs to be evaluated to ensure that the goal remains focal. Evaluation therefore needs to be formative, summative, and longitudinal.

Second, learn how to deal with feedback issues. It is key in the evaluator role to provide and receive feedback. Often, we deal with participants from different educational levels, different points of view about the necessity of interventions, and different hierarchical levels within the organization. Juggling their opinions can be trying. Focus your attention on the goal you are trying to achieve from the intervention and try not to take negative feedback personally. As one CEO suggested, there's a great deal of anxiety associated with interventions that move people out of their comfort zones; remember that what you say is just as important as how you say it.

Third, get to know your organization and the external environmental factors affecting it. WLP is not caged within the company; it affects, and is affected by, factors outside of the company as well. Keep abreast of what is going on with your customers, the legal system, your competitors, and the economy. As interventions are evaluated, modifications may have to be made. Modifications must be based on sound knowledge of what is taking place inside and outside of your organization and must be made with a consistent focus on end results.

Fourth, develop the suggested competencies associated with the role of the WLP evaluator. Again as in preceding chapters, there are worksheets to facilitate reflection on your own level of competence for each competency associated with the evaluator role (see Appendix C-24 to C-28).

Finally, learn what your CEO expects. Find out what he or she wants from you, simultaneously creating an opportunity to educate your CEO about the evaluator role. Share with your CEO the competencies associated with the evaluator role. If you have little or no experience with this role, ask your CEO for the opportunity to build the necessary competencies. This will provide an excellent opportunity to improve your CEO's perceptions about your value to the organization and enhance the image of the WLP function and the WLP field in general.

Summary

This chapter focused on CEO perceptions of WLP professionals enacting the evaluator role. Evaluators measure the results of performance improvement interventions. Too often, people think of this as happening at the end of an intervention—such as participant evaluations done upon completion of training. But growing interest focuses around continuous evaluation and continuous improvement of performance interventions. This chapter reviewed the competencies that are essential to carry out the role effectively and noted what CEOs had to say about them.

Of special note: CEOs are quite clearly paying attention to the evaluation process in their organizations. In keeping with a trend toward increased accountability in all organizational activities, CEOs want information that the organization is gaining value for its investments in performance improvement interventions. That trend is not likely to abate.

CHAPTER 9

Developing a Workplace Learning Action Plan

> I think that the ownership for knowledge and learning, and the use of information, belong across an organization and all the leadership positions, and not just in HR. Frankly, the HR person [or WLP professional] can be a catalyst, but the day-to-day behavior of an organization is driven by the people that manage the people. So I think learning has to be, from the top down, a priority—from the CEO all the way down through the organization—that learning is important and that everybody takes ownership in driving that.
>
> A CEO INTERVIEWED FOR THIS BOOK

CEOs recognize the connection between an active, integrated, broad-based learning-oriented environment and company profitability and employee motivation. This connection necessitates participation by all organizational leaders in establishing and maintaining an organization's learning climate and performance culture. Division directors, line managers, and supervisors need to model a real-time learning approach by what they do every day so that employees can see the link between learning and work.

As the CEO quotation that opens this chapter reminds us, you as a WLP professional can serve as a catalyst. But it is only through the daily management of people that behavioral changes occur. Therefore, for learning to have an impact on performance, it must become part of daily management practice. In short, it is the job of every supervisor, manager, and executive and should not be delegated to one function—such as to WLP professionals alone.

This book illuminates CEO opinions about workplace learning and performance and what CEOs perceive to be your responsibilities as a WLP leader. We made the assumption, which was verified by CEO opinions, that learning programs and other performance improvement efforts are most effective when they explicitly and clearly address business challenges. Business challenges can be found in an organization's strategic plan and emerge when serving customers, implementing new systems software, increasing productivity with fewer workers, understanding new work processes, or addressing the daily problems that arise in carrying out the organization's mission and purpose. Business challenges change each day, and the competencies that you should demonstrate must adapt to those changes. Knowing the competencies that CEOs expect from WLP professionals can help you to meet the future challenges you face and can help your organization remain successful.

Our interviews with CEOs shed light on the roles of WLP leaders. While previous studies have identified many competencies expected of WLP professionals, the results of our research focused on CEO perceptions of what competencies are essential for success in the WLP field. Whereas each chapter presented detailed information on each WLP role and their corresponding competencies, CEOs generally expect WLP professionals to participate in business decision making and apply their special knowledge of workplace learning to solving performance problems and seizing improvement opportunities. The following sections in this chapter summarize the key findings of our research on CEO expectations for WLP professionals as they enact the roles of Manager, Analyst, Intervention Selector, Intervention Designer/Developer, Intervention Implementor, Change Leader, and Evaluator (see Exhibit 9-1).

The Manager Role

CEO PERSPECTIVE

CEOs expect those enacting the WLP role of manager to orchestrate the entire workplace learning process and manage people within that process. CEOs believe that, while many competencies should be demonstrated to achieve success in this role,

EXHIBIT 9-1. WLP ROLES

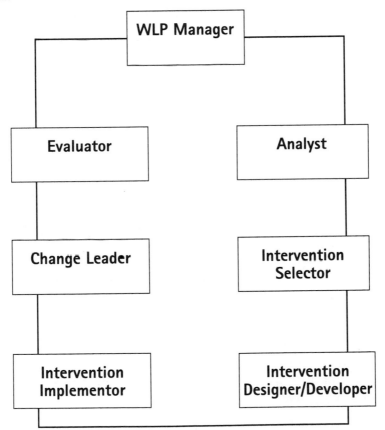

strong interpersonal competencies are essential. Although not everyone may agree with this view of the WLP manager, it is an important role to begin with, because many CEOs view this role as belonging to managers other than the WLP manager. Our research found that CEOs believe general management for workplace learning programs belongs to line (operating) managers, supervisors, and others responsible for immediate employee oversight. As a WLP professional who enacts the manager role, you will find that two issues immediately arise from these findings:

1. Your organization's managers are immediate and potential clients for you to contact, and work with, in creating WLP programs.

2. Your organization's managers are the people that you need to engage when demonstrating your competence as a WLP leader.

Given CEO opinions that management for WLP programs belongs primarily outside of WLP departments, those enacting the WLP role of manager must partner with line managers to deliver WLP programs and implement performance improvement interventions. For effective learning programs to impact performance, WLP managers must drive ownership through the organization's managers and into the organization's culture.

As a WLP professional enacting the manager role, you bring the training, experience, and content expertise for workplace learning to your organization. Your expertise in the WLP field ensures that programs are effectively targeted, designed, delivered, and evaluated. The WLP professional, acting as a manager, should be the organization's workplace learning content leader—its chief learning officer (CLO). By partnering and supporting line managers, and other immediate supervisors in your organization, you exercise your WLP manager role in the way that CEOs believe it should be exercised. Of course, it is also important that if you are a manager of people—such as staff members in a WLP or HRD Department—that you acquit all the responsibilities usually expected of managers who act in that capacity. In short, you must set an example.

COMPETENCIES

CEOs identified six competency categories: analytical, business, interpersonal, leadership, technical, and technological competencies.[1] These six categories reflect more than thirty individual competencies. Although that number may seem overwhelming, you should remember two points:

1. The relative weight for mastery of each competency for the WLP professional enacting the manager role is a function of the strength of the competencies of his or her WLP team.

2. The six competency categories overlap and can be further organized into three WLP managerial competency areas.

The first competency area CEOs recognize in WLP management is analytical/business ability.[2] Analytical abilities are reflected in the identification and organization of workforce capabilities and in the assessment of the workforce's strengths and weaknesses for meeting organizational goals. CEOs expect those who enact the WLP role of manager to analyze the current business environment, understand the organization's work processes and performance gaps within those processes, and plan for the future training needs of the organization. Against this analytical ability is balanced the ability to understand an organization's business operations and how the company makes money.

Key to demonstrating this competency effectively is aligning training programs—and, of course, other performance improvement interventions—with the organization's strategy, business goals, and work processes. Knowing the organization business model, and assessing the organization's workforce capability within the current business model, allows those who enact the WLP role of manager to target training and other efforts where most needed. CEOs want WLP managers to link learning efforts to the organization's plans.

The second area of competency CEOs recognized in the WLP manager is the interpersonal/leadership area. Interpersonal competencies reflect abilities that enable a person to interact effectively with others individually and in groups.[3] For a manager, interpersonal skills are essential for every part of the job—and may be the most crucial for success of any competency. As one CEO put it, the WLP role of manager:

- "...begins with communication. Someone who doesn't possess good communication skills in listening, speaking, and writing would not be effective in that role."

Strong interpersonal skills permit a person to participate in discussions. When combined with business competencies, interpersonal competencies give managers of WLP the opportunity to be involved in senior-level decision-making processes on an equal footing with others.

The second part of the competency area, leadership, was described by CEOs as the ability to demonstrate energy and enthusiasm for the company's learning programs. The leadership competency of those enacting the WLP role of manager is demonstrated by moving throughout the organization to meet with managers, supervisors, and others to build interest for the company's learning programs. By moving throughout the organization, WLP professionals uncover opportunities to collect information on learning needs.

Finally, CEOs want managers of WLP to interact with them directly on issues linked to training or other learning needs, business challenges facing the organization, and how the organization's learning programs are organized to increase human capacity and foster innovative, creative thinking.

The third area of competency CEOs recognized in the WLP manager is the technical/technological area. Technical competency reflects specialized abilities to facilitate group processes and provide feedback. Technological competency is reflected in keeping track of, and applying, new developments in learning technology.[4] This competency area can be considered as a bridge between the old and new worlds of HRD and WLP. Traditionally, CEOs regarded those who enacted the WLP role of manager as commanding strong abilities to lead group discussions. Since WLP professionals are usually trained facilitators, CEOs expect them to organize groups to solve business problems. In a facilitated group meeting, CEOs expect managers to provide a high level of feedback to the group.

In the new world, CEOs expect those who act as managers of WLP to discuss and apply new learning technologies. CEOs believe that e-learning tools provide a means to create new energy for an organization's workplace learning programs. While e-learning is not synonymous with innovative learning, CEOs believe that new learning technologies can offer one alluring way to interest people in their organizations' learning programs.

The Analyst Role

CEO PERSPECTIVE

The analyst role provides the foundation for all WLP activities.[5] At a basic level, the analyst identifies the root causes of performance problems. At a deeper level, the analyst identifies an organization's workforce capabilities, assesses work requirements, and works with others to build learning programs and other performance improvement interventions that support achievement of business goals. CEOs expect the analyst to know where the organization's skills currently are in relation to where the organization is planning on going. Familiarity with business challenges and organization strategy provides the analyst with a backdrop against which learning needs analyses are presented. Given ongoing changes in technology, and increased access to real-time data, demand for organization and market information in the analyst's role has increased. This increased demand forces the analyst to build interest and support for the organization's performance-oriented learning programs through focused needs analysis and increased awareness of organization goals. Although not all performance solutions are learning-based, CEOs expect the analyst to blend awareness of the organization's business needs with a sense of the corporate culture.

COMPETENCIES

CEO perceptions of the analyst role identified four competency areas: analytical, business, interpersonal, and leadership. To begin with, CEOs want to know why learning programs are being offered and how the organization will achieve a return on that investment. Return on investment for an organization's learning programs needs to be placed in the context of meeting business challenges. In our discussions, we heard CEOs speak at length about the daunting challenges they face in changing organization culture, making organization transitions, meeting financial goals in an increasingly competitive marketplace, and finding new talent for hard-to-fill positions. Analytical and business competencies allow the analyst to explain how the organization's WLP programs address business challenges and how performance gaps are being closed through interventions.

All of the analysis and business sense in the world will not get people to fully participate in programs unless they see how the programs add value. The second half of the analyst role identified by CEOs falls into the interpersonal and leadership area. Business and performance needs for training or other interventions must be packaged with personal appeal and a professional sale.

The Intervention Selector Role

CEO PERSPECTIVE

The intervention selector role requires partnership. The intervention selector chooses the appropriate learning or nonlearning intervention to address a performance gap. Whether the intervention is short or long term, CEOs believe that the intervention selector role belongs chiefly to line managers and other departmental leaders. WLP professionals should take special note of this finding and reflect on how managers are participating in the intervention selection process. Are you as a WLP professional involved prior to the intervention design phase or following its selection?

The absence of a trained WLP professional during the intervention selection phase can threaten its cost-effectiveness and success. Because choosing an appropriate intervention requires keen awareness of the job-specific context of the performers involved, historical knowledge of the department, and experience with different job demands, it makes sense to involve line managers in the process. WLP professionals, however, provide expertise with workplace learning, performance needs analysis, and intervention cost analysis. They bring valuable skills to the process. The intervention selector role is truly a shared responsibility between the WLP professional and the people in need.

COMPETENCIES

Remembering that CEOs perceive the role of the intervention selector to be owned by line managers, dominant competencies for WLP professionals fall into the areas of interpersonal and leadership.[6] To utilize your skills as a WLP professional, you need to demonstrate strong networking and consulting skills. Communication and interpersonal relationship-building behaviors must be part of your approach to creating buy-in for programs and interventions. Beyond interpersonal competencies, CEOs expect analytical and business skills to ensure that a needs assessment is documented, and that there is a logical cost/benefit approach in place. Finally, you should possess keen knowledge of adult learning principles and how new technologies can be used to deliver or support programs.

The Intervention Designer/Developer Role

CEO PERSPECTIVE

The intervention designer/developer is such a complex role that it may be most effective when divided up into distinct parts and outsourced as much as possible. CEOs perceive this role to be complex and to change rapidly. The intervention designer/developer designs, develops, leads, and evaluates learning programs. The person enacting this role must leverage internal and external resources so that learning programs are designed with the organization's business goals and strategy in mind, are developed with the aid of an adult workplace learning expert, and delivered by someone possessing the authority and authenticity of line managers. CEOs don't expect one person to successfully fill this role and would much rather see a team of internal and external partners collaborate to perform these duties.

COMPETENCIES

The competencies demonstrated by the intervention designer/developer are unlike those of other WLP roles. These competencies are unique in that they are demonstrated by deliverables, such as the types of learning programs provided and how well learning programs are designed to change employee behavior. CEOs spoke of three competency areas for the intervention designer/developer:

1. The ability to use technology creatively
2. The ability to use learning to connect the organization
3. The ability to demonstrate new behaviors

CEOs believe the intervention designer/developer needs to use new forms of technology in the development and delivery of learning programs. These programs involve people throughout the organization in the design, development, and delivery phases of the program. CEOs believe that by demonstrating an inclusive approach to program design and development, WLP professionals are positioning their interventions so that participants will have a better chance of transferring learning back to the workplace.

The Intervention Implementor Role

CEO PERSPECTIVE

Similar to the intervention selector, CEOs regard the intervention implementor role as owned by senior and line managers, but supported by WLP professionals. The definition of the intervention implementor role describes a responsibility for ensuring the effective implementation of interventions that address the specific root causes of human performance gaps. Line managers have a stronger impact on employee behaviors than instructors and facilitators. It is well within reason that CEOs see implementation as belonging to management. Also, CEOs perceive the time frame for interventions as longer term than a one-shot training event. The long-term nature of intervention implementation requires more daily oversight and operational direction than is typically expected of WLP professionals.

COMPETENCIES

The competencies associated with the intervention implementor role are dominated by analytical and interpersonal behaviors associated with process consulting. As a supporting resource to senior managers, the intervention implementor must provide performance feedback to groups and individuals and suggest ways to integrate learning tools into daily behaviors. Implicit within process consulting competencies are keen abilities to communicate, develop relationships, create support for proposed interventions, and work effectively within difficult group settings.

Given that CEOs perceive the intervention implementor as a supporting role, you as a WLP professional must constantly monitor department leaders for feedback on the effectiveness of interventions and facilitate midcourse corrections to interventions when goals are not being reached. Finally, CEOs expect the intervention implementor to recommend ways of using new learning technologies and possible ways that electronic performance support systems can be used.

The Change Leader Role

CEO PERSPECTIVE

CEOs view themselves as owners of the change leader role. Their comments reflect that they also believe that, for change to occur throughout the workplace, all management levels must reinforce it. The finding that CEOs perceive themselves as change leaders may pose a challenge to constructing an effective change management team.

We suggest that you step back and reflect on how work gets done in your organization, and consider that the CEO perception of leading change makes good sense for presenting change initiatives to a workforce and communicating support for change. CEOs can provide guidance for you on how to align your role for change within the current chain of command. Even if your organization is structured in teams, our findings suggest that senior-level managers need to own and support the change effort for it to be successful.

COMPETENCIES

Recognizing that CEOs perceive the role of change leader as belonging to the highest level of leadership, the WLP role of change leader is perhaps best characterized as a "change designer," "change facilitator," or "change architect." CEO input for the change leader suggests that four core competencies are essential:

- ❑ Drive
- ❑ Communication
- ❑ Broad perspective
- ❑ Business knowledge

Drive and communication competencies describe abilities to move throughout the organization and meet with line-managers, supervisors, and employees to discuss change and how it is impacting the organization. A key aspect of the drive competency is the ability to demonstrate energy and enthusiasm for change and discuss with others how change is planned to move the organization forward. Effectively demonstrating drive competencies requires that you communicate clearly. As you drive the message of change throughout your organization, you will facilitate large and small group settings and meetings with individuals and carry the change directives to the larger workforce.

A change leader should also incorporate other, possibly non–work-related, experiences into the change process to contribute alternative possibilities for change. Demonstrating breadth of work experience is a competency CEOs expect of change leaders. Finally, CEOs expect the change leader to be able to talk the organization's business and connect business challenges to organization strategy. Being able to converse with senior leaders as well as employees at all levels about the organization's products, services, mission, and strategy is an expectation of all change leaders.

The Evaluator Role

CEO PERSPECTIVE

Training and learning programs are, at their core, a business function; how an organization knows whether that function is meeting organizational objectives is the responsibility of the evaluator. CEOs expect evaluation of WLP programs to focus on results, not just on activities. Results of organization investments in learning programs need to be presented in financial, and nonfinancial, terms against the business needs they are intended to address. While CEOs appreciate the role of active, innovative learning programs in the recruitment and retention of employees, they are equally, if not more, concerned with the measurable level at which the programs are achieving results. Valid evaluation takes place throughout the learning intervention process. CEOs expect evaluation measures to be driven by the learning needs of the workforce, and the learning needs to be driven by the organization's business challenges. Because success at the back end requires evaluation at the front end, evaluation should take place throughout the entire learning process. The evaluator role brings the entire WLP function together by measuring the results of current programs in an attempt to identify future learning needs.

COMPETENCIES

The comprehensive nature of the evaluator role requires a unique blend of analytical, business, interpersonal, and technical competencies.[7] While the role focuses on analytical abilities involving analyzing performance, assessing work environments, systemic thinking, and identifying quality standards, it also requires abilities in strategic thinking, communication, and feedback. Evaluating immediate performance issues and measuring intervention effectiveness provides the first level of competency expected by CEOs. The evaluator should also demonstrate an ability to assess the larger business environment, customer expectations, and organization goals.

To work effectively with departments and other WLP roles, WLP professionals who enact the evaluator role must demonstrate the interpersonal competencies of listening, communication, and feedback. In the end, when changes in business challenges occur, or when it is recognized that an intervention is not working, the evaluator needs to work with others to change the intervention and identify new measures to assess.

Conclusions

CEO perceptions of workplace learning provide valuable insight into how the highest level of organizational leadership views learning programs as tools for performance improvement. Findings from our interviews provide new knowledge for WLP professionals on how CEOs perceive learning programs should address business challenges, and on the competencies CEOs want to see in WLP professionals. Clearly, CEOs are interested in knowing how learning is used to improve performance, and they seek ways to create learning cultures in their organizations. As a WLP professional, you should dialogue with your coworkers—and senior leaders—on organization business challenges and on how learning can help to meet those challenges. Senior-level feedback on workplace learning is key to strengthening the connection between learning and performance and provides immediate direction for WLP.

Feedback on the changes occurring in your organization is critical for directing your organization's learning programs. Changes occur all the time in technology, business objectives, business markets, production processes, staffing, and strategy. Dealing with change is a common business challenge, and because change is constant, employees need a process to help them understand the changes taking place and acquire new skills to meet new requirements. Change discussions can be used as a central point for building learning strategies and improving how learning programs are used to address business challenges. CEOs and other senior leaders are great sources for identifying macro-changes taking place, but WLP professionals can provide a bridge between the strategic direction for change and the organization's ability to adapt to change.

The seven WLP roles provide a foundation for building an organizational learning structure. Each role provides a distinct purpose and link to the others. Central to the structure's support are an organization's business challenges. Each role operates from the business challenge facing the organization and delivers a product to meet that challenge. The information provided in this book is intended to help WLP professionals assess how their companies' learning programs are being used to address business challenges. The dynamic relationship between business challenges and WLP competencies requires constant environmental monitoring and adaptation (see Exhibit 9-2).

EXHIBIT 9-2. THE CHALLENGE-COMPETENCY DYNAMIC

In companies that recognize the link between learning and performance, WLP has evolved into a core business process. Learning programs directed by organization mission, and targeted at helping to achieve strategic objectives, enable an organization's human resources to succeed. CEOs recognize the importance of learning programs to organization profitability, and they have strong perceptions of what WLP professionals should do. Knowing what CEOs expect, and creating a continuous feedback loop on how your organization's learning programs are meeting objectives, enables you and your interventions to provide the greatest return and directly impact performance.

As we conclude the book, we urge you to have continuing dialogue with your CEO. Meeting his or her expectations will help you be more successful in your efforts.

Use the Worksheet in Exhibit 9-3 to help you plan the next steps. Take the time to summarize the lessons you have learned from this book on the Worksheet. Then, either by yourself or as an activity with all the WLP professionals in your department or in your organization, plan specifically how you will surface, clarify, and meet the expectations of your CEO. If you are not clear about what those expectations are, then it is time you found out and took deliberate steps to satisfy this important customer/stakeholder for your efforts. Good luck on that endeavor.

Exhibit 9-3. A Worksheet for Planning Next Steps

Directions: Use this worksheet by yourself or with other WLP professionals in your organization.

For each WLP role listed in the left column below, go through the book and summarize in the middle column the key points made about CEO expectations for WLP professionals who enact that role. If you wish, also have a dialogue with the CEO in your organization about what he or she expects from you in that role. Then, in the far right column, make a list of specific action steps that you will take to help meet the CEO's expectations. There are no "right" or "wrong" answers (or proposed actions) in any absolute sense, though some answers may be better than others in one organizational setting and corporate culture.

WLP Role	Summary of the Key Points About CEO Expectations for the WLP Role from the Book and from Discussions with Your Own CEO	What Action Steps Should You Take to Meet Your CEO's Expectations?
1 Manager		
2 Analyst		

WLP Role	Summary of the Key Points About CEO Expectations for the WLP Role from the Book and from Discussions with Your Own CEO	What Action Steps Should You Take to Meet Your CEO's Expectations?
3 Intervention Selector		
4 Intervention Designer/Developer		
5 Intervention Implementor		
6 Change Leader		
7 Evaluator		

Questions to Ask Your CEO

Here are two lists of questions that you can use to interview your own CEO. If you have enough time, use the long questionnaire. If your time with the CEO is limited, use the shorter questionnaire.

Long Questionnaire

1. In the next two to three years, what are the most important business challenges facing our organization?
2. How can workplace learning contribute to meeting the challenges of our company?
3. What types of workplace learning programs would you like to see in the future?
4. In your opinion, what abilities are most important for people who bear such titles as training and development director, human resource development manager, or chief knowledge officer?

FURTHER QUESTIONS

1. What have been your perceptions about trainer roles in the past?
2. What experiences caused you to believe that?
3. Can you tell me about a time when trainers in your organ-

ization have not met your expectations?

4.   What happened in that or those example(s)?

5.   Can you tell me about a time when trainers in your organ-
     ization have met your perceptions about what you believed
     they should have done?

6.   Based upon your past experiences, if you could describe
     the "perfect" trainer, what roles do you think would be
     most appropriate for him or her?

COMPETENCY QUESTIONS

The role descriptions in this section are taken from *ASTD Models
for Workplace Learning and Performance*[1], a major study that
described what roles should be played in organizational settings
by trainers and other WLP professionals. After reading the role
descriptions, ask your CEO the following questions:

> *Manager*: Plans, organizes, schedules, monitors, and leads the
> work of individuals and groups to attain desired results; facil-
> itates the strategic plan; ensures that Workplace Learning and
> Performance is aligned with organizational needs and plans;
> and ensures accomplishment of the administrative require-
> ments of the function.

1.   How do see this particular role being carried out by the
     lead person in the training function of your organization?

2.   When you hear the word "manager" as it relates to train-
     ing, what are your perceptions about the duties of that
     role?

> *Analyst*: Troubleshoots and isolates the causes of human per-
> formance gaps or identifies areas for improving human per-
> formance.

3.   How do you see this role being carried out in your organi-
     zation?

4.   When you hear the word "analyst" as it relates to a train-
     er, what are your perceptions about the duties of that role?

> *Intervention Selector*: Chooses appropriate interventions to
> address root causes of human performance gaps.

5. How do you see this role being carried out in your organization?

6. When you hear the words "intervention selector" as it relates to training, what are your perceptions about the duties of that role?

Intervention Designer and Developer: Creates learning and other interventions that help to address the specific root causes of human performance gaps.

7. How do you see this role being carried out in your organization?

8. When you hear the words "intervention designer and developer" as it relates to training, what are your perceptions about the duties of that role?

Intervention Implementor: Ensures the appropriate and effective implementation of desired interventions that address the specific root causes of human performance gaps.

9. How do you see this role being carried out in your organization?

10. When you hear the words "intervention implementor" as it relates to training, what are your perceptions about the duties of that role?

Change Leader: Inspires the workforce to embrace change, creates direction for the change effort, helps the organization's workforce to adapt to change, and ensures that interventions are continuously monitored and guided in ways consistent with stakeholders' desired results.

11. How do you see this role being carried out in your organization?

12. When you hear the words "change leader" as it relates to training, what are your perceptions about the duties of that role?

Evaluator: Assesses the impact of interventions and provides participants and stakeholders with information about the effectiveness of the intervention implementation.

13. How do you see this role being carried out in your organization?

14. When you hear the word "evaluator" as it relates to training, what are your perceptions about the duties of that role?

15. What do you believe are the key roles of the trainers in your organization?

16. How do you see those roles being played out?

QUESTIONS ABOUT THE FUTURE ROLES OF TRAINERS

1. What do you believe are the implications for your organization when your perceptions of trainer roles differ from the perceived roles of the trainer?

2. Similarly, what do you believe are the implications for your organization when your perceptions of trainer roles match the perceived roles of the trainer?

3. What other roles do you perceive that training professionals might play to better contribute to your organization?

Short Questionnaire

1. (*Manager role*): How could I help you realize the organization's strategic objectives?

2. (*Analyst role*): What are the biggest human performance problems we face in this organization? What are the biggest opportunities for improving human performance?

3. (*Intervention Selector role*): People can learn in many ways in this organization. They can learn on-the-job and off-the-job. What one effort could we launch that might have the biggest positive impact on the performance of people in this organization?

4. (*Intervention Designer and Developer role*): If we designed and developed such a learning effort, as described in the answer to question 3 above, how do you think we should plan and organize for it? Who should do that? How?

5. (*Intervention Implementor role*):

It will take time and daily monitoring to ensure the successful implementation of the learning effort described in answer to question 3 above. What do you think my group should do to help with the continuing implementation of the effort? What should operating managers or supervisors do? In short, what should we do to help make sure that the effort is implemented as intended?

6. (*Change Leader role*):

What should we do to communicate our successes and our areas for improvement as the learning effort is implemented? How do you think we should try to keep people enthused about the change?

7. (*Evaluator role*):

What do you think we should measure to assess the relative success of the learning effort described in answer to question 3 above? How should we measure it? Who should get that feedback, and how often should they get it?

Worksheet for Recording Opinions About CEO Comments

Directions: Use this activity to help you reflect on what the opinions of CEOs might mean to you. In the left column below, you will find quotations taken directly from interviews with CEOs. In the right column, record your own reflections about what the opinions expressed in these quotations might mean to you. There are no "right" or "wrong" answers in any absolute sense. However, what you make of these opinions may reflect as much on you as on CEOs. Also consider whether the CEO of your organization might hold a comparable opinion about you in your role as a Workplace Learning and Performance (WLP) professional.

Quotation from a CEO	Record Your Own Reflections about What the Opinions Expressed in These Quotations Might Mean to You

1 "The Internet is changing—radically changing our entire business model and the way that we conduct business. Almost everything that we do has got to be reinvented over the next couple of years. And so, we need to 'A' stay on top of all of the trends that are out there, and then 'B,' figure out how it's going to change our organization and communicate that throughout the organization, because it's going to change people's jobs. So there are aspects of technical skills that need to be updated, and the way we go about processing regular transactions in our organization has got to change and get communicated."

2 "To me, the abilities that [WLP professionals] have to have—whether or not it's development director, human resource executive, or the chief knowledge officer—the ability they have to have is to do an accurate and honest assessment of what the capabilities are of the organization they're a part of. They not only have to make an honest and realistic assessment of what they have in terms of workforce knowledge and information, but they also have to make an honest assessment of what they may be missing or what they need. I think this upfront assessment is critical and all-important, because until they really have a sense of the answer to the

assessment, they can't begin to put together a realistic budget to get at the needs. And they also can't begin to decide whether some or all of these learning needs could be handled internally or whether most or all of them would have to be handled externally."

---

3 "We use a combination of outsourced workplace learning programs where we engage outside resources to come in to help develop our team in particular areas. Specifically, [there are programs on] leadership development as an example, and on sales training and education relative to the challenges that our customers are facing and how we can become more sensitive to our customers' needs and how we can uniquely fill them. So that's some of the outsourced learning that we would do. Some of the inside programs center around the development of our own organizational development function and the team of people that would work with all of our business units in order to identify some of our specific business interventions. For example, where we may have teams of people in the field who used to compete with each other, it would be a very good thing to have those people get together to develop a common agenda and to develop short-term and longer-term goals and objectives. We utilize our internal resources that come from our organizational development area to travel to these locations and conduct these types of programs."

Quotation from a CEO	Record Your Own Reflections about What the Opinions Expressed in These Quotations Might Mean to You

4 "Our programs tend to be kind of tailored to specific areas of developmental need. We tend to be more reactive right now to problem areas than really investing in being proactive. So I think that's an area we're all looking at, trying to figure out whether we as a company can do more programs, or is that unrealistic? Are we going to have to go to the outside and contract with more outside training companies and more outside universities to improve the training skills and knowledge of our workforce?"

5 "Because I use the word culture shift [as our company's business challenge] this is a very profound change to us. And our ability to use the learning systems—training systems, involvement systems—will be a major part of making this culture shift, to [our company's cultural] customer-orientation. It would be done through use of some conventional and some nonconventional, untraditional learning, such as going to the customer and learning his business and his needs and his concerns."

6 "For the manager candidates, we assess their skills in five different areas and determine where they're weak. They've got to have a minimum level of skills to even be considered, to be hired, but once they've attained that minimum then we try to focus on, well, we don't focus only on their weak-

nesses. We focus on their strengths as well. But the one area that we really hit on is interpersonal development, which is actually management of people. That, we have found in general, is the toughest skill to teach somebody. We actually found it's easier to find people who already have the skill than to try and teach it to them."

7 "They've got to be very good at systems. They've got to be good at developing systems that are easily understood by non-HR people, that are easily understood and easily implemented in the field and in an environment that is not ideal to learning. So the systems development and the systems orientation I think are critical."

8 "I think it's very important that these people truly understand the requirements of business. It's hard to understand what kind of training and people development stuff you're gonna need to do without understanding the business. So, to do the right kind of measurements, to really accurately assess the needs of the business—and that's very hard—the person has to be willing to drive change quickly. And that would be a leader, who has to be able to drive change and be a change agent."

Quotation from a CEO	Record Your Own Reflections about What the Opinions Expressed in These Quotations Might Mean to You

9 "I would say that what is critically important is for all of the individuals who are involved in [workplace learning] responsibilities, is that, number one, they have spent time understanding our customers and understanding the market that we participate in because their unique skills, their technical skills, need to be put in context of the business environment that we're operating in and that our customers are operating in. It is also very important for the workplace learning team to understand very specifically the articulated goals of the business unit that they're working with and that the unique skills that they bring to the table relative to the intervention—whether human development or technology interventions—that they are very competent in their own specific skill area that they bring to the table. But they [also need to] bring some very, very sensitive listening skills to the table to make sure that what they have brought from a technical point of view is applied very effectively from a practical point of view."

SOURCE: All quotations in Appendix B are taken from John E. Lindholm. *A Study of CEO Perceptions of the Competencies of Workplace Learning and Performance.* Dissertation Abstracts International, 2000.

Self-Assessment Worksheets

Appendix C-1. Self-Assessment Worksheet for Analytical Competencies Associated with the Role of the Manager

Directions: Use this worksheet to assess how you measure up to your CEO's expectations. After examining the analytical competencies associated with this role as presented in the chapter, indicate what you are currently doing that demonstrates each competency and what your CEO expects. Finally, think about and list the ways you could improve in the areas that you perceive need improvement. Add more paper as necessary.

Analytical Competencies	Ways I Currently Demonstrate These Competencies	My CEO's Expectations	Steps to Take to Improve My Application of These Competencies and Steps to Take to Meet My CEO's Expectations
Analytical Thinking			
Career Development Theory and Application			
Competency Identification			
Knowledge Management			
Organization Development Theory and Application			
Performance Gap Analysis			
Performance Theory			
Process Consultation			
Reward System Theory and Application			
Social Awareness			
Staff Selection Theory and Application			
Standards Identification			
Systems Thinking			
Work Environment Analysis			

Appendix C-2. Self-Assessment Worksheet for Business Competencies Associated with the Role of the Manager

Directions: Use this worksheet to assess how you measure up to your CEO's expectations. After examining the business competencies associated with this role as presented in the chapter, indicate what you are currently doing that demonstrates each competency and what your CEO expects. Finally, think about and list the ways you could improve in the areas that you perceive need improvement. Add more paper as necessary.

Business Competencies	Ways I Currently Demonstrate These Competencies	My CEO's Expectations	Steps to Take to Improve My Application of These Competencies and Steps to Take to Meet My CEO's Expectations
Ability to See the "Big Picture"			
Business Knowledge			
Cost/Benefit Analysis			
Evaluation of Results Against Organizational Goals			
Identification of Critical Business Issues			
Industry Awareness			
Knowledge Capital			
Negotiating/Contracting			
Outsourcing Management			
Project Management			
Quality Implications			

Appendix C-3. Self-Assessment Worksheet for Interpersonal Competencies Associated with the Role of the Manager

Directions: Use this worksheet to assess how you measure up to your CEO's expectations. After examining the interpersonal competencies associated with this role as presented in the chapter, indicate what you are currently doing that demonstrates each competency and what your CEO expects. Finally, think about and list the ways you could improve in the areas that you perceive need improvement. Add more paper as necessary.

Interpersonal Competencies	Ways I Currently Demonstrate These Competencies	My CEO's Expectations	Steps to Take to Improve My Application of These Competencies and Steps to Take to Meet My CEO's Expectations
Communication			
Communication Networks			
Consulting			
Coping Skills			
Interpersonal Relationship Building			

Appendix C-4. Self-Assessment Worksheet for Leadership Competencies Associated with the Role of the Manager

Directions: Use this worksheet to assess how you measure up to your CEO's expectations. After examining the leadership competencies associated with this role as presented in the chapter, indicate what you are currently doing that demonstrates each competency and what your CEO expects. Finally, think about and list the ways you could improve in the areas that you perceive need improvement. Add more paper as necessary.

Leadership Competencies	Ways I Currently Demonstrate These Competencies	My CEO's Expectations	Steps to Take to Improve My Application of These Competencies and Steps to Take to Meet My CEO's Expectations
Buy-in/Advocacy			
Diversity Awareness			
Ethics Modeling			
Goal Implementation			
Group Dynamics			
Leadership			
Visioning			

Appendix C-5. Self-Assessment Worksheet for Technical Competencies Associated with the Role of the Manager

Directions: Use this worksheet to assess how you measure up to your CEO's expectations. After examining the technical competencies associated with this role as presented in the chapter, indicate what you are currently doing that demonstrates each competency and what your CEO expects. Finally, think about and list the ways you could improve in the areas that you perceive need improvement. Add more paper as necessary.

Technical Competencies	Ways I Currently Demonstrate These Competencies	My CEO's Expectations	Steps to Take to Improve My Application of These Competencies and Steps to Take to Meet My CEO's Expectations
Facilitation			
Feedback			

Appendix C-6. Self-Assessment Worksheet for Technological Competencies Associated with the Role of the Manager
Directions: Use this worksheet to assess how you measure up to your CEO's expectations. After examining the technological competencies associated with this role as presented in the chapter, indicate what you are currently doing that demonstrates each competency and what your CEO expects. Finally, think about and list the ways you could improve in the areas that you perceive need improvement. Add more paper as necessary.

Technological Competencies	Ways I Currently Demonstrate These Competencies	My CEO's Expectations	Steps to Take to Improve My Application of These Competencies and Steps to Take to Meet My CEO's Expectations
Technological Literacy			
Computer-Mediated Communication			

Appendix C-7. Self-Assessment Worksheet for Analytical Competencies Associated with the Role of the Intervention Selector
Directions: Use this worksheet to assess how you measure up to your CEO's expectations. After examining the analytical competencies associated with this role as presented in the chapter, indicate what you are currently doing that demonstrates each competency and what your CEO expects. Finally, think about and list the ways you could improve in the areas that you perceive need improvement. Add more paper as necessary.

Analytical Competencies	Ways I Currently Demonstrate These Competencies	My CEO's Expectations	Steps to Take to Improve My Application of These Competencies and Steps to Take to Meet My CEO's Expectations
Analyzing Performance Data			
Career Development Theory and Application			
Intervention Selection			
Knowledge Management			
Organization Development Theory and Application			
Performance Gap Analysis			
Performance Theory			
Reward System Theory and Application			
Staff Selection Theory and Application			
Systems Thinking			
Training Theory and Application			

Appendix C-8. Self-Assessment Worksheet for Business Competencies Associated with the Role of the Intervention Selector
Directions: Use this worksheet to assess how you measure up to your CEO's expectations. After examining the business competencies associated with this role as presented in the chapter, indicate what you are currently doing that demonstrates each competency and what your CEO expects. Finally, think about and list the ways you could improve in the areas that you perceive need improvement. Add more paper as necessary.

Business Competencies	Ways I Currently Demonstrate These Competencies	My CEO's Expectations	Steps to Take to Improve My Application of These Competencies and Steps to Take to Meet My CEO's Expectations
Cost/Benefit Analysis			
Identification of Critical Business Issues			
Industry Awareness			
Outsourcing Management			
Quality Implications			

Appendix C-9. Self-Assessment Worksheet for Interpersonal Competencies Associated with the Role of the Intervention Selector

Directions: Use this worksheet to assess how you measure up to your CEO's expectations. After examining the interpersonal competencies associated with this role as presented in the chapter, indicate what you are currently doing that demonstrates each competency and what your CEO expects. Finally, think about and list the ways you could improve in the areas that you perceive need improvement. Add more paper as necessary.

Interpersonal Competencies	Ways I Currently Demonstrate These Competencies	My CEO's Expectations	Steps to Take to Improve My Application of These Competencies and Steps to Take to Meet My CEO's Expectations
Communication			
Communication Networks			
Consulting			
Interpersonal Relationship Building			

Appendix C-10. Self-Assessment Worksheet for Leadership Competencies Associated with the Role of the Intervention Selector
Directions: Use this worksheet to assess how you measure up to your CEO's expectations. After examining the leadership competencies associated with this role as presented in the chapter, indicate what you are currently doing that demonstrates each competency and what your CEO expects. Finally, think about and list the ways you could improve in the areas that you perceive need improvement. Add more paper as necessary.

Leadership Competencies	Ways I Currently Demonstrate These Competencies	My CEO's Expectations	Steps to Take to Improve My Application of These Competencies and Steps to Take to Meet My CEO's Expectations
Buy-in/Advocacy			
Diversity Awareness			
Ethics Modeling			

Appendix C-11. Self-Assessment Worksheet for the Technical Competency Associated with the Role of the Intervention Selector

Directions: Use this worksheet to assess how you measure up to your CEO's expectations. After examining the technical competency associated with this role as presented in the chapter, indicate what you are currently doing that demonstrates competency and what your CEO expects. Finally, think about and list the ways you could improve in the areas that you perceive need improvement. Add more paper as necessary.

Technical Competency	Ways I Currently Demonstrate This Competency	My CEO's Expectations	Steps to Take to Improve My Application of This Competency and Steps to Take to Meet My CEO's Expectations
Adult Learning			

Appendix C-12. Self-Assessment Worksheet for Technological Competencies Associated with the Role of the Intervention Selector

Directions: Use this worksheet to assess how you measure up to your CEO's expectations. After examining the technological competencies associated with this role as presented in the chapter, indicate what you are currently doing that demonstrates each competency and what your CEO expects. Finally, think about and list the ways you could improve in the areas that you perceive need improvement. Add more paper as necessary.

Technological Competencies	Ways I Currently Demonstrate These Competencies	My CEO's Expectations	Steps to Take to Improve My Application of These Competencies and Steps to Take to Meet My CEO's Expectations
Computer-Mediated Communication			
Distance Education			
Electronic Performance Support Systems			
Technological Literacy			

Appendix C-13. Self-Assessment Worksheet for Analytical Competencies Associated with the Role of the Intervention Designer/Developer

Directions: Use this worksheet to assess how you measure up to your CEO's expectations. After examining the analytical competencies associated with this role as presented in the chapter, indicate what you are currently doing that demonstrates each competency and what your CEO expects. Finally, think about and list the ways you could improve in the areas that you perceive need improvement. Add more paper as necessary.

Analytical Competencies	Ways I Currently Demonstrate These Competencies	My CEO's Expectations	Steps to Take to Improve My Application of These Competencies and Steps to Take to Meet My CEO's Expectations
Analyzing Performance Data			
Career Development Theory and Application			
Intervention Selection			
Knowledge Management			
Model Building			
Organization Development Theory and Application			
Performance Theory			
Reward System theory and Application			
Standards Identification			
Systems Thinking			
Training Theory and Application			

Appendix C-14. Self-Assessment Worksheet for the Business Competencies Associated with the Role of the Intervention Designer/Developer

Directions: Use this worksheet to assess how you measure up to your CEO's expectations. After examining the business competencies associated with this role as presented in the chapter, indicate what you are currently doing that demonstrates each competency and what your CEO expects. Finally, think about and list the ways you could improve in the areas that you perceive need improvement. Add more paper as necessary.

Business Competencies	Ways I Currently Demonstrate These Competencies	My CEO's Expectations	Steps to Take to Improve My Application of These Competencies and Steps to Take to Meet My CEO's Expectations
Industry Awareness			
Project Management			

Appendix C-15. Self-Assessment Worksheet for the Interpersonal Competencies Associated with the Role of the Intervention Designer/Developer

Directions: Use this worksheet to assess how you measure up to your CEO's expectations. After examining the interpersonal competencies associated with this role as presented in the chapter, indicate what you are currently doing that demonstrates each competency and what your CEO expects. Finally, think about and list the ways you could improve in the areas that you perceive need improvement. Add more paper as necessary.

Interpersonal Competencies	Ways I Currently Demonstrate These Competencies	My CEO's Expectations	Steps to Take to Improve My Application of These Competencies and Steps to Take to Meet My CEO's Expectations
Communication			
Communication Networks			
Interpersonal Relationship Building			

Appendix C-16. Self-Assessment Worksheet for the Leadership Competencies Associated with the Role of the Intervention Designer/Developer

Directions: Use this worksheet to assess how you measure up to your CEO's expectations. After examining the leadership competencies associated with this role as presented in the chapter, indicate what you are currently doing that demonstrates each competency and what your CEO expects. Finally, think about and list the ways you could improve in the areas that you perceive need improvement. Add more paper as necessary.

Leadership Competencies	Ways I Currently Demonstrate These Competencies	My CEO's Expectations	Steps to Take to Improve My Application of These Competencies and Steps to Take to Meet My CEO's Expectations
Diversity Awareness			
Ethics Modeling			

Appendix C-17. Self-Assessment Worksheet for the Technical Competencies Associated with the Role of the Intervention Designer/Developer

Directions: Use this worksheet to assess how you measure up to your CEO's expectations. After examining the technical competencies associated with this role as presented in the chapter, indicate what you are currently doing that demonstrates each competency and what your CEO expects. Finally, think about and list the ways you could improve in the areas that you perceive need improvement. Add more paper as necessary.

Technical Competencies	Ways I Currently Demonstrate These Competencies	My CEO's Expectations	Steps to Take to Improve My Application of These Competencies and Steps to Take to Meet My CEO's Expectations
Adult Learning			
Survey Design and Development			

Appendix C-18. Self-Assessment Worksheet for the Technological Competencies Associated with the Role of the Intervention Designer/Developer

Directions: Use this worksheet to assess how you measure up to your CEO's expectations. After examining the technological competencies associated with this role as presented in the chapter, indicate what you are currently doing that demonstrates each competency and what your CEO expects. Finally, think about and list the ways you could improve in the areas that you perceive need improvement. Add more paper as necessary.

Technological Competencies	Ways I Currently Demonstrate These Competencies	My CEO's Expectations	Steps to Take to Improve My Application of These Competencies and Steps to Take to Meet My CEO's Expectations
Computer-Mediated Communication			
Distance Education			
Electronic Performance Support Systems			
Technological Literacy			

Appendix C-19. Self-Assessment Worksheet for the Analytical Competencies Associated with the Role of the Intervention Implementor

Directions: Use this worksheet to assess how you measure up to your CEO's expectations. After examining the analytical competencies associated with this role as presented in the chapter, indicate what you are currently doing that demonstrates each competency and what your CEO expects. Finally, think about and list the ways you could improve in the areas that you perceive need improvement. Add more paper as necessary.

Analytical Competencies	Ways I Currently Demonstrate These Competencies	My CEO's Expectations	Steps to Take to Improve My Application of These Competencies and Steps to Take to Meet My CEO's Expectations
Process Consultation			
Training Theory and Application			
Workplace Performance, Learning Strategies, and Intervention Evaluation			

Appendix C-20. Self-Assessment Worksheet for the Interpersonal Competencies Associated with the Role of the Intervention Implementor

Directions: Use this worksheet to assess how you measure up to your CEO's expectations. After examining the interpersonal competencies associated with this role as presented in the chapter, indicate what you are currently doing that demonstrates each competency and what your CEO expects. Finally, think about and list the ways you could improve in the areas that you perceive need improvement. Add more paper as necessary.

Interpersonal Competencies	Ways I Currently Demonstrate These Competencies	My CEO's Expectations	Steps to Take to Improve My Application of These Competencies and Steps to Take to Meet My CEO's Expectations
Communication			
Communication Networks			
Consulting			
Coping Skills			
Interpersonal Relationship Building			

Appendix C-21. Self-Assessment Worksheet for the Leadership Competencies Associated with the Role of the Intervention Implementor

Directions: Use this worksheet to assess how you measure up to your CEO's expectations. After examining the leadership competencies associated with this role as presented in the chapter, indicate what you are currently doing that demonstrates each competency and what your CEO expects. Finally, think about and list the ways you could improve in the areas that you perceive need improvement. Add more paper as necessary.

Leadership Competencies	Ways I Currently Demonstrate These Competencies	My CEO's Expectations	Steps to Take to Improve My Application of These Competencies and Steps to Take to Meet My CEO's Expectations
Buy-in/Advocacy			
Diversity Awareness			
Group Dynamics			

Appendix C-22. Self-Assessment Worksheet for the Technical Competencies Associated with the Role of the Intervention Implementor

Directions: Use this worksheet to assess how you measure up to your CEO's expectations. After examining the technical competencies associated with this role as presented in the chapter, indicate what you are currently doing that demonstrates each competency and what your CEO expects. Finally, think about and list the ways you could improve in the areas that you perceive need improvement. Add more paper as necessary.

Technical Competencies	Ways I Currently Demonstrate These Competencies	My CEO's Expectations	Steps to Take to Improve My Application of These Competencies and Steps to Take to Meet My CEO's Expectations
Adult Learning			
Facilitation			
Intervention Monitoring			

Appendix C-23. Self-Assessment Worksheet for the Technological Competencies Associated with the Role of the Intervention Implementor

Directions: Use this worksheet to assess how you measure up to your CEO's expectations. After examining the technological competencies associated with this role as presented in the chapter, indicate what you are currently doing that demonstrates each competency and what your CEO expects. Finally, think about and list the ways you could improve in the areas that you perceive need improvement. Add more paper as necessary.

Technological Competencies	Ways I Currently Demonstrate These Competencies	My CEO's Expectations	Steps to Take to Improve My Application of These Competencies and Steps to Take to Meet My CEO's Expectations
Computer-Mediated Communication			
Electronic Performance Support Systems			
Technological Literacy			

Appendix C-24. Self-Assessment Worksheet for the Analytical Competencies Associated with the Role of Evaluator

Directions: Use this worksheet to assess how you measure up to your CEO's expectations. After examining the analytical competencies associated with this role as presented in the chapter, indicate what you are currently doing that demonstrates each competency and what your CEO expects. Finally, think about and list the ways you could improve in the areas that you perceive need improvement. Add more paper as necessary.

Analytical Competencies	Ways I Currently Demonstrate These Competencies	My CEO's Expectations	Steps to Take to Improve My Application of These Competencies and Steps to Take to Meet My CEO's Expectations
Analytical Thinking			
Analyzing Performance Data			
Performance Gap Analysis			
Performance Theory			
Standards Identification			
Systems Thinking			
Work Environment Analysis			
Workplace Performance, Learning Strategies, and Intervention Evaluation			

Appendix C-25. Self-Assessment Worksheet for the Business Competencies Associated with the Role of Evaluator

Directions: Use this worksheet to assess how you measure up to your CEO's expectations. After examining the business competencies associated with this role as presented in the chapter, indicate what you are currently doing that demonstrates each competency and what your CEO expects. Finally, think about and list the ways you could improve in the areas that you perceive need improvement. Add more paper as necessary.

Business Competencies	Ways I Currently Demonstrate These Competencies	My CEO's Expectations	Steps to Take to Improve My Application of These Competencies and Steps to Take to Meet My CEO's Expectations
Ability to See the "Big Picture"			
Cost/Benefit Analysis			
Evaluation of Results Against Organizational Goals			
Knowledge Capital			
Quality Implications			

Appendix C-26. Self-Assessment Worksheet for the Interpersonal Competencies Associated with the Role of Evaluator

Directions: Use this worksheet to assess how you measure up to your CEO's expectations. After examining the interpersonal competencies associated with this role as presented in the chapter, indicate what you are currently doing that demonstrates each competency and what your CEO expects. Finally, think about and list the ways you could improve in the areas that you perceive need improvement. Add more paper as necessary.

Interpersonal Competencies	Ways I Currently Demonstrate These Competencies	My CEO's Expectations	Steps to Take to Improve My Application of These Competencies and Steps to Take to Meet My CEO's Expectations
Communication			
Communication Networks			
Interpersonal Relationship Building			

Appendix C-27. Self-Assessment Worksheet for the Technical Competencies Associated with the Role of Evaluator

Directions: Use this worksheet to assess how you measure up to your CEO's expectations. After examining the technical competencies associated with this role as presented in the chapter, indicate what you are currently doing that demonstrates each competency and what your CEO expects. Finally, think about and list the ways you could improve in the areas that you perceive need improvement. Add more paper as necessary.

Technical Competencies	Ways I Currently Demonstrate These Competencies	My CEO's Expectations	Steps to Take to Improve My Application of These Competencies and Steps to Take to Meet My CEO's Expectations
Feedback			
Intervention Monitoring			
Questioning			

Appendix C-28. Self-Assessment Worksheet for the Technological Competency Associated with the Role of Evaluator

Directions: Use this worksheet to assess how you measure up to your CEO's expectations. After examining the technological competency associated with this role as presented in the chapter, indicate what you are currently doing that demonstrates this competency and what your CEO expects. Finally, think about and list the ways you could improve in the areas that you perceive need improvement. Add more paper as necessary.

Technological Competency	Ways I Currently Demonstrate This Competency	My CEO's Expectations	Steps to Take to Improve My Application of This Competency and Steps to Take to Meet My CEO's Expectations
Technological Literacy			

NOTES

Preface

1. Richard Tedlow, "What Titans Can Teach Us," *Harvard Business Review* 79, 11 (2001): 70–79.

2. Jack Welch and John A. Byrne, *Jack: Straight from the Gut* (New York: Warner Books, 2001).

3. Lee A. Iacocca and Sonny Kleinfield, *Talking Straight* (New York: Bantam Books, 1988).

4. Victor Kiam, *Going for It!: How to Succeed As an Entrepreneur* (New York: Morrow, 1986). See also many recent books about CEOs, such as *Bigwig Briefs: Become a CEO—Leading CEOs Reveal What It Takes to Become a CEO, Stay There, and Empower Others That Work with You* (Boston: Aspatore Books, 2002); Jeffrey E. Garten, *The Mind of the CEO* (Cambridge, MA: Perseus Books, 2001); Rakesh Khurana, *Searching for a Corporate Savior* (Princeton, N.J.: Princeton University Press, 2002); Patrick M. Lencioni, *The Five Temptations of a CEO: A Leadership Fable* (San Francisco: Jossey-Bass, 1998); Jeanne C. Meister, *Building a Learning Organization: 7 Lessons to Involve Your CEO* (New York: iUniverse, 2001).

5. See, for instance, Lloyd C. Harris and Emmanuel Ogbonna, "Strategic Human Resource Management, Market Orientation, and Organizational Performance," *Journal of Business Research* 51, 2 (2001): 157–166. See also Richard McBain, "Human Resources Management: Performance and Power," *Manager Update* 12, 1 (2001): 21–32.

6. See, for instance, Gedaliahu Harel and Shay S. Tzafrir, "The Effect of Human Resource Management Practices on the Perceptions of Organizational and Market Performance of the Firm," *Human Resource Management* 38, 3 (1999): 185–199. See also Laurie J. Bassi, "Harnessing the Power of Intellectual Capital," *Training & Development* 51, 12 (1997): 25–30.

7. Babs Bengtson, "An Analysis of CEO Perceptions Concerning Trainer Roles in Selected Central Pennsylvania Manufacturing Firms" (Ph.D. diss., Pennsylvania State University, 1994), p. 64.

8. T. E. Lawson, *The Competency Initiative: Standards of Excellence for Human Resource Executives* (Arlington, Va.: Society for Human Resources Foundation, 1989); S. C. Schoonover, *Human Resource*

Competencies for the Year 2000: The Wake Up Call (Alexandria, Va.: Society for Human Resources Foundation, 1998).

9. Robert Prescott, "The Changing Role of Human Resource Management: A Comparative Study of Importance Factors Concerning Human Resource Competencies Among General Managers" (Ph.D. diss., Pennsylvania State University, 1999).

10. See Meister, *Building a Learning Organization.*

11. But see also Bengtson, "An Analysis of CEO Perceptions."

12. William J. Rothwell, Ethan Sanders, and Jeffrey G. Soper, *ASTD Models for Workplace Learning and Performance* (Alexandria, Va.: The American Society for Training and Development, 1999).

13. See Rothwell, Sanders, and Soper, *ASTD Models*; William J. Rothwell and Henry J. Sredl, *The ASTD Reference Guide to Workplace Learning and Performance*, 3rd edition, 2 volumes (Amherst, Mass.: Human Resource Development Press, 2000); William J. Rothwell, *The Analyst: A Self-Guided Job Aid with Assessments Based on ASTD Models for Workplace Learning and Performance* (Alexandria, Va.: The American Society for Training and Development, 2000); William J. Rothwell, *The Evaluator: A Self-Guided Job Aid with Assessments Based on ASTD Models for Workplace Learning and Performance* (Alexandria, Va.: The American Society for Training and Development, 2000); William J. Rothwell, *The Intervention Selector, Designer & Developer, Implementor: A Self-Guided Job Aid with Assessments Based on ASTD Models for Workplace Learning and Performance* (Alexandria, Va.: The American Society for Training and Development, 2000); William J. Rothwell, *The Manager and the Change Leader: A Self-Guided Job Aid with Assessments Based on ASTD Models for Workplace Learning and Performance* (Alexandria, Va.: The American Society for Training and Development, 2001).

14. See the guide to academic resources found on the ASTD Web site: http://www.astd.org.

15. Alan Murray, "CEOs Need to Get Ahead of Politicians On Damage Control," *Wall Street Journal*, August 6, 2002, p. A4.

16. B. Horovitz, "Trust: Scandals Shake Public: Americans Have Great Faith in Each Other, but Their Trust in CEOs, Big Business, Priests and HMOs Is Slipping Away. *USA Today*, July 16, 2002, p. A01.

17. B. Shields, "Nature or Nurture? Why CEOs Matter," *Public Utilities Fortnightly* 139, 7 (2001):18–19.

18. W. Symonds and N. Byrnes, "Can Tyco Survive the CEO's Math?" *Business Week*, June 17, 2002, pp. 30–31.

19. A. Hilton, "Have I Got News for You," *Management Today*, January 1999, pp. 28–32.

20. W. Pietersen, *Reinventing Strategy: Using Strategic Learning to Create and Sustain Breakthrough Performance* (New York: John Wiley & Sons, 2002).

21. R. Rowden, "The Learning Organization and Strategic Change," *S.A.M. Advanced Management Journal* 66, 3 (2001): 11–16.

22. The interviews were done for John E. Lindholm, "A Study of CEO Perceptions of the Competencies of Workplace Learning and Performance" (Ph.D. diss., Pennsylvania State University, 2000), and for William G. Wallick, "CEOs' Perceptions of Trainer Roles in Selected Multihospital Health Care Systems" (Ph.D. diss., Pennsylvania State University, 2001; University Microfilms #AAT 3014717).

23. Bengtson, "An Analysis of CEO Perceptions."

24. Rothwell, Sanders, and Soper, *ASTD Models.*

25. Ibid.

26. Lindholm, "A Study of CEO Perceptions."

27. Ibid.

28. Wallick, "CEOs' Perceptions of Trainer Roles."

29. Rothwell, Sanders, and Soper, *ASTD Models.*

30. Ibid.

Chapter 1

1. William G. Wallick, "CEOs' Perceptions of Trainer Roles in Selected Multihospital Health Care Systems" (Ph.D. diss., Pennsylvania State University, 2001; University Microfilms #AAT 3014717), p. 5.

2. William J. Rothwell and Henry J. Sredl, *The ASTD Reference Guide to Professional Human Resources Development Roles and Competencies* (Amherst, Mass.: HRD Press, 1992), Vol. I, p. 5.

3. Ibid., p. 7.

4. William J. Rothwell, Ethan S. Sanders, and Jeffrey G. Soper, *ASTD Models for Workplace Learning and Performance: Roles, Competencies, and Outputs* (Alexandria, Va.: The American Society for Training and Development, 1999), p. 119.

5. Rothwell and Sredl, *ASTD Reference Guide*, Vol. II, p. 203.

6. Ibid., Vol. I, p. 9.

7. Ibid., p. 10.

8. Rothwell, Sanders, and Soper, *ASTD Models*, p. 8.

9. Ibid., p. xv.

10. Patricia A. McLagan and David Suhadolnik, *The Models for HRD Practice: The Research Report*, 4 volumes (Alexandria, Va.: The American Society for Training and Development, 1989).

11. Rothwell, Sanders, and Soper, *ASTD Models*, p. 120.

12. John E. Lindholm, "A Study of CEO Perceptions of the Competencies of Workplace Learning and Performance" (Ph.D. diss., Pennsylvania State University, 2000), p. 5.

13. See, and compare to, William J. Rothwell, Robert K. Prescott, and Maria Taylor, *Strategic Human Resource Leader: How to Prepare Your Organization for the Six Key Trends Shaping the Future* (Palo Alto, Calif.: Davies-Black Publishing, 1998).

14. John E. Lindholm, "A Study of CEO Perceptions."

15. Rothwell, Sanders, and Soper, *ASTD Models*, p. 117.

16. M. Weisbord and S. Janoff, *Future Search: An Action Guide to Finding Common Ground in Organizations and Communities*, 2nd edition (San Francisco: Berrett-Koehler, 2000).

17. G. May and B. Kahnweiler, "Shareholder Value: Is There Common Ground?" *T + D* 56, 7 (2002): 45–52.

CHAPTER 2

1. Laurence J. Peter and Raymond Hull, "The Quotations Page," http://www.quotationspage.com/search.php3.

2. David A. DeCenzo and Stephen P. Robbins, *Human Resource Management*, 6th edition (New York: John Wiley & Sons, 1999), p. 5.

3. Leonard Nadler, "A Study of the Needs of Selected Training Directors in Pennsylvania Which Might Be Met by Professional Education Institutions." Abstract in *Dissertation Abstracts International* 24, 2 (1962).University Microfilms No. 63-3766.

4. Pat Pinto and James Walker, "What Do Training and Development Professionals Really Do?" *Training and Development Journal* 32, 7 (1978): 58–64.

5. Patricia A. McLagan, *Models for Excellence* (Washington, D.C.: The American Society for Training and Development, 1983).

6. Patricia A. McLagan and David Suhadolnik, *The Models for HRD Practice: The Research Report*, (Alexandria, Va.: The American Society for Training and Development, 1989).

7. William J. Rothwell, Ethan S. Sanders, and Jeffrey G. Soper, *ASTD Models for Workplace Learning and Performance: Roles, Competencies, and Outputs* (Alexandria, Va.: The American Society for Training and Development, 1999), p. 21.

8. William G. Wallick, "CEOs' Perceptions of Trainer Roles in Selected Multihospital Health Care Systems" (Ph.D. diss., Pennsylvania State University, 2001; University Microfilms #AAT 3014717), p. 163.

9. Rothwell, Sanders, and Soper, *ASTD Models*, p. 43.

10. Ibid.

11. Ibid., pp. 53–59.

12. Ibid., p. xv.

13. Ibid., pp. 53–59.

14. Ibid., p. xv.

15. Ibid., pp. 53–59.

16. Ibid., p. xv.

17. Ibid., pp. 53–59.

18. Ibid., pp. 53–59.

Chapter 3

1. William J. Rothwell, Ethan S. Sanders, and Jeffrey G. Soper, *ASTD Models for Workplace Learning and Performance: Roles, Competencies, and Outputs* (Alexandria, Va.: American Society for Training and Development, 1999), p. 43.

2. John E. Lindholm, "A Study of CEO Perceptions of the Competencies of Workplace Learning and Performance" (Ph.D. diss., Pennsylvania State University, 2000).

3. Rosabeth Moss Kanter, *E*Volve: Succeeding in the Digital Culture of Tomorrow* (Boston: Harvard Business School, 2001), p. 321.

4. Patricia A. McLagan, *Models for Excellence* (Washington, D.C.: The American Society for Training and Development, 1983).

5. Pat Pinto and James Walker, "What Do Training and Development Professionals Really Do?" *Training and Development Journal* 32, 7 (1978): 58–64.

6. McLagan, *Models for Excellence*; Patricia A. McLagan and David Suhadolnik, *The Models for HRD Practice: The Research Report* (Alexandria, Va.: The American Society for Training and Development, 1989).

Chapter 4

1. William J. Rothwell, Ethan S. Sanders, and Jeffrey G. Soper, *ASTD Models for Workplace Learning and Performance: Roles, Competencies, and Outputs* (Alexandria, Va.: American Society for Training and Development, 1999), p. 61.

2. Thomas G. Cummings and Christopher G. Worley, *Organization Development and Change,* 7th edition (Cincinnati, Ohio: South-Western College Publishing, 2001), p. 142.

3. Rothwell, Sanders, and Soper, *ASTD Models*, p. 11.

4. Ibid., p. 16.

5. William J. Rothwell and Henry J. Sredl, *The ASTD Reference Guide to Workplace Learning and Performance*, 3rd edition, 2 volumes (Amherst, Mass.: Human Resource Development Press, 2000).

6. William J. Rothwell, *The Analyst: A Self-Guided Job Aid with Assessments Based on ASTD Models for Workplace Learning and Performance* (Alexandria, Va.: The American Society for Training and Development, 2000); William J. Rothwell, *The Evaluator: A Self-Guided Job Aid with Assessments Based on ASTD Models for Workplace Learning and Performance* (Alexandria, Va.: The American Society for Training and Development, 2000); William J. Rothwell, *The Intervention Selector, Designer & Developer, Implementor: A Self-Guided Job Aid with Assessments Based on ASTD Models for Workplace Learning and Performance* (Alexandria, Va.: The American Society for Training and Development, 2000); William J. Rothwell, *The Manager and the Change Leader: A Self-Guided Job Aid with Assessments Based on ASTD Models for Workplace Learning and Performance* (Alexandria, Va.: The American Society for Training and Development, 2001).

Chapter 5

1. See, for instance, William J. Rothwell and H.C. Kazanas, *Mastering the Instructional Design Process: A Systematic Approach*, 2nd edition (San Francisco: Jossey-Bass, 1998).

2. Patricia A. McLagan, *Models for Excellence* (Washington, D.C.: The American Society for Training and Development, 1983).

3. William J. Rothwell, Ethan Sanders, and Jeffrey G. Soper, *ASTD Models for Workplace Learning and Performance: Roles, Competencies, and Outputs* (Alexandria, Va.: The American Society for Training and Development, 1999).

4. Ibid, pp. 53–59.

5. John E. Lindholm, "A Study of CEO Perceptions of the Competencies of Workplace Learning and Performance" (Ph.D. diss., Pennsylvania State University, 2000), p. 103.

6. William G. Wallick, "CEOs' Perceptions of Trainer Roles in Selected Multihospital Health Care Systems" (Ph.D. diss., Pennsylvania State University, 2001; University Microfilms #AAT 3014717).

Chapter 6

1. William J. Rothwell, Ethan S. Sanders, and Jeffrey G. Soper, *ASTD Models for Workplace Learning and Performance: Roles, Competencies, and Outputs* (Alexandria, Va.: American Society for Training and Development, 1999), p. 5.

2. Patricia McLagan, *Models for HRD Practice* (Alexandria, Va.: American Society for Training and Development, 1989), p. 7.

3. Rothwell, Sanders, and Soper, *ASTD Models*, p. 6.

4. Ibid, p. 43.

5. Pat Pinto and James Walker, "What Do Training and Development Professionals Really Do?" *Training and Development Journal* 32, 7 (1978): 58–64.

6. Ibid.

7. Patricia A. McLagan, *Models for Excellence* (Washington, D.C.: The American Society for Training and Development, 1983).

8. Rothwell, Sanders, and Soper, *ASTD Models*, pp. 25–26.

9. Ibid., p. 97.

10. Ibid., pp. 53–59.

11. Ibid.

12. Ibid.

13. Ibid.

14. Ibid.

15. Ibid., p. 98.

Chapter 7

1. William J. Rothwell and Henry J. Sredl, *The ASTD Reference Guide to Workplace Learning and Performance*, 3rd edition, 2 volumes (Amherst, Mass.: Human Resource Development Press, 2000). Learning has become a key competency. See William J. Rothwell, *The Workplace Learner: How to Align Training Initiatives with Individual Learning Competencies* (New York: AMACOM, 2002).

2. Patricia A. McLagan and David Suhadolnik, *Models for HRD Practice: The Research Report* (Alexandria, Va.: The American Society for Training and Development, 1989).

3. Patricia A. McLagan, "Great Ideas Revisited: Creating the Future of HRD," *Training and Development Journal*, January 1996, pp. 60–67.

4. Compare McLagan and Suhadolnik, *Models for HRD Practice* to Patricia A. McLagan, *Models for Excellence* (Washington, D.C.: The American Society for Training and Development, 1983).

5. Robert Reich, "Your Job is Change," *Fast Company*, October 2000, pp. 140–160.

6. McLagan and Suhadolnik, *Models for HRD Practice*.

7. Ibid.

8. Ibid.

9. S. Sherman, "Wanted: Company Change Agents," *Fortune*, December 11, 1995, pp. 197–198.

10. Anonymous, CEO Interview, John E. Lindholm, tape recorded State College, Penn., Spring 2000.

11. Reich, "Your Job is Change."

Chapter 8

1. William J. Rothwell, Ethan S. Sanders, and Jeffrey G. Soper, *ASTD Models for Workplace Learning and Performance: Roles, Competencies, and Outputs* (Alexandria, Va.: American Society for Training and Development, 1999), p. 61.

2. Leonard Nadler and Zeace Nadler, *Designing Training Programs: The Critical Events Model*, 2nd edition (Houston, Tex.: Gulf Publishing Company, 1994), p. 15.

3. William J. Rothwell and Peter S. Cookson, *Beyond Instruction: Comprehensive Program Planning for Business and Education* (San Francisco: Jossey-Bass, 1996), p. 200.

4. William J. Rothwell, Roland Sullivan, and Gary McLean (eds.), *Practicing Organization Development: A Guide for Consultants* (San Francisco: Jossey-Bass/Pfeiffer, 1995).

5. Rothwell, Sanders, and Soper, *ASTD Models*, pp. 14–15.

6. See William J. Rothwell and H. C. Kazanas, *Human Resource Development: A Strategic Approach*, rev. edition (Amherst, Mass.: Human Resource Development Press, 1994); William J. Rothwell and H. C. Kazanas, *Planning and Managing Human Resources: Strategic Planning for Personnel Management*, rev. edition (Amherst, Mass.: Human Resource Development Press, 1994); William J. Rothwell and H. C. Kazanas, *Planning and Managing Human Resources: Strategic Planning for Human Resource Management*, 2nd edition (Amherst, Mass.: Human Resource Development Press, in press).

7. William J. Rothwell, Robert K. Prescott, and Maria W. Taylor, *Strategic Human Resource Leader: How to Prepare Your Organization for the Six Key Trends Shaping the Future* (Palo Alto, Calif.: Davies-Black Publishing, 1998).

8. Rothwell, Sanders, and Soper, *ASTD Models*, pp. 15–16.

9. See William J. Rothwell, *The Evaluator: A Self-Guided Job Aid with Assessments Based on ASTD Models for Workplace Learning and Performance* (Alexandria, Va.: The American Society for Training and Development, 2000)

10. Rothwell, Sanders, and Soper, *ASTD Models*.

11. Ibid.

12. Ibid.

13. Ibid.
14. See William J. Rothwell (ed.), *Creating, Measuring & Documenting Service Impact: A Capacity Building Resource: Rationales, Models, Activities, Methods, Techniques, Instruments* (Columbus, Ohio: The EnterpriseOhio Network, 1998).
15. Rothwell, Sanders, and Soper, *ASTD Models*.
16. Ibid.
17. Ibid.

Chapter 9

1. William J. Rothwell, Ethan S. Sanders, and Jeffrey G. Soper, *ASTD Models for Workplace Learning and Performance: Roles, Competencies, and Outputs* (Alexandria, Va.: American Society for Training and Development, 1999).
2. Ibid.
3. Ibid.
4. Ibid.
5. William J. Rothwell, Carolyn Hohne, and Stephen King, *Human Performance Improvement: Building Practitioner Competence* (Woburn, Mass.: Butterworth-Heinemann, 2000).
6. Rothwell, Sanders, and Soper, *ASTD Models*.
7. Ibid.

Appendix A

1. William J. Rothwell, Ethan S. Sanders, and Jeffrey G. Soper, *ASTD Models for Workplace Learning and Performance: Roles, Competencies, and Outputs* (Alexandria, Va.: American Society for Training and Development, 1999), pp. xv–xvi.

INDEX

ABOUT THE AUTHORS

William J. Rothwell is Professor of Human Resource Development in the Department of Adult Education, Instructional Systems, and Workforce Education and Development in the College of Education on the University Park Campus of The Pennsylvania State University. He is also President of Rothwell and Associates, Inc., a private consulting firm specializing in a comprehensive approach to human performance improvement with a client list including some 32 multinational corporations. Previously Assistant Vice President and Management Development Director for the Franklin Life Insurance Company in Springfield, Illinois, and Training Director for the Illinois Office of Auditor General, he has worked full-time in human resources management and employee training and development from 1979 to present, combining real-world experience with academic and consulting experience.

Dr. Rothwell's most recent publications include *Building Effective Technical Training* (2002); *Planning and Managing Human Resources*, 2nd ed. (2002); *The Manager and Change Leader* (2001); *Effective Succession Planning*, 2nd ed. (2000); *The Complete Guide to Training Delivery: A Competency-Based Approach* (with M. King and S. King, 2000); *Human Performance Improvement: Building Practitioner Competence* (with C. Hohne and S. King, 2000); *The ASTD Reference Guide to Workplace Learning and Performance: Present and Future Roles and Competencies*, 3rd ed., 2 vols. (with H. Sredl, 2000); *The Analyst* (2000); *The Evaluator* (2000); *The Intervention Selector, Designer and Developer, and Implementor* (2000); *ASTD Models for Human Performance Improvement*, 2nd ed. (2000); *The Competency Toolkit*, 2 vols. (with D. Dubois, 2000); *Building In-House Leadership and Management Development Programs* (with H. Kazanas, 1999); *ASTD Models for Workplace Learning and Performance* (with E. Sanders and J. Soper, 1999);

The Action Learning Guidebook: A Real-Time Strategy for Problem Solving, Training Design, and Employee Development: Sourcebook for Self-Directed Learning (with K. Sensenig, as editors, 1999); *Creating, Measuring and Documenting Service Impact: A Capacity Building Resource: Rationales, Models, Activities, Methods, Techniques, Instruments* (1998); *In Action: Improving Human Performance* (with D. Dubois, as editors, 1998); *Strategic Human Resources Leader: How to Help Your Organization Manage the Six Trends Affecting the Workforce* (with R. Prescott and M. Taylor, 1998); *In Action: Linking HRD and Organizational Strategy* (as editor, 1998); *Mastering the Instructional Design Process: A Systematic Approach* (with H. Kazanas, 2nd edition, 1998).

John E. Lindholm is the Compensation Manager at the University of Massachusetts Medical School. He has ten years effective experience working with compensation, performance management, human resources development, and financial analysis. He is a partner in Effective Organization Processes, Inc. (EEOP³I); a financial and human resources consulting firm. John is currently an adjunct faculty member at Clark University in Worcester, Massachusetts.

William G. Wallick is Assistant Professor of Human Resources and Human Resource Development in the Department of Health Administration and Human Resources in the Panuska College of Education of the University of Scranton. He is the director of the graduate human resources administration program and director of the undergraduate human resources studies program. Previously Vice President of Human Resources at the Wyoming Valley Health Care System, Wilkes-Barre, Pennsylvania; Director of Human Resources at Jersey Shore Hospital, Jersey Shore, Pennsylvania; Director of Human Resources at Allied Services, Scranton, Pennsylvania; and Training Director for the Globe Store, Scranton, Pennsylvania, he has worked full-time in human resource management and employee training and development from 1976 to the present, combining real-world experience with academic experience.